Fostering the Love of Reading: The Affective Domain in Reading Education

Eugene H. Cramer
University of Illinois at Chicago
Chicago, Illinois

Marrietta Castle
Western Illinois University
Moline, Illinois

Editors

INTERNATIONAL READING ASSOCIATION
Newark, Delaware 19714, USA

IRA BOARD OF DIRECTORS

The International Reading Association attempts, through its publications, to provide a forum for a wide spectrum of opinions on reading. This policy permits divergent viewpoints without assuming the endorsement of the Association.

Director of Publications   Joan M. Irwin
Managing Editor   Anne Fullerton
Associate Editor   Chris Celsnak
Assistant Editor   Amy Trefsger
Editorial Assistant   Janet Parrack
Production Department Manager   Iona Sauscermen
Graphic Design Coordinator   Boni Nash
Design Consultant   Larry Husfelt
Desktop Publishing Supervisor   Wendy Mazur
Desktop Publishing   Anette Schütz-Ruff
                              Cheryl Strum
Proofing   David Roberts
Cover Photo   Michael Siluk

Library of Congress Cataloging in Publication Data

Fostering the love of reading: the affective domain in reading education/Eugene H. Cramer, Marrietta Castle, editors.
   p.   cm.
Includes bibliographical references and index.
   1. Reading.   2. Reading, Psychology of.   3. Children—Books and reading—Psychological aspects.   4. Affective education.   5. Motivation in education.
I. Cramer, Eugene H.   II. Castle, Marrietta.
LB1050.2.F67   1994   94-22514
372.41—dc20   CIP
ISBN 0-87207-125-1
Second Printing, August 1996

CONTENTS

FOREWORD

●◆ This book is about the central and most important goal of reading instruction—how to foster the love of reading. It is about teachers and the critical role they play in helping children develop into motivated, active, engaged readers who read for both pleasure and information because they find it to be personally satisfying and rewarding.

Most of us would agree that the best measure of success for an instructional reading program is the enthusiasm and frequency with which students voluntarily choose to read. This goal can only be accomplished in collaboration with teachers, parents, administrators, and researchers. We must all work together to develop literacy environments that will foster students' love of reading. This book recognizes that the love of reading begins in the home, is sustained and nurtured in the classroom, and continues for a lifetime.

Fostering the Love of Reading is indeed a timely book. In 1992 the U.S. National Reading Research Center conducted a poll of International Reading Association members in the United States to determine the research areas teachers considered to be most important. Four of the top ten areas were related to reading motivation. The number one priority was creating interest in reading, followed by increasing the amount and breadth of children's reading, developing intrinsic desire for reading, and exploring the roles of teachers, peers, and parents in reading motivation. This book directly addresses these concerns and has the potential to contribute greatly to the goal of motivating students to become lifelong readers.

One of the reasons for the current interest in motivation is that teachers and researchers recognize it is at the heart of many of the pervasive problems we face in reading education. *Fostering the Love of Reading* is based on motivation theory and research that provides a body of knowledge for building the know-how we need to improve literacy learning for all students. The editors of this volume have carefully gathered a collection of articles that represent the best in current thinking about a wide range of issues related to reading motivation. The authors offer a refreshing look at how to create classroom cultures that turn students on to both the joy and value of reading. Although this book is targeted primarily at teachers, I believe it should be read by all persons with responsibility for shaping reading instruction in today's schools.

Because we want all of our students to become lifelong literacy learners, the goal of developing a love of reading must be a priority in the curriculum. This volume will serve as a rich and valuable resource for energizing teachers toward achieving this worthwhile goal.

Linda B. Gambrell
University of Maryland, College Park

CONTRIBUTORS

Camille L.Z. Blachowicz
National-Louis University
Evanston, Illinois

Marrietta Castle
Western Illinois University
Moline, Illinois

Nancy Lee Cecil
California State University
    at Sacramento
Sacramento, California

Eugene H. Cramer
University of Illinois at Chicago
Chicago, Illinois

Edward J. Dwyer
East Tennessee State University
Johnson City, Tennessee

Evelyn E. Dwyer
Walters State Community College
Morristown, Tennessee

Peter J.L. Fisher
National-Louis University
Evanston, Illinois

Cara L. Garcia
Pepperdine University
Culver City, California

Betty S. Heathington
Applied Research Associates
Knoxville, Tennessee

Jerry L. Johns
Northern Illinois University
DeKalb, Illinois

Lloyd W. Kline
LWK Publication Services
Newark, Delaware

June D. Knafle
University of Illinois at Chicago
Chicago, Illinois

Michael C. McKenna
Georgia Southern University
Savannah, Georgia

Larry Mikulecky
Indiana University
Bloomington, Indiana

Victor Nell
University of South Africa
Pretoria, South Africa

Judy S. Richardson
Virginia Commonwealth University
Richmond, Virginia

Irene Schultz
Lake Bluff, Illinois

Richard Sinatra
St. John's University
Jamaica, New York

Dixie Lee Spiegel
University of North Carolina
    at Chapel Hill
Chapel Hill, North Carolina

Peggy VanLeirsburg
Elgin Public Schools
Elgin, Illinois

Cathryn A. Wimett
National-Louis University
Chicago, Illinois

INTRODUCTION

An Overview of the Affective Domain in Reading

Increasing the proportion of children who read widely and with evident satisfaction ought to be as much a goal of reading instruction as increasing the number who are competent readers.

R.C. Anderson

Developing Lifelong Readers

Eugene H. Cramer
Marrietta Castle

●◆ Why do some people read? Why do other people who can read choose not to? Why do some people use reading as a source of information and personal pleasure throughout their lives? Why do many literate people, after completing their formal education, rarely, if ever, choose to read for personal satisfaction? How important is reading in our daily lives? What should schools do to promote lifelong reading? What can teachers do to foster the love of learning and reading? These are a few of the many questions addressed in this book about reading attitudes and motivation to read.

In the past few years there has been growing interest in the affective domain of reading. School practitioners and research scholars are addressing questions about the role of reading attitudes and reading motivation in literacy education with increasing frequency. Accordingly, we submit the following four beliefs as central to any literacy education program:

1. Affective aspects of reading are equal in importance to cognitive aspects.

2. Affective aspects of reading instruction are too often neglected.

3. Affective elements of reading can and should be measured.

4. More systematic research is needed in the affective areas of reading.

Illiteracy Is a Serious Problem

Reports of the shocking problem of illiteracy in the United States and other countries are numerous. Almost daily, news media trumpet the desperate need for increased efforts to improve U.S. literacy levels. Research studies have proliferated, and the government has invested millions of dollars in grants to literacy agencies in an attempt to stem the rising tide of illiteracy. Results are less than satisfactory. We believe that at least part of the solution to the problem of illiteracy lies in the affective domain.

Aliteracy May Be a Greater Problem than Illiteracy

While illiteracy is, without question, a very serious concern, aliteracy may be an even greater one. *Aliteracy* has been defined as a "lack of the reading habit; especially, such a lack in capable readers who choose not to read" (Harris & Hodges, 1981, p. 11). Estimates of the number of illiterates in the United States vary widely but seem to average out to about 1 in 5. That is, adults who cannot read well enough to use reading effectively in their daily lives total about 20 percent of the population. Reliable estimates of the number of aliterates in the United States are more difficult to secure. Researchers suggest that only about 20 percent of the adults who are able to read do so voluntarily with any degree of regularity. That is to say, of the 4 out of 5 Americans who can read, only 1 actually does. One authority states, "Once out of school, nearly 60 percent of all adult Americans have *never read a single book*, and most of the rest read only one book a year" (Woiwode, 1992, p. 1). Spiegel (1981) reported that a 1972 Gallup Pool estimated that 10 percent of the population accounts for 80 percent of the books read in the United States. These figures are substantiated somewhat in a 1986 Gallup Poll that found that 14 percent of U.S. adults indicated reading was one of their favorite recreational activities, compared with 21 percent who favored reading in the pre-television year of 1938.

Children educated in U.S. schools spend approximately 12 years learning how to read at increasingly sophisticated levels. In the early grades they learn the mechanical rudiments of decoding and understanding printed text. In the upper elementary grades and high school, students learn to reconstruct, comprehend, extract, assimilate, and use information from a variety of printed sources for many different purposes. After completing school, however, too many people do not voluntarily choose to read for their own personal pleasure or information.

For many years the idea of helping young readers to develop positive attitudes about the pleasures and values of reading has been an often-stated but all too frequently neglected goal of reading instruction. In 1908 Edmund Burke Huey wrote,

> The prevalent methods of teaching reading are such as cultivate wrong habits and attitudes concerning books.... Methods come and go, but all lack the essentials of any well-grounded method, viz. relevancy to the child's mental needs. No scheme for learning reading can supply this want. Only a new motive, putting the child into a

vital relation to the materials read, can be of service here.... The child
does not want to learn reading as a mechanical tool. He must have a
"personal hunger" for what is read. He must come, too, to his reading with personal experience with which to appreciate it (pp.
305–306).

A few years later, a classroom teacher wrote, "It should be the teacher's
aim to give every child a love for reading, a hunger for it that will stay with
him through all the years of his life. If a child has that he will acquire the
mechanical part without difficulty" (Mayne, 1915, p. 40).

Seventy years later, the same idea was stated in more global terms
in the landmark publication *Becoming a Nation of Readers*, a report of the
U.S. Commission on Reading: "Increasing the proportion of children who
read widely and with evident satisfaction ought to be as much a goal of
reading instruction as increasing the number who are competent readers"
(Anderson et al., 1985, p. 15). Even more recently, some researchers have
focused attention on the possible causes for the lack of motivation to read.
Following a rather comprehensive study of the problem, a researcher at the
University of Chicago concluded,

It seems increasingly clear that the chief impediments to literacy are
not cognitive in nature. It is not that students cannot learn; it is that
they do not wish to.... Literacy, numeracy, or indeed any other subject matter will be mastered more readily and more thoroughly when
the student becomes able to derive intrinsic rewards from learning
(Csikszentmihalyi, 1990, pp. 115–116).

Causes of Aliteracy

We can only speculate on the possible causes of aliteracy in the
United States. A number of reasons have been advanced that rely on historical opinion and common-sense logic. Until further research indicates otherwise, we submit the following possibilities to explain why many adults in
the United States do not choose to read.

Traditionally, Americans have tended to disapprove of classroom
teaching practices that involve indoctrination. There seems to be a fine line
between programs that motivate and programs that indoctrinate. Many
schools, therefore, have avoided any hint of possible emotional indoctrination in reading instruction, preferring the safer ground of "just teach them
to read."

Two other factors seem closely related and probably contribute to this "avoidance of indoctrination" policy. First, affective characteristics are considered private and personal and not a matter for public scrutiny or grading. Second, educators seem to believe that affective aspects are already built into our current reading programs and that children will develop positive attitudes naturally.

Further, there seems to be a common assumption among educators that affective elements of reading instruction cannot be attained in relatively short instructional periods and therefore cannot be evaluated. While this assumption may be at least partially true, there are several methods available to educators who wish to assess the reading attitudes of their students: the Estes attitude scale (Estes, 1981), the Mikulecky behavioral reading attitude measure (Mikulecky, 1978), McKenna and Kear's (1990) elementary reading attitude survey, and the Tullock-Rhody and Alexander (1980) scale for assessing attitudes toward reading in secondary school are but a few of the many instruments found to be valid and reliable in assessing students' reading attitudes. We can only speculate what use would be made of measures such as these if policy makers insisted on assessing students' reading attitudes with the same fervor now given to assessing cognitive measures.

A final reason sometimes proposed for the dearth of affective reading education is that teachers get little or no training in the affective aspects of reading instruction. Even a cursory inspection of current and popular reading methods texts reveals that affective aspects often are relegated to final chapters if they are included at all. Yet in our experience, veteran teachers usually list reading motivation as having the highest priority among potential staff-development topics.

A Brief Overview of the Book

In the following chapters we offer selected essays representing a wide range of viewpoints and ideas intended to enhance educators' understanding of the relationship between the affective domain and reading instruction. Although the 21 authors present a variety of perspectives dealing with the affective dimensions of reading, they all agree on the importance of the affective domain and the potential for teachers to increase their effectiveness in helping students develop lifelong habits of reading for pleasure and personal knowledge.

Part One is devoted to defining the role of the affective domain in reading. In Chapter 1, Lloyd Kline sets the book into the larger context of reading's place in society. His inviting overview challenges teachers to "keep the faith" in the affective domain. Michael McKenna presents in Chapter 2 an academic discussion of several theoretical models of reading attitude acquisition, which will be of special interest to teacher educators. Implications from his models are discussed throughout the book. Victor Nell's Chapter 3 has been excerpted from his work *Lost in a Book: The Psychology of Reading for Pleasure* (1988). He offers an eloquent explanation for the apparently universal craving for "stories" and a possible developmental model to suggest how some children may become avid readers.

Part Two examines student attitudes toward reading and discusses means of guiding them in the development of positive reading attitudes. Peter Fisher provides insights into reading habits of children and adults in Chapter 4 that will be of interest to practitioners. His chapter includes original research about which books are most popular with various groups of children. In Chapter 5, Edward and Evelyn Dwyer present convincing evidence establishing the relationship between teacher attitudes toward students and the reading achievement levels of those students. Their comments will reassure teachers that they can make a difference. Dixie Lee Spiegel reviews selected research from the past four decades on the roles of parents in fostering reading interest and achievement in their children. From this research she develops a portrait of parents of successful readers in Chapter 6.

Part Three deals directly with strategies that classroom teachers, reading specialists, and parents can use for motivating young readers. In Chapter 7, Jerry Johns and Peggy VanLeirsburg discuss principles of extrinsic and intrinsic motivation and examine the relative effectiveness of each. They present a wide range of classroom strategies for developmental and at-risk readers. In Chapter 8, Richard Sinatra offers a unique perspective on how literature and the visual arts may be integrated. Classroom teachers and curriculum specialists will be interested in strategies from various school programs that have blended the visual arts meaningfully with reading and writing. Nancy Lee Cecil discusses in Chapter 9 how teachers in the elementary grades can make the word—the basic ingredient of all reading and writing—come alive for children through five components of a dynamic language arts program. She gives numerous examples to demonstrate how these components may be applied successfully. Eugene Cramer describes reading and writing motivational techniques reported to him by classroom teachers. The ideas presented in Chapter 10—gathered over the past five years during workshops and inservice sessions—will be useful to teachers of all grade levels as well as special education, bilingual, and compensatory education teachers.

Part Four offers practical advice for helping students connect their reading with their lives by responding and reacting to what they read. In Chapter 11, Marrietta Castle stresses the role of teachers in helping children choose books through modeling, providing ready access to reading material, and setting up incentives for reluctant readers. Throughout the chapter there is an emphasis on fostering constructive choices in positive, interactive, social settings. June Knafle in Chapter 12 analyzes the interrelationships among values presented in books for children and adolescents. She unlocks a number of cultural and political issues that could stimulate spirited discussions between students and teachers. Chapter 13 offers a fresh view on an important but usually unaddressed issue: preservice teachers who have not been readers. Camille Blachowicz and Cathryn Wimett present ways to broaden preservice teachers' exposure to literature for children and adolescents while helping them gain insight into reading processes and instructional strategies.

Part Five concerns the development of affective reading programs. Betty Heathington provides a series of scenarios in Chapter 14 that demonstrate some of the choices teachers have to make between curriculum concerns and their role in fostering positive attitudes toward reading. She also presents specific teaching strategies to develop and maintain students' positive attitudes. In Chapter 15, Judy Richardson makes a strong case for reading aloud to high school students. She describes a procedure for integrating content area instruction with teacher read-alouds and gives specific examples of the technique and of students' reactions. Children's author Irene Schultz presents a workable and accessible formula for creating materials for discouraged readers in Chapter 16. Her advice may be useful not only to classroom teachers but to parents and high school students as well. Cara Garcia discusses factors affecting inservice education and offers advice regarding "client-centered" changes necessary when instituting an affective reading program. In Chapter 17, she describes a process of nondirective, informal staff development in a series of dialogues that demonstrate this technique.

In the **Epilogue**, Larry Mikulecky presents a strong case for the need for a literate society that not only *can* read but *does* read with understanding and commitment. His words remind teachers at all levels of the vital need to attend to the affective dimensions of reading instruction espoused throughout this book.

We believe that now, at long last, the affective domain may be emerging from the shadows of reading education. Reading motivation is becoming more than just the frosting on the academic cake. No longer should the affective domain be the inevitable last chapter in reading methods texts. There is a growing realization among many educators that affective elements of reading instruction are essential to the development of readers.

The message in this book was clearly anticipated more than 75 years ago in a reference work for teachers (Aiton, 1916, p. 61), and it is just as clearly pertinent today:

> Your work as a teacher of reading is not done until you have taught the children three things:
>
> 1. How to read
> 2. What to read
> 3. To read.

References

Aiton, G.B. (1916). *Standard reference work for the home, school, and library*. Minneapolis, MN: Welles Brothers.

Anderson, R.C., Hiebert, E.H., Scott, J.A., & Wilkinson, I.A.G. (1985). *Becoming a nation of readers: The report of the Commission on Reading*. Washington, DC: U.S. Department of Education.

Csikszentmihalyi, M. (1990). Literature and intrinsic motivation. *DAEDALUS, Journal of the American Academy of Arts and Sciences, 119*(2), pp. 115–116.

Estes, T.H. (1981). *The Estes attitude scales*. Austin, TX: Pro-Ed.

Harris, T.L., & Hodges, R.E. (Eds.). (1981). *A dictionary of reading and related terms*. Newark, DE: International Reading Association.

Huey, E.B. (1968). *The psychology and pedagogy of reading*. Cambridge, MA: MIT Press. (Original work published 1908)

Mayne, E. (1915). The object of teaching reading. In W.J. Beecher & G.B. Faxon (Eds.), *Methods, aids, and devices for teachers*. Danville, NY: E.A. Owen.

McKenna, M.C., & Kear, D.J. (1990). Measuring attitude toward reading: A new tool for teachers. *The Reading Teacher, 43*, 626–639.

Mikulecky, L. (1978). A behavioral reading attitude measure. In C.B. Smith, S.L. Smith, & L. Mikulecky (Eds.), *Teaching reading in secondary school content subjects: A book-thinking process* (pp. 100–104). New York: Holt, Rinehart.

Nell, V. (1988). *Lost in a book: The psychology of reading for pleasure*. New Haven, CT: Yale University Press.

Spiegel, D. (1981). *Reading for pleasure: Guidelines*. Newark, DE: International Reading Association.

Tullock-Rhody, R., & Alexander, J.E. (1980). A scale for assessing attitudes toward reading in secondary schools. *Journal of Reading, 23*, 609–614.

Woiwode, L. (1992). Television: The cyclops that eats books. *Imprimis, 21*(2), 1.

PART ONE

Defining the Role of Affect in Reading

The student who can read, but chooses not to, is probably the most crucial concern confronting our educational institutions today. It is not illiteracy we are combating, but aliteracy.

K. Thomas & G. Moorman

Chapter 1

Reading and Society: Lessons from the World out There

Lloyd W. Kline

●◆ I was a classroom teacher for 13 years, then a writer, editor, and publisher for teachers for another 13 years. For the better part of the past decade, I have been earning my keep as a "self-employed independent," writing, editing, designing, and producing things in print for various clients. I devote many of my efforts to serving clients in the "world out there"—marketers, service agencies, suppliers, producers—as well as people in and around education. The priorities of the people out there tend to be much different from the classroom teacher's. For one thing, none of them has the luxury of looking at a clean slate each September. They are on the hook day after day from one budget year to the next—no breaks, no fresh starts. They can't even console themselves with the professional folklore that if they have taught one child one thing in one year, their efforts have been successful.

How do I see the notion of "affective reading" at work in that world out there? Have I learned anything that might be worth passing along to those who labor faithfully in the classroom? I think I have: namely, you're doing far better than you probably think you're doing, and certainly much better than you've too often been told!

Fact or Falsehood? Nobody Reads Anymore

You know that's false! When 40 percent of the waste that overwhelms U.S. landfills is made up of paper—most of it carrying one set of printed messages or another—it is pure nonsense to declare that society is on the path to irreversible illiteracy. *What* people are reading and *why* they are reading it is certainly undergoing change. But that kind of change has been underway since Gutenberg.

Urban graffiti, bumper stickers, and boardwalk T-shirts carry messages almost exclusively in print. It is true that, most are lavishly illustrated or illuminated, but many are also pure poetry, and a marvelous few are even profound in their vernacular wisdom and insight.

True, magazines have evolved drastically into marketing tools rather than the treasure troves of fiction and enlightenment some of them once were. But most children's magazines fulfill their goal of engaging and entertaining young readers, and *Sassy* matured enough in just a few years to merit nomination as one of the five best magazines in the United States. Periodicals in general have proliferated so much that there is not a newsstand big enough to hold them all.

True, prophets of electronic nirvana continue to envision a paperless society. Computer keyboards, however, remain standardized to the 26 letters of the alphabet. Printouts cascade into ever-larger binders and shredders, and so-called desktop publishing has turned anyone who works on user-friendly menus into an instant Gutenberg.

Book lists burgeon; rock groups continue to adopt names, themes, and titles out of classical mythology; and library use per year surpasses attendance at all professional sporting events put together—in Philadelphia, at least, my nearest "big city".

Fact or Falsehood? To Read Is Good; Not to Read Is Bad

The old moral-imperative trick! Put the notion that reading is inherently good out of your head. If the idea is not false, it is at least misleading. With very few exceptions, there is nothing inherently good about reading. Neither is there anything inherently bad about not reading. What, why, and how somebody reads is a whole lot more important than *whether* or *when*. True, we all know that you court disaster if you fail to read and heed the stop sign at the dangerous intersection, but none of us believes that bookworms are morally superior—and are also safer drivers.

All of us—*especially* those of us who consider ourselves readers—choose often and wisely not to read, and morality has nothing to do with it. The first time I tried to read an entire Sunday edition of *The New York Times*, I wasn't halfway through by the following Wednesday. I threw out the entire bundle and couldn't bring myself to pick up another copy of the Sunday *Times* for the next quarter century. Absorbing every inch of *any* newspaper or magazine is more than I will attempt, even today. Most of us who are habitual readers read *much*, but skip *most* of just about anything we pick up, and we are not condemned for doing so.

How many of us read the supermarket tabloids, if only the headlines, and then mostly to kill time in the checkout line? I marvel at the infinite flexibility of the English language as it is manipulated by the perverse but agile imaginations of those who write and edit those tabloids! But that makes my reading no more moral or immoral than that of the woman who once stood behind me in line, trying to devour the contents of both *Star* and *Enquirer* even as she hushed her fussing child. The child was restive mainly because he was reading and responding to the candy wrappers, an activity that was at the moment neither more or less virtuous than either of our "adult" reading.

Do you honestly believe that every student in every class is morally obligated to become excited over each word in today's required reading lesson? Let's not shortchange reading with the belief that there is some magical goodness about it. Reading is good if it puts people and their ideas and feelings together—with themselves or with others. With few exceptions, if you find out where a person is coming from, you will find a motivation for reading. Find the person and you will know what makes reading worth the effort for that person.

Fact or Falsehood? Teaching in the Affective Domain Is Important Because It Will Make Students Like to Read

Wait a minute! I have not met many people who *like* to read disaster reports, obituaries of dearly loved friends, unfavorable job reviews, bank audits, or painful medical reports. But they read them nonetheless, as they should, *because they care very much.*

Many of us say we want students to like to read, and liking to read is a commendable goal. But a love a reading isn't the only area in the affective domain, nor does it explain most of our day-to-day reasons for reading.

During an interview on pesticide use, an agrichemist told me, "We say we want a natural environment, but we really don't mean that. What most of us want is a *controlled* natural environment. We like rabbits but not rats, buttercups but not thistle burrs, mushrooms but not mildew." As teachers, we say we want our students to like to read, but we really do not mean that. We really want our students to like books better than billboards, poetry rather than pornography, literature instead of license plates.

Now, *you* have to decide if the approach used by the agrichemist should be applied to reading. I suggest that *choosing* to read is more important than liking it, and choice is very circumstantial. *Liking* to read may not be important at all. Watch students fight to get hold of secret notes they think their "enemies" have written about them. Similarly, I have seen company executives turn white at the knuckles during interviews, wondering what the interviewer will say about them in print. That anxiety guarantees they will read the copy when it is finally delivered, although and there is no guarantee that they will like what they read.

There are many things that are easy to like in this world—much easier to like than to read about. Which of us liked Chaucer or, for that matter, *Chicken Little* the first time we tried to read them? I still prefer Zeffirelli's filmed version of *Romeo and Juliet* to reading Shakespeare's text alone and in silence. I have been reading—20 or 30 minutes at a time—Churchill's histories of World War II and of the English-speaking peoples, choosing to read, laboring, but hardly *liking* every detailed minute by minute of these years of working my way through all ten volumes.

From my experience writing copy for employee newsletters, I have found that people do not like to read long articles at work, but they do enjoy reading about co-workers or events relevant to their lives. An alumni newsletter that I write carries a crowded, unattractive, lined questionnaire about three inches tall, placed inconspicuously in each issue. It asks personal information of all who receive the paper. It never fails to draw hundreds of responses from people planning marriages, getting promotions, opening businesses, or seeking classmates. Readers? Yes, yes! Believing that others are readers, too? Yes. Because, like it or not, they are uniquely and personally involved? Yes. Yes!

If you have read this far, I suspect I know what you are thinking: "How will this help me on Monday morning?" Remember, I was there myself on many Monday mornings for many years.

The affective domain is so vast and complex. If you mean to work in it, you must believe in it. Try to conceptualize its vastness and complexity, then accept it all the way to its infinite ends. It is not words we read; it is joy and pain, exhilaration and despair, hate and love, wisdom and stupidity, facts and fiction, and fantasy and faith.

Keep the faith. You might think you are losing the fight; I suspect you are winning the world.

When I was a young teacher of English, I tried to take a class of ninth graders into *Julius Caesar*. Few of them could make their way unerringly into even a single line of blank verse. Most of the time, I read aloud to them, hoping that Boaz, the most terrifying roughneck in the group, was indeed asleep at his desk as he appeared to be. I would not have wanted to wake him for the world as long as even just one or two of his classmates seemed to be listening and as long as I was not for the moment in fear of my life during one of his periodic rampages. Rampages emanate in some small corner of the affective domain that I do not know how to handle very well.

Years later, long after Boaz had dropped out of school, one of the guidance counselors told me that I had been Boaz's favorite teacher.

"Get serious," I said.

"I am serious," the counselor replied. "Boaz told me you're the only one who taught him anything."

"Like what?" I roared in disbelief.

"Boaz said you taught him that not crossing a 't' is like not tying your shoes."

Now, I don't know if I ever really said that, but it's not all that bad a statement. It certainly is not a line from *Julius Caesar*. But even if it wasn't my statement to Boaz's class, I'll still be glad to take credit for it. Maybe Boaz wasn't really sleeping at his desk, after all. Maybe somewhere, in all my fevered, frustrating attempts to get through anything—sentences, "t"-crossing, lesson plans, the day—somehow, Boaz, the moment, and just the right message came together. And I was there to get credit for it, even though I hadn't even known what happened.

Now *that's* keeping faith in the affective domain.

Chapter 2

Toward a Model of Reading Attitude Acquisition

Michael C. McKenna

●◆ No teacher would deny the importance of fostering a positive attitude toward reading. Numerous factors, however, conspire to make this goal an elusive one in the case of many students. Forces outside the teacher's control (in the home and in peer groups, for example) may undermine the teacher's efforts. Pressure to focus first on cognitive growth may cause affective concerns to be addressed haphazardly or not at all, as Cramer and Castle mentioned in their introduction. Poor conceptualization of what Athey (1985) has called the "shadowy variables" of affect (p. 527) may reinforce the notion that school time is best devoted to the pursuit of reading proficiency. Unless a teacher appreciates how attitudes develop and under what conditions they can be expected to change, reading instruction will be unlikely to realize its potential for shaping attitudes in positive ways.

Attitude and the Forces that Shape It

Consider the following situations in terms of the likelihood that the child in each case will elect to read:

- A 17-year-old boy with poor reading ability receives, as a gift, a book devoted to a subject he dislikes.

- The same boy receives a note from a girl he finds attractive but whom he does not know very well.

- Upon opening his textbook after school, an inner-city minority student is chided by a friend for his interest in academics.

- A 13-year-old girl picks up an unfinished book but decides to consult the TV listings before resuming her reading.

• A girl who reads in bed each evening finds the opening chapter of a new novel disappointing. The next night she reaches again for the book, then hesitates.

In each of these cases psychological factors are at work to influence the decisions of students who have options other than reading. Such factors include self-concept, expectations of success, expectations of pleasure or utility, social and cultural pressures, and so forth. Understandably, they do much to shape an individual's overall *attitude,* which Alexander and Filler (1976) define as "a system of feelings related to reading which causes the learner to approach or avoid a reading situation" (p. 1). This overall predisposition, is slow to form and somewhat resistant to change. To shape (or reshape) it positively, a teacher's best hope of success is to address factors that can be brought to bear in classroom settings. Recent models can help us conceptualize how these factors operate to affect students' attitudes and how teachers can effectively intervene to influence them.

Models of Reading Attitude

In the case of an activity as complex as reading, it is hardly surprising that corresponding psychological models tend to be complex. Because in reading nearly all model building to date has been undertaken by cognitive psychologists interested in the reading process, intriguing models of reading have emerged that have nothing to say about affective factors (see, for example, Just & Carpenter, 1987; Rayner & Pollatsek, 1989; see also Stanovich, 1991). A few theorists, however, have attempted to incorporate affective factors into useful models with highly practical implications for teaching.

The Mathewson Model

Mathewson (1994) has proposed a model in which affective factors interact with cognitive processes during reading. This model represents an extension of an earlier version (Mathewson, 1985) and makes a considerable contribution to the theory of attitude in reading. Mathewson's chief concern is with the role of attitude as a causal agent during the act of reading and during the period when one learns to read. His model therefore has less to say about how attitude is affected by other factors and how it develops over time. It is nevertheless an excellent starting point in the construction of such a model.

The Mathewson model (see Figure 1) represents attitude as one of three principal factors influencing one's intention to read (or keep reading);

Figure 1
The Mathewson Model

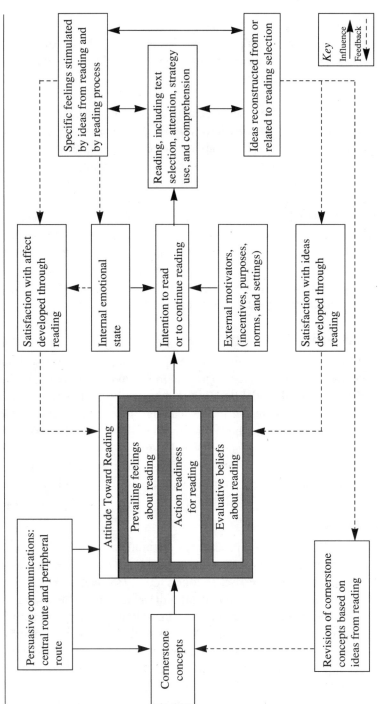

From G.C. Mathewson, "Model of Attitude Influence upon Reading and Learning to Read" (p. 1149). In R.B. Ruddell, M.R. Ruddell, & H. Singer (Eds.), *Theoretical Models and*

the others are external motivators and one's emotional state. These causal relationships are indicated by arrows. Of primary concern in developing a model of attitude acquisition, however, are the factors theorized as causally linked to attitude in such a way that attitude is an effect rather than a cause (denoted by arrows leading *to* the attitude box). Mathewson has postulated two major factors (solid arrows) and two minor ones (broken arrows). The latter represent feedback (cognitive and affective) from individual reading experiences. The former are *cornerstone concepts*, which include personal values, goals, and self-concepts, and *persuasive communications*, which can reach the reader through a central route (for example, when a teacher touts reading) or peripherally (when reading materials are attractively formatted, for instance).

An important aspect of Mathewson's model is its three-component definition of attitude. It includes not only feelings about reading but action readiness for reading and evaluative beliefs about reading. Mathewson acknowledges that psychologists are not of one mind on this point: some prefer a more limited definition in which attitude is conceptualized primarily in terms of emotion, which was the view suggested by Alexander and Filler (1976), cited earlier. In addition, this limited definition has an important advantage in constructing a model of reading attitude *acquisition*. By separating beliefs about reading from attitude toward reading, a model can postulate a causal relationship between the two, a relationship that is now well established, but which the Mathewson model does not articulate.

Another important aspect of the Mathewson model must be reconsidered as well: the role proposed for subjective "norms," or the beliefs and expectations held by significant others in the reader's environment. Mathewson envisions these as influencing one's intention to read in a given situation. As an example, he suggests that "junior high school students in a library may not read because they perceive that conversation is expected by their reference group. In this case, the students are attending to a peer subjective norm rather than the one advocated by librarians" (1994, p. 1136). There is no question that norms influence behavior in this way. What the Mathewson model avoids, however, is the notion that such normative beliefs can also have a direct influence on attitude. Such an influence has been suggested by other theorists and represents a central consideration in any model of attitude acquisition.

The Ruddell–Speaker Model

Ruddell and Speaker (1985) proposed a view somewhat different from that of Mathewson though comparable in important ways. One difference is the specificity devoted by Ruddell and Speaker to word-recognition subprocesses in an effort to provide a truly comprehensive model of reading.

The Ruddell–Speaker model comprises four major components that interact during reading. The *reader environment* component involves the immediate context of the reading act, including features of the text being read, "conversational" aspects (such as the varying roles of the reader and the writer), and instructional factors that may influence a given reading situation (see also Ruddell & Unrau, 1994). The *knowledge utilization and control* component includes both the reader's representation of a text's meaning and the "goals and expectation, plan of action, and ability to monitor and evaluate" the reading process (p. 751). This component involves not only the cognitive and metacognitive dimensions of a reader's thinking but the "affective state" as well. This element accounts for "the reader's interests, attitudes, and values which determine goals and objectives for the reading of a passage" (p. 756). Ruddell and Speaker acknowledge that a reader's initial expectations will influence both affect and comprehension as those expectations are either confirmed or refuted during reading:

> The affective state serves to establish the reader's goal direction and expectations for content, processing time, and product. Highly interesting text or text that has been judged as important to the reader's goal will receive maximum processing and persistence. With less interesting text or text judged to be of little importance, the reader will be less persistent, and limited processing will occur (p. 757).

Therefore, as reading proceeds, a reader's goals and expectations (a part of the affective state) interact both with the cognitive strategies the reader uses and with feedback from metacognitive strategies used to "monitor the product of reading and evaluate it against the goals and time expectations set in the affective state" (p. 759).

The *declarative and procedural knowledge* component includes decoding, language ability, and general knowledge. Finally, the *reader product* component comprises a variety of changes brought about by a specific incidence of reading. Some of these changes (for example, in comprehension and new knowledge) are largely cognitive in nature, but Ruddell and Speaker also include changes to the affective state.

Figure 2 illustrates the model's interactive dimensions, denoted by connecting lines. Because the affective state connects with virtually all other dimensions of the model, it is easy to see the importance that Ruddell and Speaker ascribe to it. Commenting on interactive changes in the affective state, Ruddell and Speaker offer the following description:

Figure 2
The Ruddell–Speaker Model

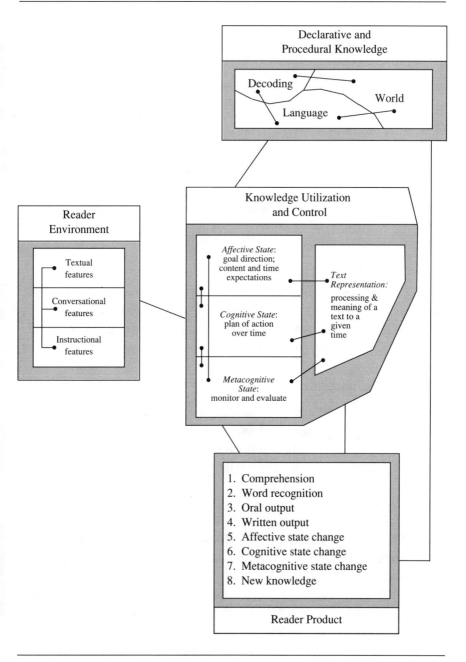

From R.B. Ruddell & R.B. Speaker, Jr., "The Interactive Reading Process: A Model" (p. 752). In H. Singer & R.B. Ruddell (Eds.), *Theoretical Models and Processes of Reading*, 3rd ed., 1985. Reprinted by permission of the International Reading Association.

> In the affective state, the reader sets goal direction, expectations for a product, and expectations for the time needed to create the product. These expectations are based on the text to be read, its situational context in the reader environment, and the declarative and procedural knowledge already activated and located in the text representation. The affective state can be modified during the reading process based on the metacognitive evaluation of the fit between the goals and expectations of the affective state and the product of the text representation. If the overriding feature of the environment is instructional, say the reading is assigned, the affective state will be based on external rather than internal expectations. Completing the assignment within the allotted time becomes the goal. If the environment is not instructional, say the reader has selected a highly interesting text for pleasure reading, the affective state will be based on internal expectations using knowledge from the declarative and procedural knowledge component (p. 774).

The Ruddell–Speaker model, like the Mathewson model, accounts for slow changes in attitude toward reading partly through the notion that feedback is cumulative from each individual act of reading to overall attitude toward reading. Precisely how this process works, however, is not well detailed.

Extending the Models

Both models take immense strides toward describing the role of affective factors in reading. Certainly they go far beyond the tendency of cognitively oriented models to represent affective factors "as a 'box,'" in Athey's (1985) words, with "little elaboration or explication" (p. 527). In addition, both models add unique features to our conceptualization of the role of affective factors. The Mathewson model, for example, adds the notion of one's intention to read and the importance of internal and external factors in this intention. The Ruddell–Speaker model provides for the metacognitive monitoring of a reader's expectations and its effect on the affective state.

At the same time, however, because both models focus on an individual act of reading, they are limited in their power to explain the affective impact of environmental factors that transcend the immediate reading context. The Mathewson model comes nearer by acknowledging, for example, the role of personal values, goals, and self-concept. As stated earlier, however, it fails to account for additional factors that clearly influence long-term, cumulative changes in attitude.

General Models of Attitude Acquisition

One of the most influential attempts to produce a general model of how attitudes are acquired was that of Fishbein and Ajzen (1975; Ajzen, 1989; Ajzen & Fishbein, 1980). Based on their extensive review of theory, they began with the following definition of *attitude*: *"a learned predisposition to respond in a consistently favorable or unfavorable manner with respect to a given object"* (Fishbein & Ajzen, 1975, p. 6). They acknowledge that this definition entails certain ambiguities, such as whether the "predisposition" is to be considered general or specific.

Like Mathewson (1985), Fishbein and Ajzen trace the concept of attitude to its 18th-century roots. During that era, three psychological components of attitude were postulated: affect (emotion), cognition (thought), and conation (desire). Fishbein and Ajzen translated these constructs into more workable modern counterparts. Attitudes involve "affective evaluations," cognition is reflected in an individual's system of beliefs about the object in question (for our purposes, reading), and conation is represented in terms of "behavioral intentions." These concepts are causally linked in a general depiction of how attitudes are acquired and how they influence behavior.

Figure 3 presents the Fishbein–Ajzen model. Causation proceeds in general from beliefs to attitudes to intentions to behaviors. Tracing the model from left to right, we first see that two important kinds of beliefs are recognized: those about the consequences of a given behavior and those "of a normative nature, that is, beliefs that certain referents think the person should or should not perform the behavior in question" (Fishbein & Ajzen, 1975, p. 16). The latter kind of belief is predicted to have little if any effect on attitude toward a behavior (the position taken by the Mathewson model), while beliefs about the consequences of the behavior (and whether the individual evaluates them as favorable or unfavorable) are seen as the primary determiner of attitude. Fishbein and Ajzen see normative beliefs as helping to shape, along with attitude, one's intention to engage in the behavior. Note the feedback pathway (denoted by the dotted line at the base of the diagram), indicating that every occurrence of a given behavior will influence an individual's belief structure. In this way, an individual's set of beliefs is seen to be strengthened or modified as a result of each incidence of engaging in a particular behavior. Strengthened or altered beliefs about the consequences of engaging in the behavior will consequently lead to small changes in one's attitude toward that behavior.

Figure 3
The Fishbein–Ajzen Model

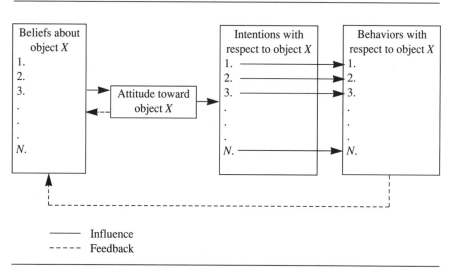

────── Influence
- - - - - Feedback

Let's apply this general model to reading. Suppose a third grade teacher asks students to read a chapter of their social studies text at home. Knowledge of this teacher's expectation enters the students' set of normative beliefs and helps shape their subjective appraisal of outside influences on the possibility of actually reading the chapter. Joe, a poor reader, brings to the situation a set of beliefs about what will occur if he attempts the assignment. Such beliefs may include an expectation of frustration, fatigue, and the fact that he will be unable to engage in more desirable actions (watching TV or playing with friends, perhaps) during the attempt. His attitude has been largely shaped by previous experiences and the beliefs that they have engendered. These beliefs, together with his teacher's expectations, will determine his intent to read the chapter. Because in Joe's case the beliefs do not uniformly support a positive intention, his eventual decision will be hard to predict and will involve his own resolution of the conflict. If he elects to read, the experience will alter or strengthen his pre-existing beliefs. A successful experience may improve his attitude slightly; another instance of frustration and failure will reinforce his already negative outlook.

If beliefs are causally related to the development of attitude, it is important to understand how we can influence them. Fishbein and Ajzen identify three basic types of beliefs, which they classify according to their origins. *Descriptive* beliefs come from direct personal observation ("This book is boring"). *Inferential* beliefs involve logical conclusions based on existing beliefs ("Because this book is boring, others may be"). *Informational* beliefs are acquired from outside sources that an individual regards as significant ("My friends say books are boring"). Each type of belief is associated with a level of strength, or "salience," ranging from those that are firmly held to those that are tentative and weak.

According to Fishbein and Ajzen, attitude can be improved by changing an individual's belief structure. A teacher interested in fostering a positive attitude toward reading should first determine a student's salient beliefs by asking the student to rate various statements about reading (see, for example, McKenna & Kear, 1990) or by eliciting completions of open-ended comments, such as, "Reading is...," Once key beliefs are known to the teacher, three avenues to change are available. One is to weaken or eliminate existing beliefs by providing contrary evidence. A child who believes reading is boring might be exposed to books carefully selected on the basis of high interest. Another method is to introduce new beliefs. A student raised on a steady diet of literature might profit from experiencing how reading can also be useful in solving problems and answering questions. Finally, perhaps the most difficult way beliefs can be altered is by changing how a student evaluates an object's attributes. For example, a student may come to associate reading with work—more work than certain competing alternatives such as watching TV. If this student were to alter the personal value of work and reach a judgment that it is sometimes desirable, attitude toward reading would improve.

Limitations of the Fishbein–Ajzen Model

As useful as these predictions are, they are based on an overly narrow view of how attitudes develop and change. Fishbein and Ajzen maintain what is essentially an information-processing view of attitude acquisition. Their model indicates that attitude is the result of beliefs alone and that beliefs in turn depend on information available to the individual.

Cothern and Collins (1992) have called attention to Liska's revision of the model and its implication for reading attitude development. Liska (1984) has argued that the original Fishbein–Ajzen model is too simplistic. The lock-step causal chain from beliefs to attitude to intentions to behaviors (see Figure 3) does not allow for other causal relationships, which research now clearly indicates exist. Figure 4 presents Liska's revision of the Fishbein–Ajzen model. The revised version is based on two sets

Figure 4
Liska's Revision of the Fishbein–Ajzen Model

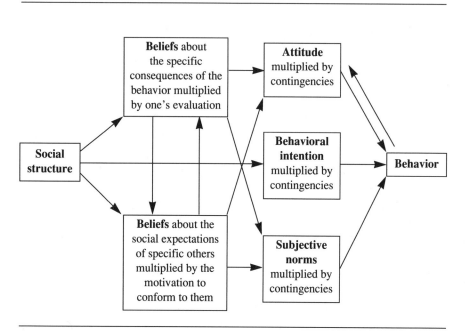

From A.E. Liska, "A Critical Examination of the Causal Structural of the Fishbein–Ajzen Attitude-Behavior Model" in *Social Psychology Quarterly*, *47*, 61–74. Copyright 1984. Reprinted by permission of the publisher and the author.

of considerations: the first involves how the four basic components of the original model are related; the second involves the influence of other variables.

Liska reaches four key conclusions regarding how beliefs, attitudes, intentions, and behaviors are causally linked. First, he suggests that intentions are not enough to account for many behaviors, especially where skill and social interaction are needed. It is easy to see that certain skill deficits and the embarrassment their exposure might bring could thwart the best-intentioned reader (note the central horizontal arrow indicating that an individual's intentions are determined by elements in the social structure). Second, Liska cites research evidence that attitude affects behavior directly, without being mediated through intentions, which are often vaguely formed and unstable (note the arrow from attitude to behavior). Third, he argues that findings also indicate that attitude does not serve as a mediator between beliefs and intentions (note the absence of an arrow connecting attitude and intentions). Fourth, he contends that behavior does not directly affect beliefs in the causal loop suggested by Fishbein and Ajzen (see Figure 3). Rather, Liska views the influence of behavior on attitude as a direct one—and the only causal relationship that begins with behavior (note the arrow from behavior to attitude).

Regarding additional variables, Liska views the three-way classification of Fishbein and Ajzen as useful. They characterized these as independent variables, variables presenting important contingencies, and background variables. Liska, however, disputes how certain variables are classified in this scheme. For example, the Fishbein–Ajzen model indicates that normative beliefs act independently to influence intentions. Research evidence, on the other hand, suggests that such beliefs and beliefs about the behavior itself are causally linked (note the two vertical arrows in Figure 4). Moreover, research also indicates that attitude, intentions, and subjective norms are all contingent on other variables. Liska's revised model accounts for these contingencies while the original model does not. Finally, Fishbein and Ajzen see social structure as a background variable: its effects on behavior are seen only after influencing beliefs, then attitude, and then intentions. Liska suggests that social structure affects intentions directly, as noted earlier.

What does Liska's revised model say about the development of reading attitude? As Figure 4 indicates, three factors affect attitude. As with the original Fishbein–Ajzen model, one of these factors is the reader's beliefs about the act of reading and its outcomes. Thus, our conclusions discussed earlier about influencing these beliefs are essentially unaltered by the revision. A second factor influencing attitude is the act of reading itself. Since the route is more direct than that of the original version, the new model underscores the importance of providing children with numerous reading experiences that are successful, on the one hand, and interesting or useful on the other. The third factor is the reader's beliefs about the social expectations of others and the motivation to conform to them. This is a complex factor that would appear to allow many opportunities for successful intervention by teachers. For example, cooperative learning settings might exert positive peer expectations while parental involvement programs might create beneficial expectations at home.

A Proposed New Model

Can these various models be integrated into one coherent model of reading attitude acquisition that accounts for the influence of specific incidents of reading? Careful inspection of Liska's revision of the Fishbein–Ajzen model, the Mathewson model, and the model developed by Ruddell and Speaker readily indicates that the three cannot be simply patched together into a consistent whole because their features overlap greatly. Combining them into one coherent model requires several conclusions about where the overlapping occurs. First, it seems clear that Ruddell and Speaker's idea of the affective state is largely incorporated into the concepts of subjective norms, intention to read, and attitude. Second, the Liska revision is at odds with the Mathewson model in terms of accounting for the role of subjective norms. Third, Ruddell and Speaker's idea of reader product can be inferred from the cumulative interaction of various model components (which can be indicated by arrows passing in both directions). Finally, Ruddell and Speaker's notion of reader environment is partially comparable to Liska's idea of social structure and can be accounted for adequately in terms of factors on which the intent to read is contingent.

Figure 5 presents an integrated model based on these conclusions. Liska's revision is preserved largely intact, though with two exceptions. First, reading-related contingencies are suggested. Second, Liska appears to have gone too far in eliminating all feedback from behavior to beliefs. This loop from the original Fishbein–Ajzen model has been restored. Overall, however, Liska's revision of the general Fishbein–Ajzen model moves toward specifying how affective factors interact during reading. The Mathewson and Ruddell–Speaker models indicate that interactions take place, but Liska adds much-needed specifics.

The proposed model preserves Mathewson's original notion (1985) of a decision to read, which is a consequence of subjective norms, intent, and attitude—all three of which are conditioned by contingencies. Because reading is, usually, an ongoing process rather than a discrete act, the initial decision becomes a decision to continue reading once the process begins. Feedback from the metacognitive state, together with subjective norms, intent, and attitude, will determine at each moment whether the process will continue.

Metacognitive control (in terms of comprehension monitoring) is also seen as central to the development of text representation and to consideration of whether that representation has satisfied the reader's purpose. In view of increasing evidence that fluent reading largely entails automatic decoding (Rayner & Pollatsek, 1989; Stanovich, 1991), metacognitive oversight of decoding is not built into the model as a normal function. Liska's feedback from behavior to attitude (see Figure 4) is reflected here

Figure 5
Proposed Model of Reading Attitude Acquisition

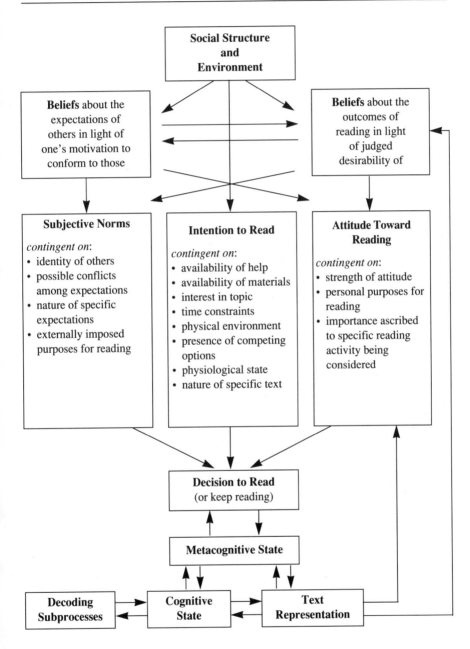

in the arrow leading from the metacognitive state to attitude. The influence of attitude, however, is directed at the decision to read or continue reading.

Support for the Model

Each arrow of Figure 5 postulates a causal relationship. Many such relationships have been discussed in a context broader than reading (Ajzen & Fishbein, 1980; Fishbein & Ajzen, 1975; Liska, 1984), while several that involve reading subprocesses have also been examined in some detail (Just & Carpenter, 1987; Rayner & Pollatsek, 1989; Stanovich, 1991). The goal here is to examine existing support for changes in reading attitude indicated by the model. This goal requires examination of beliefs about subjective norms, beliefs about the outcomes of reading, and each specific act of engaging in reading—all of which affect attitude, as shown by arrows in the model.

Beliefs About Subjective Norms

The influence of culture, home, peer group, and other environmental factors leads to beliefs about how much reading is valued by significant others. A separate question involves how strongly an individual feels compelled to conform to these values. It is easy to imagine a reader surrounded by positive environmental forces who nevertheless chooses to discount them, or another reader who, by reading, defies strong values held by peers or parents.

Sex differences. An important source of influence on normative expectations is a reader's sex. Environments may, for various reasons, exert different expectations about the reading behavior of boys and girls. Children's perceptions of these expectations may well facilitate or hinder attitude development. In the United States, evidence abounds that girls tend to harbor more positive attitudes toward reading than do boys (Anderson, Tollefson, & Gilbert, 1985; Ross & Fletcher, 1989; Shapiro, 1980; Smith, 1990; Stevenson & Newman, 1986; Wallbrown, Levine, & Engin, 1981). Moreover, the observed tendency of attitudes to be more positive in classrooms with male teachers (Shapiro, 1980) would seem to support the notion of a subjective norm at work. The fact that a similar pattern of females having more positive attitudes than males has been observed in other cultures, such as Ireland (Greaney & Hegarty, 1987) and Japan (Ishikawa, 1985), may simply indicate a value shared cross-culturally.

It may, however, be an oversimplification to conclude that children come to believe at an early age that reading is an activity more feminine than masculine in character. The pattern of girl dominance may also be related to achievement. Evidence that girls establish and sustain an early advantage in reading ability (Mullis, Campbell, & Farstrup, 1993) suggests that sex-based differences in attitude may derive from differences in ability. Certainly the relationship of ability to attitude is well documented (Anderson, Tollefson, & Gilbert, 1985; Lipsky, 1983; Martin, 1984; Richards & Bear, 1986; Swanson, 1982a; Walberg & Tsai, 1985). If sex-based advantages in reading ability do in fact lead to better attitudes among girls, the proposed model would account for that result by means of a different channel: the effect of beliefs about the outcomes of reading. That is, because girls are more likely to believe reading will be a successful experience, their attitudes are naturally better.

It is important to realize that these two hypotheses are not mutually exclusive. It may well be that societal pressures lead to the quicker emergence of literate behavior in girls (see Johnson, 1973), which in turn affects attitude. Thus, attitude may grow differentially stronger among girls both because of societal values *and* because these values lead to an early edge in ability.

Other environmental factors. The proposed model suggests that subjective norms are complex and that an individual's set of normative beliefs may include many that are unconnected to sex differences. Available evidence generally supports this view. Ross and Fletcher (1989) reported significant differences among students in grades three to five depending on whether they lived in a university town, the inner city, or a rural setting. (Mean attitude scores were successively lower in this order.) Morrow (1983) found that kindergartners had already reached relatively well-formed attitudes even before schooling could possibly have had much of an effect. Environmental correlates included the frequency of being read to at home and the extent to which parents modeled reading as a leisure activity. Swanson (1982b) reported a positive correlation coefficient between reading attitude and socioeconomic status, though the relationship may be subordinate to sex differences. Saracho and Dayton (1991) reported significant differences in attitude according to ethnic group membership. These relatively recent studies are indicative of the range of environmental pressures that affect reading attitude acquisition.

Beliefs About the Outcomes of Reading

The proposed model suggests that attitude is influenced by beliefs about what will happen if an individual engages in reading. Some of these beliefs have environmental origins; others come from actual reading experiences. Of particular importance is the latter relationship (indicated in Figure 5 by the arrow leading from the metacognitive state to beliefs about reading outcomes). This recursive, cumulative process suggests that the recurrence of dissatisfying results will lead to successively worsened attitudes. Conversely, a succession of positive experiences may result in more positive attitudes, but only if environmental factors are positive. As children grow older, more and more leisure alternatives are open to them, and reading must compete with these. Thus, the attitude of even the successful reader may be subject to decline (Anderson, Tollefson, & Gilbert, 1985; Martin, 1984). In any event, the model predicts a general worsening of reading attitude with age for readers with problems. Evidence generally confirms this developmental trend (Ishikawa, 1985; Ross & Fletcher, 1989; Shapiro, 1980). Some studies have shown no significant declines between some grade levels (Wallbrown, Levine, & Engin, 1981) and even significant increases at certain grade levels (Parker & Paradis, 1986).

Contrary evidence may be due to small samples in which other variables, such as instructional practices, counteract the effects of students' beliefs about their abilities. It is clear that certain practices can be effective in halting or reversing the decline. Such a result is generally predictable from the model, and a highly productive line of research entails identifying techniques that tend to have positive effects on attitude. Promising methods include reading aloud to students (see, for example, Herrold, Stanchfield, & Serabian, 1989), using high-quality literature (Morrow, 1983), avoiding denigrating reading-group placement (Wallbrown, Brown, & Engin, 1978), providing metacognitive training (Payne & Manning, 1992), openly discussing students' beliefs (Hudley, 1992), stressing links between literature and students' lives (Guzzetti, 1990), and using questions to activate prior knowledge (Jagacinski & Nicholls, 1987).

Finally, what might the model predict for prereaders? Because they cannot yet read themselves, their attitudes toward reading are limited to essentially vicarious experiences in which others read aloud to them. Since reading failure has not yet begun to exert a cumulative negative impact, it is reasonable to hypothesize that attitudes will improve in an environment where reading is modeled by adults and where interesting books are often read aloud. These findings were in fact among those of a study by Saracho and Dayton (1991). The fact that many beginning readers despite their lack of proficiency harbor positive attitudes has been attributed by Paris (1991) to "optimism, poor self-evaluation, or naiveté" (p. 681). This may be another way of saying that the effects of failure have not yet begun to accumulate. Even among these children, however, positive attitude scores are far from universal (McKenna & Kear, 1990), so that assessment by means of rating scales is apt to be both useful and discriminating.

Direct Effect of Reading Experiences

The proposed model suggests two ways in which attitude may be influenced by a specific reading experience: one indirect and the other direct. In the indirect method, a reading encounter affects the individual's beliefs about the probable outcomes of reading. The altered beliefs then lead to alterations in attitude. The direct route involves immediate impact on attitude without the cognitive mediation of belief change. Liska (1984) summarizes evidence for such a link, but it is not specific to reading. Currently, this causal link in the proposed model relies on this general evidence for support.

Indirect Effects on Reading Attitudes

So far we have discussed only the three direct factors that are indicated by the model, denoted by the arrows leading to attitude from (1) beliefs about the expectations of others, (2) beliefs about the outcomes of reading, and (3) individual reading experiences. Because each of these proximate causes is the result of more remote causes, the proposed model also predicts that a teacher can influence attitude positively in indirect ways. For example, a teacher who establishes a library corner in the classroom and provides students with opportunities to use it is altering the environment favorably (see the topmost box in Figure 5). The model suggests that such a change will not *directly* affect attitude. However, it does predict that the improved availability of books will influence children's intentions to read, which may lead to more decisions to read, which should ultimately influence attitude. Morrow (1985) summarizes studies that support this prediction.

Another example of an indirect route to attitude improvement involves the use of tangible incentives. The prospect of rewards transforms the student's environment and can have a direct impact on intentions, which are contingent on the appeal of other behavioral options. A potential reward for reading serves to reduce the attractiveness of competing options and increase the probability that a student will decide to read. The reading experience itself is then relied on to influence attitude, both directly and by its effect on a student's beliefs about the outcomes of reading. Little evidence exists concerning the efficacy of incentive programs in changing reading attitudes. There is little doubt, however, that they can change behavior and induce students to read. Whether reading brought about in this manner will strengthen attitudes depends, as with all incidents of reading, on whether the outcome has been a successful one in terms of decoding and comprehension and on whether the experience has proved interesting or useful to the student. The model predicts that incentives will accomplish the goal of improved attitude only when the materials read meet these requirements. (See also Chapter 7 for a complete discussion of intrinsic and extrinsic motivation.)

Implications for Teachers

What advice does the proposed model offer teachers? While each of the following suggestions for teachers to use in fostering positive attitudes derives from the model, some are more thoroughly validated than others, and some may seem more intuitive than others. (See also Chapters 5 and 14 on the attitudes and role of teachers.)

1. *Assess students' beliefs about reading.* Use projective techniques, rating scales, or both to garner useful information about how students regard reading. Rating scales that yield composite scores (see, for example, McKenna & Kear, 1990) should be inspected for responses to particular items so that the nature of the beliefs underlying each child's attitude can be better appreciated.

2. *Work to instill positive beliefs.* Challenge the negative beliefs of individual students by discussing them privately. For all students, convey the positive value of reading by using it as a reward, by providing books as gifts where feasible, and by implementing student publishing and sharing.

3. *Create an environment that promotes reading.* A print-rich classroom abounding with literacy opportunities can do much to overcome the negative or neutral environments that surround many students outside school.

4. *Plan a varied program.* Expose students to a variety of genres and topics. Help them realize early that reading can serve many purposes. Employ quality literature, but avoid the use of fiction only—a shortcoming of many literature-based programs (Hiebert & Fisher, 1990).

5. *Ensure early success.* Preempt the cumulative effects of reading failure by making certain each student comes to a quick grasp of the alphabetic principle. Where difficulties persist, early

intervention programs should be made available, such as Reading Recovery (see Pinnell, Fried, & Estice, 1990) and restructured compensatory education programs of established effectiveness (for example, see Hiebert et al., 1992).

6. *Strive to show students the relevance of reading.* Relate the actions, problems, and circumstances of characters to students' own lives. Endeavor to show them links, and encourage them to bridge from books to the decisions they face. Be on the lookout for nonfiction sources that can help answer real-life questions, and be prepared to recommend them wherever appropriate.

7. *Provide positive adult models.* Expose students to adults who show that reading is useful, relaxing, or fun. Teachers can provide one kind of model, but others should be sought. Posters of sports and entertainment figures engaged in reading, for example, can convey subtle cultural messages.

8. *Provide positive student models.* Challenge negative culturally normative beliefs by providing counter examples. Comments from respected peers can help, as can input from older students during cross-age tutoring or sharing sessions. Cooperative learning, in which good and poor readers collaborate to achieve common goals, provides another potential source of positive peer modeling.

9. *Seek parent involvement.* Effect positive change in the home environment by working with parents. Counsel them on read-aloud techniques, book selection, and the importance of serving as models. Look for ways to reach parents of preschoolers through community agencies, volunteer groups, preschools, and daycare centers. Early belief formation is critical.

10. *Read aloud to students.* The effectiveness of this perennial suggestion is well recognized (Anderson et al., 1985) but haphazardly followed. Be systematic in developing a read-aloud program, and be sure to include a variety of materials on many topics (see Chapter 15 in this work).

11. *Facilitate learning through text.* The cumulative impact of reading failure on attitude is never more threatening than in content areas. By the middle and secondary grades, poorer readers rank the prospect of reading content materials lower

....

than any other topic (McKenna, 1986). Do more than assign textbook reading. Assist students by properly introducing materials to read and by providing content literacy guides that focus thinking and encourage active engagement (McKenna & Robinson, 1993; Wood, Lapp, & Flood, 1992).

12. *Recommend books on the basis of student opinion rather than yours alone.* Subjective norms are often reflected in children's choices (see Carter & Harris, 1981).

References

Ajzen, I. (1989). Attitude structure and behavior. In A.R. Pratkanis, S.J. Brecker, & A.G. Greenwald (Eds.), *Attitude structure and function* (pp. 241–274). Hillsdale, NJ: Erlbaum.

Ajzen, I., & Fishbein, M. (1980). *Understanding attitudes and predicting social behavior.* Englewood Cliffs, NJ: Prentice Hall.

Alexander, J.E., & Filler, R.C. (1976). *Attitudes and reading.* Newark, DE: International Reading Association.

Anderson, M.A., Tollefson, N.A., & Gilbert, E.C. (1985). Giftedness and reading: A cross-sectional view of differences in reading attitudes and behaviors. *Gifted Child Quarterly, 29,* 186–189.

Anderson, R.C., Hiebert, E.H., Scott, J.A., & Wilkinson, I.A.G. (1985). *Becoming a nation of readers: The report of the Commission on Reading.* Washington, DC: U.S. Department of Education.

Athey, I. (1985). Reading research in the affective domain. In H. Singer & R.B. Ruddell (Eds.), *Theoretical models and processes of reading* (3rd ed., pp. 527–557). Newark, DE: International Reading Association.

Carter, B., & Harris, K. (1981). The children and the critics: How do their book selections compare? *School Library Media Quarterly, 10,* 54–58.

Cothern, N.B., & Collins, M.D. (1992). An exploration: Attitude acquisition and reading instruction. *Reading Research and Instruction, 31*(2), 84–97.

Fishbein, M., & Ajzen, I. (1975). *Belief, attitude, intention, and behavior: An introduction to theory and research.* Reading, MA: Addison-Wesley.

Greaney, V., & Hegarty, M. (1987). Correlates of leisure-time reading. *Journal of Research in Reading, 10,* 3–20.

Guzzetti, B.J. (1990). Enhancing comprehension through trade books in high school English classes. *Journal of Reading, 33,* 411–413.

Herrold, W.G., Jr., Stanchfield, J., & Serabian, A.J. (1989). Comparison of the effect of a middle school, literature-based listening program on male and female attitudes toward reading. *Educational Research Quarterly, 13*(4), 43–46.

Hiebert, E.H., Colt, J.M., Catto, S.L., & Gury, E.C. (1992). Reading and writing of first-grade students in a restructured Chapter 1 program. *American Educational Research Journal, 29,* 545–572.

Hiebert, E.H., & Fisher, C.W. (1990). Whole language: Three themes for the future. *Educational Leadership, 47*(6), 62–64.

Hudley, C.A. (1992). Using role models to improve the reading attitudes of ethnic minority high school girls. *Journal of Reading, 36*, 182–188.

Ishikawa, K. (1985). Developmental study of school children's attitudes toward reading. *The Science of Reading, 29*, 89–98.

Jagacinski, C., & Nicholls, J. (1987). Confidence and affect in task involvement and ego involvement: The impact of social comparison information. *Journal of Educational Psychology, 79*, 107–114.

Johnson, D.D. (1973). Sex differences in reading across cultures. *Reading Research Quarterly, 9*, 67–86.

Just, M.A., & Carpenter, P.A. (1987). *The psychology of reading and language comprehension.* Boston, MA: Allyn & Bacon.

Lipsky, J.A. (1983). A picture-story technique to uncover covert attitudes associated with reading failure. *Reading Psychology, 4*, 151–155.

Liska, A.E. (1984). A critical examination of the causal structure of the Fishbein/Ajzen attitude-behavior model. *Social Psychology Quarterly, 47*, 61–74.

Martin, C.E. (1984). Why some gifted children do not like to read. *Roeper Review, 7*, 72–75.

Mathewson, G.C. (1985). Toward a comprehensive model of affect in the reading process. In H. Singer & R.B. Ruddell (Eds.), *Theoretical models and processes of reading* (3rd ed., pp. 841–856). Newark, DE: International Reading Association.

Mathewson, G.C. (1994). Model of attitude influence upon reading and learning to read. In R.B. Ruddell, M.R. Ruddell, & H. Singer (Eds.), *Theoretical models and processes of reading* (4th ed., pp. 1131–1161). Newark, DE: International Reading Association.

McKenna, M.C. (1986). Reading interests of remedial secondary school students. *Journal of Reading, 29*, 346–351.

McKenna, M.C., & Kear, D.J. (1990). Measuring attitude toward reading: A new tool for teachers. *The Reading Teacher, 43*, 626–639.

McKenna, M.C., & Robinson, R.D. (1993). *Teaching through text: A content literacy approach to content area reading.* White Plains, NY: Longman.

Morrow, L.M. (1983). Home and school correlates of early interest in literature. *Journal of Educational Research, 76*, 221–230.

Morrow, L.M. (1985). Developing young voluntary readers: The home–the child–the school. *Reading Research and Instruction, 25*, 1–8.

Mullis, I.V.S., Campbell, J.R., & Farstrup, A.E. (1993). *NAEP 1992: Reading report card for the nation and the states.* Washington, DC: U.S. Department of Education.

Paris, S.G. (1991). Portfolio assessment for young readers. *The Reading Teacher, 44*, 680–682.

Parker, A., & Paradis, E. (1986). Attitude development toward reading in grades one through six. *Journal of Educational Research, 79*, 313–315.

Payne, B.D., & Manning, B.H. (1992). Basal reading instruction: Effects of comprehension monitoring training on reading comprehension, strategy use and attitude. *Reading Research and Instruction, 32*, 29–38.

Pinnell, G.S., Fried, M.D., & Estice, R.M. (1990). Reading Recovery: Learning how to make a difference. *The Reading Teacher, 43*, 282–295.

Rayner, K., & Pollatsek, A. (1989). *The psychology of reading.* Englewood Cliffs, NJ: Prentice Hall.

Richards, H.C., & Bear, G.G. (1986, April). *Attitudes toward school subjects of academically unpredictable elementary school children.* Paper presented at the meeting of the American Educational Research Association, San Francisco, CA.

Ross, E.P., & Fletcher, R.K. (1989). Responses to children's literature by environment, grade level, and sex. *Reading Instruction Journal, 32*(2), 22–28.

Ruddell, R.B., & Speaker, R. (1985). The interactive reading process: A model. In H. Singer & R.B. Ruddell (Eds.), *Theoretical models and processes of reading* (3rd ed., pp. 751–793). Newark, DE: International Reading Association.

Ruddell, R.B., & Unrau, N.J. (1994). Reading as a meaning construction process: The reader, the text, and the teacher. In R.B. Ruddell, M.R. Ruddell, & H. Singer (Eds.), *Theoretical models and processes of reading* (4th ed., pp. 996–1056). Newark, DE: International Reading Association.

Saracho, O.N., & Dayton, C.M. (1991). Age-related changes in reading attitudes of young children: A cross-cultural study. *Journal of Research in Reading, 14*, 33–45.

Shapiro, J.E. (1980). Primary children's attitudes toward reading in male and female teachers' classrooms: An exploratory study. *Journal of Reading Behavior, 12*, 255–257.

Smith, M.C. (1990). A longitudinal investigation of reading attitude development from childhood to adulthood. *Journal of Educational Research, 83*, 215–219.

Stanovich, K.E. (1991). Word recognition: Changing perspectives. In R. Barr, M.L. Kamil, P.B. Mosenthal, & P.D. Pearson (Eds.), *Handbook of reading research::* Volume II (pp. 418–452). White Plains, NY: Longman.

Stevenson, H.W., & Newman, R.S. (1986). Long-term prediction of achievement and attitudes in mathematics and reading. *Child Development, 57*, 646–657.

Swanson, B.B. (1982a). The relationship between attitude toward reading and reading achievement. *Educational and Psychological Measurement, 42*, 1303–1304.

Swanson, B.B. (1982b). The relationship of first graders' reading attitudes to sex and social class. *Reading World, 22*, 41–47.

Walberg, H.J., & Tsai, S.L. (1985). Correlates of reading achievement and attitude: A national assessment study. *Journal of Educational Research, 78*, 159–167.

Wallbrown, F.H., Brown, D.H., & Engin, A.W. (1978). A factor analysis of reading attitudes along with measures of reading achievement and scholastic aptitude. *Psychology in the Schools, 15*, 160–165.

Wallbrown, F.H., Levine, M.A., & Engin, A.W. (1981). Sex differences in reading attitudes. *Reading Improvement, 18*, 226–234.

Wood, K.D., Lapp, D., & Flood, J. (1992). *Guiding readers through text: A review of study guides.* Newark, DE: International Reading Association.

Chapter 3

The Insatiable Appetite

Victor Nell

> It seems incredible, the ease with which we sink through books quite
> out of sight, pass clamorous pages into soundless dreams (Gass,
> 1972, p. 27).

> We are not now in possession of a complete list of components of
> reading skill, but the information we now have is converging toward
> such a catalog.... Furthermore, it is now possible to state how the
> components of reading skill interact, and how they form a hierarchy
> leading to effective total reading performance (Carroll, 1981, p. 18).

●◆ Reading for pleasure is an extraordinary activity. The black
squiggles on the white page are still as the grave, colorless as the moonlit
desert; but they give the skilled reader a pleasure as acute as the touch of a
loved body, as rousing, colorful, and transfiguring as anything out there in
the real world. And yet, the more stirring the book the quieter the reader;
pleasure reading breeds a concentration so effortless that the absorbed reader of fiction (transported by the book to some other place and shielded by it
from distractions), who is so often reviled as an escapist and denounced as
the victim of a vice as pernicious as tippling in the morning, should instead
be the envy of every student and every teacher.

These are the paired wonders of reading: the world-creating power
of books, and the reader's effortless absorption that allows the book's frag-
ile world, all air and thought, to maintain itself for a while, a bamboo and
paper house among earthquakes; within it readers acquire peace, become
more powerful, feel braver and wiser in the ways of the world.

Absorption may sometimes deepen to become entrancement, the
signs of which are greater resistance to interruption and the returning reader's momentary bewilderment, as of someone waking from a dream. "Oh,"

From *Lost in a Book: The Psychology of Reading for Pleasure* by Victor Nell. Copyright
©1988. Reprinted with permission from Yale University Press, New Haven, CT.

says the reader, half-apologetically, "I was so deep in the book!"—and indeed, a person emerging from a reading trance does appear to be surfacing from a depth or returning from another place. Absorption seems to accompany all pleasure reading, but trance is less common and resembles an altered state of consciousness: reverie, or dreaming, or perhaps even hypnosis. Neither absorption nor trance is restricted to fiction: the final entries in Captain Scott's journals can transport a reader to the icy Antarctic wilderness as surely as any novel or short story; and a newspaper account of a tankcar derailment that sends poisonous fumes creeping toward a sleeping community can entrance as fully as any imaginary disaster story. Nor does narrative nonfiction (travel, biography) seem to be in any way distinct from fiction in the effects it produces on the reader. But fiction is the most common vehicle of pleasure reading and will accordingly occupy most of our attention.

Pleasure reading is playful: it is free activity standing outside ordinary life; it absorbs the player completely, is unproductive, and takes place within circumscribed limits of space and time (Caillois, 1958; Huizinga, 1938/1950). "Ludic reading," from the Latin *ludo*, meaning "I play" (Stephenson, 1964), is therefore a useful characterization of pleasure reading, reminding us that it is at root a play activity, intrinsically motivated and usually paratelic, that is, engaged in for its own sake (Apter, 1979; Deci, 1976). Ludic readers often describe themselves as reading addicts, and they do indeed spend a great deal of time reading a great many books. Some read ten books a week, others even more. As a convenient rule of thumb, the term *ludic reader* is here reserved for those who read at least one book a week.

Reading as Consciousness Change

Like dreaming, reading performs the prodigious task of carrying us off to other worlds. But reading is not dreaming because books, unlike dreams, are subject to our will: they envelop us in alternative realities only because we give them explicit permission to do so. Books are the dreams we would most like to have, and, like dreams, they have the power to change consciousness, turning sadness to laughter and anxious introspection to the relaxed contemplation of some other time and place.

The newspaper reader is absorbed and transported as readily as the fiction reader (though usually for a shorter time and to a disjointed succession of places), and my own curiosity about the nature of the reader's experience goes back to 1974, when I returned to journalism after a long break.

I soon began to wonder how it was that even the least experienced of our number in the copy editor's room of a provincial morning newspaper were repeatedly able to demonstrate perfectly correct newsworthiness judgments in distinguishing big stories from small ones, and small stories from non-stories. In 1949, Wilbur Schramm, the doyen of mass media researchers, wrote that no aspect of communication is as impressive as the enormous number of choices and discards that have to be made between communicator and receiver (p. 289). To me, there are two much more impressive phenomena. The first is the extraordinary agreement among journalists about news-value rankings, which seems to have nothing to do with experience or formal knowledge of news criteria (Nell, 1978b); for example, when I first began work as a journalist (I was a news editor on Israel Radio during the heady days of the Eichmann trial), I could rank stories for newsworthiness as accurately as 30-year veterans. The second phenomenon is the nature of the public appetite for news, "a crying primal want of the mind, like a hunger of the body" (Will Irwin in Boorstin, 1964). To me, this news hunger can best be seen as a variant of story hunger, the appetite that drove our ancestors to listen, rapt, to tribal storytellers, and that drives us today to theaters and television shows, to libraries and newsstands. To me, this insatiable appetite is the most impressive aspect of communication, not only because of its economic importance (it underpins the entertainment industry), but also in purely psychological terms, as the provider of reinforcements sufficiently strong to sustain many consecutive hours of attention (to anecdotal conversation and informal storytelling as well as to books, radio, and television programs) on every day of every normally functioning person's life.

Entertainment is that aspect of play which stands within the economic sector, and the huge and immensely lucrative entertainment industry has consciousness change as its entire stock in trade. We pay handsomely for the spectacles, titillations, and close-ups of catastrophe that take us out of ourselves by taking over consciousness. But books—the most portable and ubiquitous product of the entertainment industry—often come to us free or nearly free, from libraries, used-book exchanges, and friends. Pleasure reading thus straddles two sets of boundaries: it stands between the entertainments we pay for and those adult play activities for which no money changes hands—chatting and visiting, backyard games, willing sexuality, and the like. Next, within the play domain, reading is both a spectator and a participant activity. It is participant because, until the reader's eye lights on the page, the book does not exist. Nonetheless, the reader, like other spectators, is acted on by the world rather than primarily acting on it.

The permeability of these boundaries is underscored by bearing in mind that the fundamental distinction between activities performed for their own sake (paratelic) and those we labor at because of external rewards (telic) is itself reversible. As mood and intention change, the chore I begin this morning (reading *Pride and Prejudice* to prepare for an examination) becomes a delight by afternoon.

The Elitist Fallacy

Critics and literary historians have traditionally subscribed to the view that readers are either lowbrow or highbrow and, as a corollary, that trained and untrained minds do not share the same tastes. If this division correctly reflects the way in which culture is produced and consumed, can this book accommodate the richness and diversity of the ludic reading experience of those who read intently and deeply, or will it, on the contrary, focus on the lumpenproletariat, the "ignorantly contented lower orders" (Oxford, 1976) who flourish on the fecund dung heap of popular fiction? If my concern is with "the effect of cheap novels on the minds of uneducated people" (Sterba, 1939), this book will have little interest for sophisticated readers because it will offend them by its implied arrogance while failing to reflect their own experience of ludic reading.

My intentions are neither highbrow nor lowbrow, because the two classes of reader as defined by the elitist critics do not exist; the view that they do contains a fundamental error so common that it deserves to be labeled "the elitist fallacy"—the belief that as sophistication grows, coarser tastes wither away. If today I delight in Milan Kundera's *The Unbearable Lightness of Being* or *Foe* by Jim Coetzee, I cannot tomorrow return to *Biggles and the Blue Moon* by William Earl Johns or *Just William* by Richmal Crompton, which I enjoyed as a child, or lose myself in the Harlequin romance offered by the airplane passenger in the next seat.

On the contrary: though sophisticated readers have the capacity and the desire to enjoy deeply felt and delicately wrought literature, and habitually do so, they continue, on occasion and if their consciences allow them, to delight in the childlike triumphs of "His Majesty the Ego" (Freud, 1908/1957) and in the stereotyped narratives that recount the endless victories of invincible heroes and heroines.

For example, 33 ludic readers, among whom trained minds were well represented, rated an average of 42.6 percent of their own pleasure reading as "trash"; the highest individual rating, 90 percent, came from a person working on a doctoral dissertation in English literature. Among the nearly 300 other subjects were many readers of equal depravity. A correspondent of austere tastes, who does not trouble to conceal her contempt for the dolts, oafs, and freaks who trade subtlety for stereotypes—and worse, do so in great quantity—confesses to enjoying "good trash—good enough for airplane or before-sleep reading, not for one's permanent library or for bothering to remember."

Of course, the fallacy is unidirectional, because, for untrained or unwilling minds, much reading matter must remain inaccessible. In the sense that there is a class of lowbrow readers who avoid the products of elite culture, the critics are correct; but, as even fleeting examination of culture consumption in the world around us shows, the doors from high culture to low remain open, and earlier tastes do not wither and die as more refined appetites develop. At least metaphorically, evolutionary theory, which teaches that ontogeny recapitulates phylogeny (Haeckel's "fundamental biogenetic law," 1867) and that new systems do not replace older ones but are superimposed on them (see, for example, McLean, 1973), prepares the grounds for the suggestion that more primitive cultural levels remain accessible despite later accretions. Psychoanalysis, in Freud's careful archeological metaphor for the structure of consciousness (for example, 1909/1984, p. 57)—and quite specifically in his account of literary creation—also suggests that earlier and more primitive needs and desires are not rooted out by maturation and education but merely overlaid and that they remain active in disguised or flamboyant ways throughout life.

The arrogant dismissiveness with which elite critics have studied the workings of lower class minds since the birth of the mass reading habit thus appears to rest on the faulty premise that the critics' own minds have nothing of cultural importance in common with those of the lower classes they study. A humility that derives from the realization that elite and lowbrow minds share a multitude of drives and gratifications, in literature as in life, might be more appropriate, and would certainly be more productive. Moreover, the new trends in literary criticism make it increasingly difficult to defend the premises on which the elitist fallacy is founded.

Of course, it may be that I have substituted a populist fallacy for the elitist error; time will tell. Nonetheless, ideology has of course molded my method. I have not stratified my subjects by taste culture because I believed from the beginning of these studies ten years ago that within every elite reader lurks a vestigial or fully formed lumpenprole, so that both classes are contained in one.

About ourselves: the elitist fallacy has a moral variant, which encourages its proponents to believe that people who behave in morally reprehensible ways—police torturers, Eichmann, Conrad's Kurtz (on the last two, see Nell, 1981)—are abnormal and, comfortingly, less than human; escapists and reading addicts, the tipplers at literature's tuppeny dram shops, are tarred by the same brush. There is by now a great body of literature affirming that at least the capacity to behave in brutal and immoral ways is part of the fabric of our humanity: Milgram's *Obedience to Authority* (1974), Arendt, 1963; Jones, 1976; and the Stanford simulated prison study (Haney, Banks, & Zimbardo, 1973). Accordingly, the aberrant readers may be "abnormal" but are not less human, or less interesting, for it.

Readers startled by this assertion might like to look back at one of psychology's early texts, Henry Murray's *Explorations in Personality* (1938). In the concluding study of this clinical study of "50 men of college age" (all were students at Harvard), Murray remarks:

> Most of our subjects were carrying what seemed to us a heavy load of crippling anxiety, inferiority feelings, guilt feelings, or dejection.... They doubted that they could live up to their own standards or to the expectations of their parents. Frequently, they suffered from memories of stinging humiliations, and when they went to their books in the evening, overriding apprehensive thoughts of future failure or depressing feelings of separateness and forsakenness prevented concentration. A basic sense of insupport aggravated by dissensions with one or both parents was a frequent finding (pp. 730–731).

And this of a group representative of the most talented and high achieving of America's youth!

Escapists, Addicts, or Otherwise Maladjusted

Over the past ten years I have talked with hundreds of ludic readers on two continents, singly and in groups, and the extent to which they share concerns that derive from the elitist and moral fallacies is quite striking. They wonder whether the way they enjoy books is unique or shared by other readers; if they read inordinate quantities, or at exceptional speed; why they enjoy good literature as well as reading matter they know to be trash, and why they can be equally moved by both; why they reread old favorites with undiminished enjoyment; why reading in bed is so enjoyable, and why reading books seems to give a deeper pleasure than watching television or going to the theater; and, finally, whether they are escapists, or addicts, or otherwise maladjusted.

In Western society, in which ludic reading is so commonplace that it passes largely unnoticed, the opportunities readers have to talk about their personal experience of reading are strangely circumscribed. When a group of ludic readers is brought together to talk about reading, they respond first with amazement and then with delight. They soon discover that they have a great deal in common (whether as a precondition for ludic reading or as a consequence of it, ludic readers are articulate, well informed, and endlessly curious), and there is a great deal of unembarrassed self-disclosure about childhood fears, reading matter that touches raw places, and authors that speak most deeply to them.

The following pages are devoted to answering some (though not all) of the questions readers ask about their reading and the ways in which it soothes and captivates them.

A Motivational Model of Ludic Reading

The inquiry that follows is complex, as it needs to be in order to describe the complex route readers follow from the printed page to reading enjoyment. The simplest way of introducing these complexities is by means of a model of ludic reading that will accommodate all aspects of the subject in orderly fashion. (I use "model" in the sense of a careful analogy that displays the relations of the part to the whole. Models, note English and English, 1958, are useful for discovering hypotheses, which admirably suits our purpose in this exploratory study.) Both the preliminary and elaborated models are motivational in the sense that they relate reading to the reward systems that set it in motion and determine whether it will be continued or terminated in favor of another activity.

The figure shows that the point of entry to the model is a person—we do not know yet whether he or she is going to be a ludic reader.

Certain preconditions must be met before ludic reading can begin. In the first place, ludic readers seem by and large to be skilled readers who rapidly and effortlessly assimilate information from the printed page. It seems likely that this skill can be expressed as a minimum reading speed below which reading books or other long, continuous texts will be too slow and tedious to be rewarding.

The second antecedent is the expectation that reading will be a pleasurable experience. First exposure to the delights of storytelling takes place in early childhood; later, the child reader may find that books offer similar delights and learn to turn to them for the kind of consciousness change that narrative produces so readily. The third antecedent is selection of an appropriate book. I shall show that readers develop great skill in

A Preliminary Model of Ludic Reading

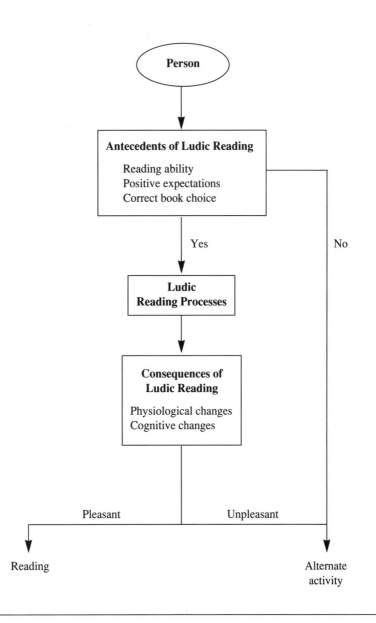

selecting the kind of book that promises "a good read." Of course, this is a very personal preference: my good read will likely end up in another reader's garbage pail. For this reason, the ludic readers who participated in the laboratory study were not all given the same book to read but were asked to bring along with them books of which they had sampled the first 50 pages and which they felt sure they would enjoy.

In the absence of any one of these antecedents, ludic reading is either not attempted or fails. If all three are present, and reading is more attractive than the available alternatives, reading begins and is continued as long as the reinforcements generated are strong enough to withstand the pull of alternative attractions. These reinforcers appear to be of two kinds. One is a series of physiological changes in the reader mediated by the autonomic nervous system, such as alterations in muscle tension, respiration, heart beat, electrical activity of the skin, and the like. These events are by and large unconscious and feed back to consciousness as a general feeling of well-being.

The second kind of reinforcer is cognitive changes, which are numerous and profound. Reading changes the focus of attention from self to environment. Because of the heavy demands reading makes on conscious attention, the reader is effectively shielded from other demands, whether internal or external. At the same time, the intense attention brought to bear by the entranced reader may have the effect of transfiguring both book and reader. The absolute control readers exercise over their reading with regard to pace, content, initiation, and duration means that reading can be used to accomplish two very different goals, to dull consciousness or heighten it. I argue that readers' personality dispositions and current concerns determine which of these goals is pursued: for most readers, most of the time, it is likely that one of these two modes will consistently be preferred.

Between the antecedents of ludic reading and its consequences is the reading process itself, in which meaning is extracted from the symbols on the page and formed into inner experience. The quotes from Gass and Carroll at the beginning of this chapter allude to these two processes: one is meaning extraction, addressed by the tough-minded empiricism of Carroll's approach; the other is the mystery of reading, the "otherness" of the reader's experience, the easy sinking through the pages into soundless dreams. However, the skills and the otherness are not disjunctive. The simplest definition of reading, and the one on which most opinion now converges, is the extraction of meaning from a printed or written message. In this sense, both Gass and Carroll are concerned with meaning, one with how the reader extracts it, and the other with what he or she does with it once it has been extracted.

Taxonomy

Of course, reading, like play (Berlyne, 1969, p. 843), means too many things to too many people to be a useful category for psychology. A commuter reads the billboards and road signs that flash by, and a preschool child, paging through a well-loved book, "reads" the story by interpreting the pictures; a student, heavy with effort, reads a statistics text and a moment later, with a sigh of relief, settles down with a Somerset Maugham anthology. Any attempt to devise a model that accommodates all these diverse activities will produce statements of high generality and low heuristic value (Nell, 1978a), and the literature contains some lurid examples of the results that emerge from an inadequately defined approach to reading. Bernard Berelson, for example, produced an essay with the resounding title: "Who Reads What Books and Why" (1958). The findings are rather less resounding: "Some Americans read books frequently, some read them occasionally, some seldom, and some not at all" (p. 120); or "People read what interests them" (p. 124); or "The general moral of this tale...is that the state of popular reading is complicated, uneven, shifting, sometimes obscure" (p. 125).

Such generalizations are not helpful, and some arise in faulty taxonomies of reading. Data gathering must be preceded by an act of classification (otherwise data overwhelm us), and interpretation cannot begin until we know what it is that we are interpreting (otherwise meaning eludes us).

Berelson's study and others similar to it exemplify the communications research tradition, which Lewis (1978) characterizes as "productive in the accumulation of data [but] much less successful in the interpretation of this complex material" (p. 47). Some of these problems can be avoided by carefully circumscribing the investigation and restricting it to ludic reading only—that is, the reading of fiction and near-fiction for pleasure by skilled readers.

A Precipitous Landscape

The first chapter of Huey's pioneering 1908 study of reading is entitled "The Mysteries and Problems of Reading": 80 years later, these mysteries are still the subject of diligent investigation. But that "acme of a psychologist's achievements," the complete analysis of what we do when we read, which "would be to describe very many of the most intricate workings of the human mind" (p. 6), seems even more remote today than it must have appeared to Huey, if only because the length of the road and the difficulty of the terrain are clearer now than they were at the beginning of the century. We follow a route through this precipitous landscape that leads us through some rather beautiful and mysterious parts of the ludic reader's world and allows us, here and there, between peaks we shall not attempt to scale, to catch a glimpse of distant countries that have not yet been explored.

References

Apter, M.J. (1979). Human action and theory of psychological reversals. In G. Underwood & R. Stevens (Eds.), *Aspects of consciousness* (vol. 1) London: Academic.

Arendt, H. (1963). *Eichmann in Jerusalem: A report on the banality of evil*. London: Faber & Faber.

Berelson, B. (1958). Who reads what books and why. In B. Rosenberg & B.H. White (Eds.), *Mass culture: The popular arts in America* . Glencoe, IL: Free Press.

Berlyne, D.E. (1969). Laughter, humor, and play. In G. Lindzey & E. Aronson (Eds.), *Handbook of social psychology* (vol. 3). Reading, MA: Addison-Wesley.

Boorstin, D.J. (1964). *The image: A guide to pseudo-events in America*. New York: Harper-Collins.

Caillois, R. (1958). *Man, play, and games*. Glencoe, IL: Free Press.

Carroll, J.B. (1981, April). *New analyses of reading skills*. Paper presented at the 26th annual convention of the International Reading Association, New Orleans, LA.

Deci, E.L. (1976). *Intrinsic motivation*. New York: Plenum.

English, H.B., & English, A.C. (1958). *A comprehensive dictionary of psychological and psychoanalytical terms*. London: Longman.

Freud, S. (1957). The relation of the poet to daydreaming. In *Collected papers* (vol. 4). London: Hogarth. (Original work published 1908)

Freud, S. (1984). Notes upon a case of obsessional neurosis. In A. Dickson (Ed.), *The Pelican Freud Library (Vol. 9): Case histories*. London: Penguin. (Original work published 1909)

Gass, W.H. (1972). *Fiction and the figures of life*. New York: Vintage.

Haney, C., Banks, C., & Zimbardo, P.G. (1973). Interpersonal dynamics in a simulated prison. *International Journal of Criminology and Penology 1*, 69–97.

Huey, E.B. (1968). *The psychology and pedagogy of reading*. Cambridge, MA: MIT Press. (Original work published 1908)

Huizinga, J. (1950). *Homo ludens*. Boston, MA: Beacon. (Original work published 1938)

Jones, R. (1976). The third wave. In A. Pines & C. Maslack (Eds.), *Experiencing social psychology* (2d ed.). New York: Knopf.

Lewis, G.H. (1978). The sociology of popular culture. *Current Sociology, 26*.

McLean, P.D. (1973). *A triune concept of the brain and behaviour*. Toronto, Ont. University of Toronto Press.

Milgram, S. (1974). *Obedience to authority: An experimental view*. London: Tavistock.

Murray, H.A. (1938). *Explorations in personality*. New York: Oxford.

Nell, V. (1978a). Kinds of reading and kinds of motivation: Reflections on the psychology of the reading habit. *Mousaion, 2*(5).

Nell, V. (1978b). News value rankings and power motive scores. *Communicatio, 4*, 40–43.

Nell, V. (1981). At the heart of darkness: Eichmann and *Apocalypse Now*. *Critical Arts, 1*(4), 28–40.

Oxford. (1976). *The concise Oxford dictionary* (6th ed.). Oxford, England: Author. University Press.

Schramm, W. (1949). The nature of news. *Journalism Quarterly, 26,* 259–269.

Stephenson, W. (1964). The ludenic theory of newsreading. *Journalism Quarterly, 41,* 367–374.

Sterba, R.A. (1939). The significance of theatrical performance. *Psychoanalytic Quarterly, 8,* 335–337.

PART TWO

Examining Attitudes Toward Reading

*We do not need to burn books
to kill our civilization; we need
only to leave them unread for a
generation.*

R.M. Hutchins

Chapter 4

Who Reads What and When?

Peter J.L. Fisher

●◆ In 1945, after the increase in books sold during World War II, U.S. publishers commissioned a study of reading habits to determine how to continue the high volume of sales. Link and Hopf's (1946) now classic study interviewed 4000 people in 106 cities and towns throughout the United States. One of the major questions the 235 interviewers asked could be summarized as "Who reads what and when?" They concluded that only 50 percent of the population were active readers, that 70 percent of all books were read by 21 percent of the population, and that there was enormous variety in the reading material of adults. Twenty years earlier, Terman and Lima (1925) collected data from 2000 school-age children about their reading habits and interests; they concluded that the "individual reading interests of children are difficult to control" (p. 49). Historically the question "Who reads what and when?" has been of interest to many researchers, and it is somewhat surprising that we do not know much more now than we did when these studies were conducted. I will attempt to begin to answer this question by reviewing selected research, particularly that relating to children.

Personal Testimony

As children our access to particular books may be limited or our selection encouraged by our families or schools. As we become adults our reading habits become more stable but also idiosyncratic. The reasons we choose certain materials and books to read may be governed more by personal dictates than those of our physical and social environments. One continuing source of information on what and when people read and how reading affects them is the personal testimonies of people who have become readers.

Over 30 years, Carlsen and Sherrill (1988) collected reflections about childhood reading from students who were in training to be librarians or English teachers. From thousands of these recollections, they distilled some thoughts about what children like to read and when. Preschool memories of being read to by mother and having favorite books reread were common. The early elementary years were characterized by children wanting to read favorite books that had been read to them and, for these mainly avid readers, the discovery of the library as a source of books. The accounts of these students indicated that even in the late elementary years the family continued to provide a model for young readers. Often during these years "respondents discovered some subject that nearly became an obsession with them" (p. 15). Horses, wolves, pioneers, airplanes, and many other topics were mentioned, as was addiction to series and comic books; Nancy Drew, the Hardy Boys, and Superman were part of the reading diet of even these college-bound students for some time.

By the junior high school years, many respondents recalled keeping some sort of record of what they read. Favorite books mentioned centered on adventure and mysteries, with a beginning interest in biographies for some, while many girls sampled teenage romance novels. Not surprisingly, many respondents mentioned passing around sexually explicit books among peers at this age. The authors note that during the high school years, students became more "earnest" in their reading and deliberate in their selection of what to read. In these years the "classics" were approached or particular authors devoured. The reflections of the students suggested that in high school, reading literature began to be more than entertainment: it became also an intellectual activity. Once in college, these students read to understand the author's craft, which may have been required of them by their professors.

Carlsen and Sherrill (1988), in their discussion of how books affect readers, also mention "watershed books," which had a major impact on or changed the direction of a respondent's life.

Sabine and Sabine (1983) asked 1400 U.S. citizens, "What book made the greatest difference in your life?" People from all walks of life responded in ways that demonstrated the power of books. They told how books had influenced their careers, places of residence, involvement in political and social organizations, religion, and marriages. They noted how books had helped with such things as bereavement, overcoming handicaps, and child rearing. Some people identified with characters; others noted that reading just made them feel better. The authors conclude that books certainly do make a difference in peoples' lives but that the experience, purpose, and result of reading are so personal that no one book can be identified as being a "common" book. Sabine and Sabine argue that people whose lives are affected by books are not distinguishable by any characteristic, such as race or sex. They also believe that most books that appear to have had a strong influence on people would be classified as literature and have "never appeared on a bestseller list" (p. 127).

May (1992) collected personal literacy statements from members of her community as part of a school-community project. She notes that the statements show that "the rewards of reading are so deeply imbedded in these individuals' lives and in such a positive way, that it is difficult for them to imagine a life without reading" (p. 3). The respondents demonstrated an interest in reading on diverse subjects and in various genres. What perhaps is more significant is that many connected their reading and writing; they wrote about the power of communicating on paper with great intensity and emotion. Researchers, in the past, have focused on what readers read and when and have not searched for connections between reading and writing in people's lives.

Personal testimonies demonstrate the great variety of what is read at all ages and in all situations. What significantly affects one person may not be important for another. Yet some behaviors, such as interest in series books and library use, are mentioned frequently by adult readers as having been important in their childhoods.

Library Use

As documented in testimonies such as those mentioned earlier, the research on library use suggests that adult library use for leisure purposes is often established in the preteen years (see also Berelson, 1949; Luckham, 1971; Razzano, 1985). This emphasizes the importance of an early introduction to the library as a source of reading material. While sex, race, income, and level of education have traditionally been used to explain variations in library use (see, for example, Mendelsohn & Wingerd, 1967), Kling (1982) argued that these factors explain only a small percentage of the differences in adult reading habits. He contended that reading habits tend to be idiosyncratic: why, what, or when an adult chooses to read is affected by personal factors, rather than being predictable from sex, income, educational level, or race.

However, it remains true through the years and in different cultures that a major part of public library use is by people under 18 years of age and by mothers with young children (Mendelsohn & Wingerd, 1967; Ward, 1977; Westerhein, 1986). These sources indicate that a high proportion of the circulation figures at public libraries is juvenile, which means that books are finding their way from the libraries and into the hands of children. Robinson and Sulzby (1984) suggested that preschool children may spend considerable time reading with parents and that the books used for this activity come from many sources, with the library being only one.

How then can studies of library use inform the answer to our question? Surveys conducted over the last 50 years have suggested that library use decreases with age, that more women than men use the library, that public libraries are used more by lower income groups, but that individuals from higher income groups visit more frequently (Berelson, 1949; Davies, 1986; Gallup, 1978; Mendelsohn & Wingerd, 1967). A further consistent finding is that incidence of library use increases with level of education attained. We can see, therefore, that these groups are more likely to have books at hand when needed for recreational and informational reading.

Bestseller Lists

Despite the fact that influential books may rarely appear on bestseller lists, such lists are good indicators of what the public is willing to pay to read. Roback (1992) noted the increased book buying of children's books in the United States during the 1980s continued through 1990, despite a slowdown in the economy. Publishers' combined title output rose 73.3 percent from 1980 to 1988. Retailers allocated more space to children's books, and more titles were carried in stores that sell children's books. Interestingly, however, the bestsellers of publishing houses were often older titles—10 to 15 years old—and retailers report that customers want the "classics." This is not because grandma is buying all the books. In fact, mother is the main buyer (over 40 percent of sales), with children accounting for about 15 percent of purchases. This means that the lists of best-selling children's books need to be understood from the perspective that these books are often chosen by adults, although children may still read them.

Maryles (1989) listed the best-selling hardcover children's books of all time. At the top of the list was *The Tale of Peter Rabbit*, with *Pat the Bunny* next, and in the top ten there were four Dr. Seuss books, in addition to the Bible. The paperback bestsellers were dominated by books for older students (beyond the primary grades). Here, S.E. Hinton's *The Outsiders* headed the list, with classics in the top ten including *Charlotte's Web*, *Where the Red Fern Grows*, *The Little Prince*, and two titles by Laura Ingalls Wilder. Judy Blume was represented by three titles, and Hinton had a second. Both these lists suggest that there are perennial favorites, but perusal of monthly lists indicates fluctuations in sales that occur for a variety of reasons.

The children's bestsellers for December 1991, February 1992, and March 1992 from *Publishers Weekly* show that seasons, movies, and trends all affect sales. For example, *The Jolly Christmas Postman* was top of the picture book list for December, but by March it had been replaced by the classic *Goodnight Moon*. In February, Walt Disney's *Beauty and the Beast* was a hit at the box office and the book tie-in topped the list for younger readers. For older readers the new Roald Dahl offering of *Matilda* maintained first place. The paperback series bestseller lists for all three months were dominated by Baby-Sitters Club selections. Engelhardt (1991) notes, "Company handouts claim an astonishing 65 million Sweet Valley and 43 million Baby-Sitters books in print" (p. 60). He also shows that the top three best-selling paperback books for 1990 were part of the Teenage Mutant Ninja Turtle series (with 6 more titles in the top 20). The predominance of series titles in bestseller lists for a particular year is not new—50 years ago it was Nancy Drew and the Hardy boys—but the frequency with which they change may be a reflection of the increased juvenile market and of the increased volume of sales for which publishers are competing (see also Chapters 11 and 12).

Bestseller lists clearly indicate that the classics are still being sought and bought and that movies, series, and seasonal aspects all influence what people choose to buy. One is left wondering if all those series books are being bought by mothers—the major buyers of children's books, and whether children really prefer series books to all other types.

Children's Reading Preferences

No article on reading interests and preferences would be complete without mentioning Norvell's classic studies (1950, 1958), if only for their size. In the first study, 625 teachers collected data from more than 50,000 adolescents in over 200 schools, and in the second, 960,000 opinions were obtained from 24,000 children in grades 3–6. The studies highlight the energy and resources that have been devoted to trying to evaluate children's interests and preferences. Monson and Sebesta's (1991) review of the historical and current literature can serve as one source of information on what we know after nearly 100 years of research.

The ways in which reading interests and preferences have been investigated vary but fall into three broad categories. Researchers have looked at what children *actually read*, what they say they *like to read*, and which books, of some number of choices, they *prefer to read*. Methods have included diaries, logs, surveys, interviews, lists of topics, lists of real and imaginary titles (both annotated and unannotated), paired comparisons, silent reading of excerpts, and reading aloud to subjects. What remains common to most studies is that children's reading interests and preferences are influenced by sex and age (Monson & Sebesta, 1991). Some researchers have also found a racial influence on interests (Fisher, 1988; Wolfson, Manning, & Manning, 1984), but the similarities in interests between racial groups seem to be stronger than the differences. This also appears to be true in international comparisons (Fisher & Ayres, 1990; Kirsch, Pehrsson, & Robinson, 1976). Johnson and Greenbaum (1982), concluded that in general boys prefer to read adventure, science, sports, and information books, while girls choose mystery, romance, fairy tales, and books about home and school life and animals. Similar results have been found in many studies since 1982, although interests in adventure, mysteries, humor, and fantasy seem to be common for both sexes at most ages.

Since 1974, Children's Choices—a joint project of the Children's Book Council and the International Reading Association—has elicited responses from 10,000 elementary-age children to 500 newly published trade books each year. Primary grades chose funny books over make-believe, with people and animal stories in second place. Intermediate grades chose adventure, humor, and informational books first, with fantasy, mystery, sports, and the supernatural in second place. The author acknowledges that these differences from other research could be due to the number of books available in each category, but the Children's Choices lists (published in the *The Reading Teacher*) do provide good information about what students actually enjoy reading.

If, then, the results are fairly consistent across studies, why is there a continuing interest in studying children's preferences? The interest seems to be motivated by a desire to match children and books so that they are encouraged to read more and develop a lifelong love of reading. As the number and nature of books change, so, some might suppose, will the interests of children. This supposition is probably false. Beyond ephemeral interests, such as Mutant Ninja Turtles, any teacher can tell that a good story is more important than the genre. In addition, good stories may cross more than one genre. Is the ever-popular Narnia series an adventure, fantasy, or animal story? It has elements of each. Moreover, each child may be "turned on" by a different book, much as adults relate being influenced by different literature. Certain books do seem to last, however, and, as suggested earlier, publishers rely heavily on the classics in their lists. Do children read these classics because they like them, or are they "good literature" that children should pay homage to as adults do to Shakespeare?

Wilson (1985) investigated whether fifth and sixth graders liked reading the classics. She developed a list of 27 titles based on expert opinion from which 374 students read 3 or more books and voted for their favorites. *Charlotte's Web, Little House in the Big Woods*, and *The Secret Garden* were the first three choices. Surprisingly, Wilson did not find any statistically significant differences in the classics that boys and girls chose to read, nor in their preferences. Because this finding opposed the strong trend in other research, I wanted to find out if children actually read the classics on this list without prompting, and if so, if boys and girls differed in what they chose and what they liked. I was also curious to see if adults recalled reading and enjoying the same books.

I asked 157 fifth and sixth graders from 2 schools which of the 27 titles they had read. I then asked them to rank their enjoyment of the books they had read on a five-point Likert scale. In addition, 123 teachers (mainly female) in graduate education classes completed the same tasks. The table on the next page shows the highest rated books on average for boys and girls and for adults over and under 30 years of age. Only those books that were read by more than 30 percent of the respondents were included. The only book that appears on all four lists is *Charlotte's Web*. Four books, *The Lion, the Witch, and the Wardrobe, A Christmas Carol, Mary Poppins*, and *The Little House in the Big Woods* appeared on three of the lists. The boys and girls had four common books in their top ten: *The Lion, the Witch, and the Wardrobe, A Christmas Carol, Mary Poppins*, and *Tom Sawyer*. This suggests that boys and girls do differ somewhat in the classics they read and enjoy, with boys focusing more on adventure. Both groups appeared to enjoy fantasy but of differing kinds. Both liked the Narnia book, but the boys liked *Rip Van Winkle* and *The Hobbit*, while the girls liked *Alice in Wonderland, The Just So Stories, Peter Pan*, and *Mary Poppins*. The adults over and under 30 had 6 books in common in their top 10 choices, so the similarities may be greater than the differences. Both adult groups, which comprised mainly women, had six books in common with the girls' list as well, suggesting that many titles have stood the test of time. The books rated highly by adults that were not on the children's top ten included *Little Women* (which may be read by older girls), *Heidi*, and *The Borrowers*.

Also in the table is the percentage of respondents who said they read each of the highest rated books. *Charlotte's Web* was again the highest in this category. On average, the pupils said that they had read 9 books of the 27, while adults had read 12 of the titles. It appears, therefore, that chil-

The Ten Highest Rated Books for Boys and Girls
in Fifth and Sixth Grade and for Adults

Boys	Who Read	Girls	Who Read
1. *Tom Sawyer*	52	1. *Alice in Wonderland*	73
2. *Rip Van Winkle*	34	2. *Just So Stories*	30
3. *Wind in the Willows*	44	3. *The Secret Garden*	58
4. *King Arthur & His Knights*	33	4. *The Lion, the Witch, and*	
5. *The Lion, the Witch, and*		*the Wardrobe*	58
the Wardrobe	72	5. *Charlotte's Web*	89
6. *Robin Hood*	53	6. *Tom Sawyer*	32
7. *Treasure Island*	52	7. *Peter Pan*	57
8. *A Christmas Carol*	50	8. *A Christmas Carol*	45
9. *The Hobbit*	47	9. *Mary Poppins*	48
10. *Charlotte's Web*	78	10. *The Little House in the*	
		Big Woods	39

Adults <30 years	Who Read	Adults >30 years	Who Read
1. *The Secret Garden*	40	1. *Little Women*	76
2. *Little Women*	55	2. *Heidi*	74
3. *Charlotte's Web*	89	3. *Peter Pan*	75
4. *The Lion, the Witch, and*		4. *Mary Poppins*	53
the Wardrobe	49	5. *Charlotte's Web*	66
5. *Heidi*	56	6. *The Little House in*	
6. *Mary Poppins*	49	*the Big Woods*	43
7. *The Little House in the*		7. *Tom Sawyer*	78
Big Woods	53	8. *The Borrowers*	34
8. *A Christmas Carol*	55	9. *Just So Stories*	37
9. *The Borrowers*	31	10. *Robin Hood*	59
10. *Alice in Wonderland*	57		

dren are still being exposed to the classics and reading many of them with considerable enjoyment. Although this survey cannot examine which version of the classic was read, it seems unlikely that *Rip Van Winkle and the Legend of Sleepy Hollow* was read by all the boys in its original version. Similarly, *The Adventures of Robin Hood* has appeared in many versions, some of which might be popular while others are not. Nevertheless, this small piece of research suggests that the classics that adults read and enjoyed are still being read and enjoyed by children.

Preference and interest research indicates that there are differences in what boys and girls choose to read and that there are age-level differences. Neither of these results will surprise teachers and parents. Book flood experiments, such as those described by Ingham (1981) and Anderson, Wilson, and Fielding (1988) in which classrooms are "flooded" with many books, indicate that local factors in classrooms and homes influence what particular books a child chooses to read, rather than global factors such as age or sex. The influence of parents and teachers on choosing to read and choosing what to read overrides any other global influences (see also the following two chapters).

Reflections

In attempting to address the question of who reads what and when, I have drawn on four types of research. There are many other areas I have not touched on, such as the research into reading and leisure-time activities (see, for example, Greaney & Hegarty, 1987; Taylor, Frye, & Maruyama, 1990) or what affects newspaper readings (see Lain, 1986). What becomes clear from all the areas of research is that while we may be able to predict influences on what sort of materials adults and children will read and when, any individual may react differently in any given situation. Sex and age characteristics have the greatest influence on choices of reading material, and interest in reading for pleasure declines with age. Beyond that, individuals may be influenced by different books and use literacy in various ways in their lives. Baldwin (1914) described the way literacy influenced his life while growing up in Indiana in the middle of the last century. He recalled sitting on a three-legged stool by the fireside, surrounded by all his family, while his father read from the scriptures. Reading (and listening) was associated with warmth and family. In reality, it may have been the only activity that all the family could engage in on an isolated farm at that time of night. I am encouraged, when I am in situations where there is little to do but read, by the sight of so many others also reading. Just look around next time you are on a train or a plane—those are times when most people choose to read.

References

Anderson, R.C., Wilson, P.T., & Fielding, L.G. (1988). Growth in research and how children spend their time outside of school. *Reading Research Quarterly, 23*, 285–303.

Baldwin, J. (1914). *In my youth*. Indianapolis, IN: Bobbs-Merrill.

Berelson, B. (1949). *The library's public*. New York: Columbia University Press.

Carlsen, G.R., & Sherrill, A. (1988). *Voices of readers: How we come to love books*. Urbana, IL: National Council of Teachers of English.

Davies, C. (1986). Use of the public library: A lifelong habit? *Current Studies in Librarianship, 10*, 17–25.

Engelhardt, T. (1991). Reading may be harmful to your kids. *Harper's, 282*(1693), 55–62.

Fisher, P.J.L. (1988). The reading preferences of third, fourth, and fifth graders. *Reading Horizons, 29*, 62–70.

Fisher, P.J.L., & Ayres, G.A. (1990). A comparison of the reading interests of children in England and the United States. *Reading Improvement, 27*, 111–115.

Gallup Organization. (1978). *Book reading and library usage: A study of habits and perceptions.* Princeton, NJ: Author.

Greaney, V., & Hegarty, M. (1987). Correlates of leisure-time reading. *Journal of Research in Reading, 10*, 3–20.

Greenlaw, M.J. (1983). Reading interest research and children's choices. In N. Roser & M. Frith (Eds.), *Children's Choices: Teaching with books children like* (pp. 90–92). Newark, DE: International Reading Association.

Ingham, J.L. (1981). *Books and reading development: The Bradford books flood experiment.* Portsmouth, NH: Heinemann.

Johnson, C.S., & Greenbaum, G.R. (1982). Girls' and boys' reading interests: A review of research. In E.M. Sheridan (Ed.), *Sex stereotypes and reading: Research and strategies.* Newark, DE: International Reading Association.

Kirsch, D., Pehrsson, R., & Robinson, H.A. (1976). Expressed reading interests of young children: An international study. In J.E. Merritt (Ed.), *New horizons in reading* (pp. 45–56). Newark, DE: International Reading Association.

Kling, M. (1982). Adult reading habits. *Reading Psychology, 3*, 59–70.

Lain, L.B. (1986). Steps toward a comprehensive model of newspaper readership. *Journalism Quarterly, 63*, 69–74, 121.

Link, H.C., & Hopf, H.A. (1946). *People and books: A study of reading and book-buying habits.* New York: Book Manufacturers' Institute.

Luckham, B.L.G. (1971). *The library in society: A study of the public library in an urban setting.* London: Library Association.

Maryles, D. (1989). All-time best-selling children's books. *Publishers Weekly, 236*(17), 28–29.

May, M. (1992). *The literacy connection.* Unpublished paper, National-Louis University, Evanston, IL.

Mendelsohn, H., & Wingerd, K. (1967). *The use of libraries and the conditions that promote their use: A report to the National Advisory Commission on Libraries.* New York: Academy for Educational Development.

Monson, D.L., & Sebesta, S. (1991). Reading preferences. In J. Flood, J.M. Jensen, D. Lapp, & J.R. Squire (Eds.), *Handbook of research on teaching the English language arts* (pp. 664–673). New York: Macmillan.

Norvell, G.W. (1950). *The reading interests of young people.* Boston, MA: Heath.

Norvell, G.W. (1958). *What boys and girls like to read.* Morristown, NJ: Silver Burdett.

Razzano, B.W. (1985). Creating the library habit. *Library Journal, 110*(3), 111–114.

Roback, D. (1992). In space, titles, sales, the trend is still up. *Publishers Weekly, 239*(3), 26–31.

Robinson, F., & Sulzby, E. (1984). Parents, children, and "favorite" books: An interview study. In J.A. Niles & L.A. Harris (Eds.), *Changing perspectives on research in reading/language processing and instruction* . Thirty-third Yearbook of the National Reading Conference, (pp. 54–59). Rochester, NY: National Reading Conference.

Sabine, G., & Sabine, P. (1983). *Books that made the difference: What people told us.* Hamden, CT: Library Professional Publications.

Taylor, B.M., Frye, B.J., & Maruyama, G. (1990). Time spent reading and reading growth. *American Educational Research Journal, 27*, 351–362.

Terman, L.M., & Lima, M. (1925). *Children's reading: A guide for parents and teachers.* New York: Appleton.

Ward, M.L. (1977). *Readers and library users: A study of reading habits and public library use.* London: Library Association.

Westerhein, I. (1986). Young people and the library. *Scandinavian Public Library Journal, 19*, 107–108.

Wilson, P.J. (1985). *Children's classics: A reading preference study of fifth and sixth graders.* Unpublished doctoral dissertation, University of Houston, TX.

Wolfson, B.J., Manning, G., & Manning, M. (1984). Revisiting what children say their reading interests are. *Reading World, 24*(2), 4–10.

Chapter 5

How Teacher Attitudes Influence Reading Achievement

Edward J. Dwyer
Evelyn E. Dwyer

●◆ "Can we read when we get back?" Sean asked his teacher even as he left with his first grade class to go to one of his favorite activities, physical education. What made Sean like to read and become a "good" reader? Sean had not been considered a "good" reader by anyone the previous year. In fact, he read so poorly he had had to repeat first grade.

Did Sean bloom during the summer? Did he become involved with a fantastic new program? Did he simply mature? Did he realize the importance of lifelong learning and the critical role of literacy in the pursuit of success? Did the virtues of hard work and diligence come as gifts on his seventh birthday? All of these might be true, to some extent. We have no way of knowing for sure what changed Sean's reading attitude or ability, but we believe it had more to do with his teacher than any other factor or combination of factors. Sean's teacher inspired him to try. Her teaching competence coupled with her positive attitude and other affective qualities brought a light to his eyes and a smile to his face. Sean succeeded.

Educational Reforms

Educational reform is often thought of as a goal of national consequence, but, in stories like Sean's, we see "educational reform" as a very local and even a very personal issue. We might even say, "Sean reformed," but, far more likely, he was in a learning environment where he felt appreciated and capable of learning.

The news media are replete with information on the efforts of many different political groups, which demand what is loosely described as "reform" in education. Television and radio stations clamor for attention in presenting their perspective on what should be done to improve education.

66

"What's wrong with public schools" is a staple among subjects discussed on talk shows where listeners call to express their views. In this light, researchers Hesson and Weeks (1991) concluded that "not since the wave of education reforms that followed Sputnik in the late 1950s and early 1960s has there been so much pressure on education in the United States" (p. 339).

Perhaps much of the attention to schools began with the much publicized report of the U.S. National Commission on Excellence in Education (1983) titled *A Nation at Risk: The Imperatives for Educational Reform*. This report focused primarily on what appeared to the authors as academic deficiencies among U.S. school children as compared with children in other developed nations. The commission suggested the following:

> If an unfriendly foreign power had attempted to impose on America the mediocre educational performance that exists today, we might well have viewed it as an act of war.... We have, in effect, been committing an act of unthinking, unilateral educational disarmament (p. 5).

Walberg (1986) compared U.S. students to those from other developed countries by examining survey data from the International Association for the Evaluation of Educational Achievement. His findings led him to the unfortunate conclusion that "results are even more worrisome than those reported in *A Nation at Risk*" (p. 8).

Reform and Affective Considerations

Hesson and Weeks (1991) contended that reports such as *A Nation at Risk* encouraged the first wave of reforms. However, they found a preponderance of quick-fix proposals such as increasing the amount of time spent in school, adding to requirements for high school graduation, and assessing student achievement more frequently and comprehensively. (See also Chapter 14 for a complete discussion of teachers' struggles to teach both the cognitive and affective aspects of reading.) In contrast to these reform prospects, Hesson and Weeks described more comprehensive "second wave" (p. 352) reforms not only emphasizing cognitive development but also recognizing the importance of affect in teaching and learning. Hesson and Weeks encouraged wider implementation of reforms promoting improved school environments where "personalization and trust" (p. 353) are evident. The researchers further stressed the importance of teacher expectations concerning levels of achievement and attitudes toward the learning ability of students as critical factors in fostering learning.

Further support for the contention that reform should originate from teachers and school administrators was expressed by the American Association of School Administrators (1986), which synthesized the research on effective schools and teachers reported from 1970 through 1985. Their report emphasized the importance of affective considerations among teachers, specifically listing

1. high expectations for students and for themselves as teachers;

2. warm and caring attitudes demonstrated to students;

3. teaching focused on needs of students rather than on specific content;

4. highly flexible, enthusiastic, and imaginative instruction; and

5. high levels of personal comfort during interactions with students.

The association found that school leaders want teachers to possess the qualities necessary to convey to their students that they can learn effectively (see also Chapter 17 on staff development).

In a similar vein, Staver and Walberg (1987) reviewed research on effective teaching that led them to conclude that characteristics such as the following substantially affect performance of both students and teachers: (1) clarity in presenting directions, expectations, and information; (2) ability to deal flexibly with instructional programs to meet individual student needs; and (3) enthusiasm for both subject matter and teaching. These researchers found consistently superior performances among students in classrooms where teachers provided students with psychological as well as academic support. Specifically, psychological support was noted through reinforcing desirable behavior, recognizing quality work, and emphasizing achievement while avoiding criticism whenever possible.

Odden (1987) also found schools moving toward greater effectiveness when teachers demonstrated a combination of positive attitudes and high expectations for students, good classroom management strategies, and effective instructional practices. Odden reported agreement among researchers that when teachers demonstrate positive attitudes toward their students as capable learners, their students will, in fact, perform more successfully.

An extensive review of literature accompanied by data-based survey research led Christophel (1990) to propose that the most prominent "teacher behaviors contributing to student learning were found to be vocal expressiveness, smiling, and a relaxed body position" (p. 325). This re-

searcher further concluded that even if students bring low levels of motivation to the classroom, teachers can help students substantially improve their
motivation levels through their communicative behaviors. Conclusions
reached by Christophel and Odden are consistent with those of numerous
other researchers, notably, Guskey (1982), Good and Brophy (1978), and
Eccles and Wigfield (1985).

The Pygmalion Principle

The affective studies of Rosenthal and Jacobson (1968) were for
educators what landing an astronaut on the moon was for space scientists.
Their goal was to determine if teacher attitudes affected learning among
first and second graders. The researchers informed teachers that, based on
test scores, some students were likely to blossom academically during the
school year, while in fact, the researchers had randomly assigned high test
scores to some students and mediocre scores to an equivalent group. Analysis of data indicated that students designated as likely to demonstrate substantial academic growth, to "bloom," significantly outpaced their untarget-
ed counterparts who were not expected to make above average gains. This
led Rosenthal and Jacobsen to conclude that teacher's positive attitudes
toward the learning capabilities of students designated as likely to make
substantial gains did, in fact, help teachers provide a learning environment
wherein those students prospered. The researchers concluded that teacher
expectations also played a major role in the mediocre achievement of the
control group.

Shrank (1968), like Rosenthal and Jacobson, advised teachers that
some classes had high-ability students while others had students with low
learning potential, but the students were, in fact, placed randomly in classes. The results were similar to those of Rosenthal and Jacobson. That is,
students who were expected by teachers to achieve at higher levels
appeared to learn substantially more than students viewed as having lower
levels of learning potential.

Robeck and Wallace (1990) also studied the effects of school environment on achievement and self-concept. Through a comprehensive
review of literature, they concluded that students develop a self-concept
based largely on how they compare themselves to a variety of others
including siblings, classmates, and significant adults, such as teachers.
Robeck and Wallace further contended that children must experience success, especially when learning to read—"the major cognitive task of the
elementary years" (p. 37). Like Rosenthal and Jacobson, Shrank, and others

researching the effects of school environment on learning, Robeck and Wallace suggested that school personnel must emphasize the worth and dignity of all students, thus encouraging positive attitudes toward learning. This appears particularly apropos of reading: belief in their ability to succeed in mastering the printed page is particularly important for children as they undertake reading to accomplish their own purposes. Ford (1992), in a tribute to his late mother, a reading teacher in Iowa, remembered the "intangible, personal factors" (p. 513) she brought to her classroom to encourage children to feel good about themselves. Ford's own work with children, he reported, is heavily influenced by memories of the affective qualities demonstrated by his mother, both as a parent and a teacher.

Further supporting the importance of the learning environment relative to student achievement, Good and Brophy (1978) and Weiner (1971) found a powerful positive relationship between teacher attitudes toward student achievement and eventual success of students. In fact, these researchers found teacher attitudes toward students the most critical factor in influencing student achievement.

More specific to reading, Bettelheim and Zelan (1982) found learning to read the most important experience of elementary school children— so important as to largely determine levels of success or failure throughout the school years. Bettelheim and Zelan discovered that the way children are taught to read is vital to their success. They proposed that teachers can and must present reading as a valuable, meaningful, and entertaining activity. Further, Bettelheim and Zelan proposed that teachers' competencies coupled with affective considerations are the most important factors relative to learning to read "irrespective of what the child brings from home" (p. 5).

Agony at the Chalkboard

The literature cited earlier represents only a small portion of the abundant research describing nuturing classroom environments and educators who consistently and constantly affirm every child as a worthy and successful human being. We all can remember times, however, when the classroom did not appear to be a place where we were appreciated. How we longed for our day in the sun when we would shine, only to fall short, not so much because we did not know but because we just could not come up with the clever words at the time. Storyteller Garrison Keillor (1989) described an all too common memory of school days:

> In fall when I was young, I thought, this year I will do better in
> physics. Study hard, listen, take good notes, and when he calls on

me, I'll give the answer in a loud clear voice, and not just a good answer but a brilliant one, possibly an answer that illuminates some dark corner of physics. I'll not only be a good student, I'll be a genius....

Then October came and I didn't understand anything. I was scared that he'd call on me and fear made the air around me hot and dry, creating teacher suction, and he drew close to me and said, "Go up and see what you can do," so I stood at the blackboard, looked at the problem, and thought, "God, take this chalk and write the answer. Or make the blackboard fall off and kill me. Please." I wrote a few faint numbers and the smart kids laughed. He said from the back of the room, "We talked about this last week, Mr. Keillor! I assumed you were paying attention! Your eyes were open, as I recall! Your head was up off the desk!" (p. 137).

All the research cited earlier and much more related research comes to a focal point in Keillor's story. The physics teacher was not a bad person and perhaps he believed his admonitions would inspire the young Mr. Keillor to greater effort and eventual accomplishments. On the other hand, the dismal failure encountered by Keillor undoubtedly left scars— painful reminders of teachers and schools. While young Mr. Keillor's teacher demonstrated belittling behavior, we as reading teachers must do much more than simply condemn such actions. Neutrality of disposition is not enough or even defensible. Positive affirmation of each and every student is essential.

Enhancing Affective Environments

The foundation of any learning environment is a warm invitation to learn. Teachers constantly struggle to maintain this kind of environment for students, particularly those who are uncomfortable in the typical school setting. In this light, Juel (1991) determined to find a way to help at-risk and primarily African American children feel successful in their elementary school learning environment. Juel engaged the children in learning through a tutoring program that matched them with student athletes from a nearby university. The children's mentors, both male and female, helped create an atmosphere that made the children feel truly important. Their confidence increased, and they felt "special" because someone cared enough about them to come and work with them (p. 183). African American male athlete role models provided an "especially powerful" (p. 184) influence on the children with whom they worked. Further, Juel found many of the student athletes so moved by their experiences that they expressed interest in teaching careers. Juel also reported remarkable gains in test scores, which should not be overlooked when emphasizing affective dimensions. When the tutoring program began, it appeared likely that none of the 20 students who participated would be ready to progress to second grade; after the program, only 2 of the 20 students had to be retained in first grade.

Like Juel, Gaskins (1992) studied the effects of close individual contact between caring adults and students who demonstrated learning difficulties. Gaskins described a mentoring program in which professional and nonprofessional adults, were matched one-on-one with children not only to provide help in academic areas but also to demonstrate advocacy for the child through a "caring attitude toward and commitment to the child" (p. 569). Gaskins stressed the importance of "emotional engagement" (p. 568) wherein the learner is encouraged to develop self-confidence, independence, and a willingness to learn. Gaskins found mentors extremely helpful in promoting among students the concept of self-regulation, which involved students in developing independence and assuming more responsibility for their own learning.

Bill Martin Jr (1987) described how his marvelous fifth grade teacher ushered him from being a nonreader to developing a love of literature—a love so strong as to ignite his career as one of North America's best-loved authors of children's literature. Martin credited his teacher with having the power to infuse her students with a love of literature, a quality he termed a "blessed thing" (p. 15). Like Gaskins, who focused on the power students generate for themselves through self-regulation, Martin found the self-generated power a love of reading can bring to an individual, a power he called "the literary touchstone that has sustained my life" (p. 16).

Positive Teachers Create Enthusiastic Readers

Teachers must create within each classroom a positive atmosphere, a way of life conducive to promoting reading through positive affect. Positive teachers are realistic but always looking for the best in their students. Positive teachers are competent teachers, constantly striving to better their skills. They realize that positive affect coupled with a high level of teaching ability promotes maximum achievement from their students.

We almost forgot to finish the story at the beginning of this chapter. Sean's teacher answered him with a smile: "Yes, you can read when you get back." And she did not make a grammatical error—she knew what she was talking about when she said Sean *can* read.

References

American Association of School Administrators. (1986). Effective teaching: Observations from research. Arlington, VA: Author.

Bettelheim, B., & Zelan, K. (1982). On learning to read. New York: Knopf.

Christophel, D.M. (1990). The relationship among teacher immediacy behaviors, student motivation, and learning. Communication Education, 39, 323–340.

Eccles, J.S., & Wigfield, A. (1985). Teacher expectations and student motivation. In J. Dusek (Ed.), Teacher expectancies (pp. 185–217). Hillsdale, NJ: Erlbaum.

Ford, M.P. (1992). A single rose: Remembrances of a good teacher. The Reading Teacher, 45, 512–513.

Gaskins, R.W. (1992). When good instruction is not enough: A mentor program. The Reading Teacher, 45, 568–572.

Good, T.L., & Brophy, J. (1978). Looking in classrooms. New York: HarperCollins.

Guskey, T.R. (1982). The effects of change in instructional effectiveness on the relationship of teacher expectations and student achievement. Journal of Educational Research, 75, 345–348.

Hesson, R.F., & Weeks, T.H. (1991). Introduction to the foundations of education (2nd ed.). New York: Macmillan.

Juel, C. (1991). Cross-age tutoring between student athletes and at-risk children. The Reading Teacher, 45, 178–186.

Keillor, G. (1989). Leaving home. New York: Penguin.

Martin, B., Jr. (1987). The making of a reader: A personal narrative. In B.E. Cullinan (Ed.), Children's literature in the reading program (pp. 15–19). Newark, DE: International Reading Association.

National Commission on Excellence in Education. (1983). A nation at risk: The imperatives for educational reform. Washington, DC: U.S. Government Printing Office.

Odden, A. (1987). School effectiveness, backward mapping, and state education policies. In J. Lane & H. Walbert (Eds.), Effective school leadership. Berkeley, CA: McCutchan.

Robeck, M.C., & Wallace, R.R. (1990). The psychology of reading: An interdisciplinary approach (2nd ed.). Hillsdale, NJ: Erlbaum.

Rosenthal, R., & Jacobson, L. (1968). Pygmalion in the classroom: Teacher expectation and pupils' intellectual development. New York: Holt, Rinehart.

Shrank, W. (1968). The labelling effect of ability grouping. Journal of Educational Research, 62, 51–52.

Staver, J.R., & Walberg, H.J. (1987). Educational research and productivity. In J. Lane & H. Walberg (Eds.), Effective school leadership (pp. 109–125). Berkeley, CA: McCutchan.

Walberg, H.J. (1986). What works in a nation still at risk. Educational Leadership, 44, 7–10.

Weiner, B. (1971). Achievement motivation and attribution theory. Morristown, NJ: General Learning Press.

Chapter 6

A Portrait of Parents
of Successful Readers

Dixie Lee Spiegel

●◆ Parents play a crucial role in the development of children who have positive attitudes toward reading and who become successful readers. Anderson et al. (1985) baldly state: "Reading begins at home." Reviews of research, studies of early readers, and investigations of emergent literacy uniformly conclude that parents' beliefs, aspirations, and actions affect their children's literacy growth.

Children's interest and attitudes are affected by two major factors: first, the climate in the home, which surrounds the child from birth and carries explicit and implicit messages about the value of reading; and second, the child's own competence in reading. Thus, research about children's reading achievement is intertwined with information about parental roles in the development of children's interest in reading. Some environmental factors can be altered, such as availability of literacy materials in the home, frequency of home literacy events, and, more difficult to change, the nature of parent-child literacy interactions and parents' attitudes toward their roles in their children's literacy development. However, two factors cannot be changed or are at best extremely difficult to change: socioeconomic status (SES) and race.

Clearing the Air: Socioeconomic Status, Race, and Reading Achievement and Interest

When researchers have investigated the relationship between socioeconomic status or race and reading, the results have often been conflicting. For many years it was assumed that individuals of low SES levels would also have lower levels of reading achievement and would provide impoverished literacy environments for their children. Indeed, a great deal of research supports a positive relationship between SES and various reading measures: high SES is associated with high reading achievement and vice versa. For example, Walberg and Tsai (1984) looked at National Assessment of Educational Progress data for 13-year-olds in the United States and found a significant relationship between reading achievement and SES. When studying data from 15 nations, Thorndike (1976) came to a similar conclusion. Neuman (1986) reported that children in higher SES homes had more books, spent more time reading, and participated in more family discussions about books and magazines than did children at lower SES. Race has also been found related to reading achievement and parental expectations in that membership in different ethnic groups has been reported to be associated with different levels of reading achievement (see Walberg & Tsai, 1984).

On the other hand, a comparable body of research has not found a relationship between SES and a variety of reading measures. Socioeconomic status has not been found to affect early reading (Torrey, 1979; White, 1982), attitude toward reading (Wigfield & Asher, 1984), or affective characteristics in general (Marjoribanks, 1979), type or amount of parental reading (Southgate, Arnold, & Johnson, 1981), or overall reading achievement (Dunn, 1981). Further, increasing evidence indicates that low SES parents do and can provide rich literacy environments for their children (Ingham, 1981; Teale, 1986).

In examining the role of race in literacy environments, Anderson and Stokes (1984) found wide variation within ethnic groups. Where they did find trends, they were in parent-child interactions. For example, they noted that low-income Anglo-American parents initiated literacy interactions more frequently than did low-income African American or Mexican American parents. (This finding corresponds to Heath's results in 1982.) However, African American and Mexican American parents tended to spend more time in individual interactions with their children. Thus, the amount of time spent in parent-child literacy interactions was similar across ethnic groups. On the other hand, in comparing literacy materials and events in the home of Anglo-, African, and Mexican American preschoolers, Teale (1986) found no clear ethnic differences in literacy practices.

What can these contradictory findings mean? These results call into question the utility of simply correlating race or various SES factors, such as parental level of education or family income, with reading achievement. Increasingly, and especially as alternate research methods gain credibility, literacy investigators are suggesting that SES is at best what Clarke-Stewart and Apfel (1978) call "only a crude shorthand index of presumed differences in home environment" (p. 57) and that ethnicity is not an automatic indicator of culture. We are coming to understand that it is not what parents have as resources or what they "are" but what they do in their homes—the literacy environment—that has the most effect on their children's literacy development.

Literacy Environments that Value and Encourage Reading

Ample evidence exists that parents in general are interested in their children's success in school, particularly in reading. A constant theme in Downing's (1973) international survey of literacy was the high degree of interest parents in most countries typically display in their children's reading and writing success. Williams and Stallworth (1983–1984) found parents eager to play a variety of roles in their children's literacy development; Fitzgerald, Spiegel, and Cunningham (1991) found both high- and low-literacy parents of entering kindergarten students to be very positive about their roles.

However, having an interest in the literacy development of one's child is apparently not enough to nurture that development. Parents of less successful readers have often been identified as valuing education and hoping that their children will do well (Heath, 1982; Ingham, 1981). Interest alone cannot be the determining variable. Other aspects of parental beliefs and attitudes must also be important.

A Profile of Beliefs and Attitudes of Parents of Successful Readers

Parents of successful readers—defined here as children who score well on reading achievement measures, who learn to read early, or who show high interest in reading as a leisure-time activity—have the following characteristics.

They want their children to succeed. Parental concern about their children's success in reading has been found to be strongly related to reading achievement in Japan (Sakamoto, 1976), Scotland (Goodacre, 1973), England (Ingham, 1981), and the United States (Anderson & Stokes, 1984; White, 1982). However, this does not mean that parents of less successful readers are necessarily disinterested in their children's success. Heath (1982) paints a profile of two mill town communities of the Carolina Piedmonts in the United States. In both Roadville, a white community, and Trackton, a black community, school success is valued, but rarely achieved. Ingham (1981) describes parents of less successful readers as caring but mired in a sense of helplessness, of lacking any sense of control over their children's success.

Parents of successful readers impart a sense of the importance of education to their children. They also impart high expectations to their children. Parents of successful readers let their children know that it is important to do well in school and that they are confident their offspring indeed will do well. Clay (1976) found that this emphasis on the importance of education was the distinguishing factor between the homes of Samoan children in New Zealand, who generally succeeded in learning to read, and those of Maori children, who had a better command of English but were often less successful readers. Dave (1963), in a U.S. study, and Marjoribanks (1979), in a summary of international studies, both concluded that parents' expressed desire that their children do well was the important variable in children's reading achievement.

On the other hand, parents of less successful readers often have high aspirations for their children, but low expectations (Ingham, 1981; Scott-Jones, 1984; Wigfield & Asher, 1984). They hope that their children will do well but do not really believe that they will.

Parents of successful readers impart a love of reading and a sense of the value of reading to their children. Several researchers have noted the relationship between parents' enjoyment of reading and the likelihood that their children will also learn to enjoy reading (Neuman, 1986; Sauls, 1971). Ingham (1981) expresses the relationship as follows:

> It is as though the parent experiences so much joy in reading that he or she tries to make available the same experiences to the child and also causes the child to seek the experiences that give so much pleasure to a loved and respected person. Also, it is likely that the child receives a further reward in terms of the parents' satisfaction and admiration if the child reads well and shares the parents' excitement about books (p. 176).

These parents like, enjoy, and respect their children, and they are willing to spend time, money, and effort to nurture their literacy. According to Ingham (1981), "the main strand that runs throughout all these aspects of the home lives of avid readers is that they know they are wanted, respected, cared for, and considered" (p. 232). She found that lower income parents of avid readers often made personal sacrifices to provide their children with nurturing literacy environments. Teale (1978) concluded that parents of early readers were concerned enough about their children to take the time needed to answer their questions and meet their emerging literacy needs.

By contrast, Ingham also reported that parents of infrequent readers often considered money used to buy books ill spent.

Parents of successful readers believe that they are their child's first teacher. Dunn (1981) concluded that the most critical variable in kindergartners' reading achievement was a parental "teaching set." Durkin (1966) found that fewer mothers of early readers believed that reading instruction ought to be left to the schools than did mothers of nonearly readers, in spite of the fact that the prevailing wisdom of the time was that parental teaching of preschoolers might "damage" children. Plessas and Oakes (1964) reported that 80 percent of the parents of early readers in their sample had intentionally set out to teach their preschoolers to read.

Mothers of avid readers in Ingham's (1981) study did not seem to think that this intentional nurturing of literacy was noteworthy. Ingham reports that the mothers tended to mention introducing their children to books in much the same way that they discussed providing them with a balanced diet or a warm room. Thus, to these mothers, providing for their children's literacy development was a natural part of nurturing their children.

However, parents of less successful readers tend not to believe that their own interventions as teachers or coaches of their children will have any impact, and they tend to be less actively involved in their children's literacy development than parents of successful readers. Heath (1982) summarizes the Trackton community's (mentioned earlier) viewpoint of parents as casual providers of experiences from which the child may or may not learn. She gives a particularly poignant quotation from a Trackton mother:

> "Ain't no use tellin' 'im: Learn this, learn that, what's this, what's that? He just gotta learn, gotta know; he sees one thing one place one time, he know how it go, see sumpin' like it again, maybe it be the same, maybe it won't" (p. 67).

Parents know what is happening in the literacy lives and schooling of their children. Sutton (1964) found a strong correlation between early reading and parents' interest in their children's school progress. Ninety-six percent of the parents of early readers maintained a high degree of contact with the school, whereas only 56 percent of nonearly readers' parents did in this U.S. study. Sakamoto (1976) relates the high rate of literacy success in Japan to parental interest; he reports that 45 percent of parents in one study knew every book that their children were currently reading and another 47 percent knew nearly all. Feitelson (1973) described a similar high degree of awareness among Israeli parents. On the other hand, Ingham (1981) reports that in her sample not one parent of an infrequent reader had ever talked to the child about his or her schooling.

Parents of successful readers believe that they can have an impact on their children's literacy development and are aware of the impact they are having. Ingham (1981) reports that without exception, parents of avid readers believed their efforts had an effect on their children's development of literacy. When Kastler, Roser, and Hoffman (1987) asked parents of successful first grade readers to describe their home literacy environments, four of the six most frequently mentioned events were parent structured and three of the five most common attributions for children's success involved parental actions or beliefs.

Literacy Environments: What Goes on in the Home

What parents believe and their attitudes toward literacy are reflected in the literacy environments of their homes. An impressive body of research over several decades and in many countries has established the importance of those environments in children's literacy development. Home literacy environments have several components, which are discussed in ascending order of importance: artifacts, events, and the nature of parent-child interactions.

Artifacts

One way to examine home literacy environments is to look at the presence of literacy artifacts in the home: books, newspapers, pencils and paper, letters, junk mail, and other print-related materials. Anderson and Stokes (1984) echo Teale's (1978) warning that literacy artifacts should not be equated solely with books, especially when discussing homes of the urban poor. Anderson and Stokes report that in such homes book-related literacy experiences are not common literacy events.

In spite of these findings, most research has concentrated on the presence of published literacy materials, such as books, newspapers, and magazines, with some attention to writing materials. Parents do think having books available to children is important. For example, when parents of incoming kindergartners were asked to rate the importance of various home literacy materials, children's books received the highest ratings (Fitzgerald, Spiegel, & Cunningham, 1991).

However, not all parents do provide books in the home. In Heath's (1982) Trackton community, which was lower SES and black, there were no children's literacy artifacts other than occasional religious materials. McCormick and Mason (1986) found extreme group differences when comparing the number of alphabet books in homes of professional parents, university staff and student parents (designated midlevel SES), and parents on public aid. Forty-two percent of public-aid parents estimated that they had no alphabet books in the house, whereas the estimates were 13 percent for midlevel parents and 3 percent for professionals.

Writing materials seem to be available in most homes, although Teale (1986) found that in many of the low-income homes that he visited writing materials were often not readily accessible. Parents in the Fitzgerald, Spiegel, and Cunningham (1991) study rated pens, pencils, and markers second only to children's books and magazines in importance for preschoolers' literacy development. Paper was rated as next most important.

"Instructional" materials—workbooks, flashcards, computer toys for reading and spelling—are valued by some parents but not by others. Fitzgerald, Spiegel, and Cunningham (1991) found that parents with low literacy levels had a higher opinion of instructional materials than did parents with high literacy levels.

Adult reading materials are available in most homes, although not all parents are aware of the role of these materials in developing children's literacy. All the low-income homes in Teale's (1986) study had newspapers and adult magazines, although several did not have many. *TV Guide* was a common fixture in most homes. However, low-literacy parents in the Fitzgerald, Spiegel, and Cunningham study ranked adult literacy materials far behind children's in importance, whereas the high-literacy parents gave them almost equal rankings. To extend our portrait of parents of successful readers, we therefore add that *parents of successful readers tend to provide literacy artifacts, especially children's materials, in their homes.*

Two final points need to be made about literacy artifacts:

1. The literacy artifacts described are often very simple, inexpensive materials. Children's books, although often bought, need not be; they are readily available at little or no cost from public or school libraries. Thus low SES should not be considered an obstacle to having literacy materials in the home;

2. Both Teale (1978) and the parents in the Fitzgerald, Spiegel, and Cunningham (1991) study concluded that it is not what you have in the home that is important—it is what is done with the materials.

Literacy Events

Recent research into home literacy environments has emphasized the social nature of literacy events. Parents often set up activities or events primarily designed to teach their children something about literacy. Early research focused primarily on these formal literacy interactions and events and found that they were (and are) apparently quite common in the lives of children who learn to read early (Durkin, 1966; Plessas & Oakes, 1964).

However, Teale and Sulzby (1989) report that by far the "vast majority of literacy experienced by young children is embedded in activities directed toward some goal beyond literacy itself" (p. 3). Most literacy events in homes are informal rather than formal. Indeed, because these kinds of literacy interactions are so much a part of everyday life, parents may not even be aware of the frequency of these events.

An emphasis on the importance of informal literacy events should not be construed as suggesting that naturally occurring literacy events are by themselves likely to be sufficient for a child to develop literacy. Teale (1982) suggests that social interactions with literacy might serve as inducers, as triggering events for the development of literacy. Durkin (1966) emphasizes the importance of both kinds of interactions: "Early interest in becoming a reader is as much 'caught' as 'taught'" (p. 95).

Children learn functions of literacy by observing literacy events in their environment. In fact, Teale and Sulzby (1989) assert that the key role parents play in literacy development is demonstration of uses of literacy. What children may learn from these observations is shown by Southgate, Arnold, and Johnson's (1981) research with average readers. The results indicated that young children are aware of the functional purposes of reading but do not necessarily perceive it as a source of pleasure.

Research has often substantiated the impact of adults as literacy role models for their children (Guthrie & Greaney, 1991; Ingham, 1981; Manning & Manning, 1984). Although many parents do read in front of their children, some parents are not aware of the importance of this modeling. None of the low-literacy parents in the Fitzgerald, Spiegel, and Cunningham (1991) study ever mentioned any adult literacy event as important when responding to open-ended questions about preschoolers' literacy development.

Although adult role modeling is important, the most frequently researched home literacy event has been reading to children. The research is clear that reading to children is related to reading achievement, early development of literacy, and interest in reading (Ingham, 1981; Kastler, Roser, & Hoffman, 1987; Neuman, 1986; Teale, 1984). Most parents are aware of the importance of reading to their children. Forty-four of the 49 parents in Durkin's (1966) sample said that their children's curiosity about reading came from being read to at home, and all of the parents of early readers in her New York sample read to their children. For both high- and low-literacy parents in the Fitzgerald, Spiegel, and Cunningham (1991) study, listening to stories read was the most highly rated and most frequently mentioned literacy event.

However, even if most parents are aware of the value of reading to their children, not all do. Only 73 percent of the parents of nonearly readers in Durkin's study (1966) read to their children. Thomas (1985) found a similar pattern of less frequent reading to children among parents of nonearly readers. Heath (1982) reports that in Trackton there was no bedtime story; parents rarely if ever read to their children. Ingham's (1981) infrequent readers and their parents both reported that the parents never read to the children. Rossman (1974), who investigated remedial high school readers, and Ryan (1977), who looked at first-year college students in remedial English classes, both reported parents had not read to their subjects as children.

This review of literacy events adds more to our portrait of parents of successful readers: *they read to their children often; they serve as role models as readers themselves.*

The Nature of Effective Literacy Interactions

Earlier I suggested that it was not what you had in the home that made a difference in literacy development but what you did with what you had. There are two complementary perspectives that explain the nature of effective literacy interactions: viewing interactions as facilitating construction of meaning versus viewing them as precursors or preparation for school interactions.

The constructivist vewpoint. This viewpoint draws on the work of Bloome (1985), Snow (1983), and Thomas (1985), among others. Thomas uses Snow's model for parent-child interactions for language development to suggest a framework for examining parent-child interactions that help children learn to construct meaning from text. Snow suggests that three parental procedures facilitate language development: semantic contingency, scaffolding, and accountability.

Semantic contingency involves an adult (or other knowledgeable individual) expanding on topics introduced by the child and answering the child's questions. Thomas (1985) found that early-reader studies consistently report that someone answered early readers' questions about text. Through *scaffolding* adults adjust their demands of the child to match what the child can do, thus reducing uncertainty and providing what Mason and Allen (1986) describe as "just enough support...to enable [the child] to succeed, but no more" (p. 28). It is through scaffolding that the adult models mature performance of the task. Scaffolding has often been associated with successful development of literacy (Mason & Allen, 1986; Teale & Sulzby, 1989). By contrast, Heath (1982) found that Roadville and Trackton parents, whose children often were less successful in school, did not provide scaffolding during parent-child interactions, whereas Maintown (a mainstream, middle-class Carolina Piedmont community) parents did.

Accountability means that parents require children to complete literacy tasks of which they are capable. Several researchers suggest that parents are uniquely qualified for this role because they are likely to be keenly aware of their children's needs and abilities and serve as responsive mediators between children and text (Clarke-Stewart & Apfel, 1978; Sulzby & Teale, 1991; Teale, 1978).

Thus, a picture emerges of interactions in which the child is an engaged, active participant in the construction of meaning from text. The child and parent are involved in joint problem solving through guided participation.

Parent-Child Interactions as Precursors of School Interactions. A second perspective is that effective parent-child literacy interactions serve to prepare the child for the kinds of interactions that take place in and are rewarded in school. Heath's (1982) work has been seminal in viewing parent-child interactions during story reading as preparation for school. She describes what Maintown children learn from interactions in two ways. First, Heath identifies a pattern of interaction called "what-explanations" which involves "asking what the topic is, establishing it as predictable, and recognizing it in new situational contexts by classifying and categorizing it in our mind with other phenomena" (p. 54). This pattern, Heath claims, is exactly the pattern that is "replayed" in schools daily. Maintown children are exposed to "what-explanations" before school during story reading; Trackton children are not.

The second set of Maintown findings Heath describes concerns rules for literacy events. Starting in infancy, children gradually learn to give attention to books and information in books and to ask questions about books. Again, these are the kinds of rules and book interactions that will be rewarded in school; Roadville and Trackton children come to school with a different set of rules. Thus, *parents of successful readers provide effective literacy interactions that assist their children in learning how to construct meaning from text and interact successfully in school settings.*

Reflections

Two portraits have emerged from this examination of parents' role in literacy development and interest. The first is a picture of a home literacy culture that immerses the child in reading and writing, both by design and by the circumstances of everyday living. Resnick (1987) contends that learning to read is a sociocultural process and that children develop literacy and an understanding of the purposes and pleasures of reading through serving apprenticeships while immersed in literacy environments. We have seen that some literacy environments are more effective than others and that the richness of a literacy environment has less to do with money and socioeconomic status than with parental beliefs, attitudes, and actions.

The second portrait is that of parents of successful readers. Parents whose children learn to read well and who love reading have generally created rich literacy environments. These parents value reading and education, and hope and expect that their children will develop the same values. These high expectations reflect the love and respect that the parents have for their children. Further, parents of successful readers are aware of the importance of their efforts in creating effective literacy environments. Because of the value they place on reading and on their children, these parents are willing to make the effort needed to create rich literacy environments.

The parental role in the development of children who both can and will read is enormous. As literacy educators, we now have an understanding of this role. It is heartening that so many parents play this role well. It is also encouraging to find that income level and race are not necessarily determinants of how well parents play this role. Still, a great deal needs to be done to assist many parents in providing more effective home literacy environments. A place to start is with parental beliefs and attitudes, especially in their understanding of their own role in their children's literacy development.

References

Anderson, A.B., & Stokes, S.J. (1984). Social and institutional influences on the development and practice of literacy. In H. Goelman, A. Oberg, & F. Smith (Eds.), *Awakening to literacy* (pp. 24–37). Portsmouth, NH: Heinemann.

Anderson, R.C., Hiebert, E.H., Scott, J.A., & Wilkinson, I.A.G. (1985). *Becoming a nation of readers: The report of the Commission on Reading.* Washington, DC: U.S. Department of Education.

Bloome, D. (1985). Bedtime story reading as a social process. In J.A. Niles & R.V. Lalik (Eds.), *Issues in literacy: A research perspective.* Thirty-fourth yearbook of the National Reading Conference, (pp. 287–294). Rochester, NY: National Reading Conference.

Clarke-Stewart, K.A., & Apfel, N. (1978). Evaluating parental effects on child development. In L.A. Shulman (Ed.), *Review of research in education* (Vol. 6, pp. 47–119). Itasca, IL: American Educational Research Association.

Clay, M.M. (1976). Early childhood and cultural diversity in New Zealand. *The Reading Teacher, 29*, 333–342.

Dave, R. (1983). *The identification and measurement of environmental process variables that are related to educational achievement.* Unpublished doctoral dissertation, University of Chicago, IL.

Downing, J. (1973). *Comparative reading: Cross-national studies of behavior and processes in reading and writing.* New York: Macmillan.

Dunn, N.E. (1981). Children's achievement at school-entry age as a function of mothers' and fathers' teaching sets. *Elementary School Journal, 81*, 245–253.

Durkin, D. (1966). *Children who read early.* New York: Teachers College Press.

Feitelson, D. (1973). Israel. In J. Downing (Ed.), *Comparative reading: Cross-national studies of behavior and processes in reading and writing* (pp. 426–439). New York: Macmillan.

Fitzgerald, J., Spiegel, D.L., & Cunningham, J.W. (1991). The relationship between parental literacy level and perceptions of emergent literacy. *Journal of Reading Behavior, 23*, 191–213.

Goodacre, E.J. (1973). Great Britain. In J. Downing (Ed.), *Comparative reading: Cross-national studies of behavior and processes in reading and writing* (pp. 360–382). New York: Macmillan.

Guthrie, J.T., & Greaney, V. (1991). Literacy acts. In R. Barr, M.L. Kamil, P.B. Mosenthal, & P.D. Pearson (Eds.), *Handbook of reading research: Volume II* (pp. 68–96). White Plains, NY: Longman.

Heath, S.B. (1982). What no bedtime story means: Narrative skills at home and school. *Language in Society, 2*, 49–76.

Ingham, J. (1981). *Books and reading development: The Bradford book flood experiment.* Portsmouth, NH: Heinemann.

Kastler, L.A., Roser, N.L., & Hoffman, J.V. (1987). Understandings of the forms and functions of written language: Insights from children and parents. In J. Readence & R.S. Baldwin (Eds.), *Research in literacy: Merging perspectives* (Thirty-sixth yearbook of the National Reading Conference, pp. 85–92). Rochester, NY: National Reading Conference.

Manning, M.M., & Manning, G.L. (1984). Early readers and nonreaders from low SES environments: What their parents report. *The Reading Teacher, 38*, 32–34.

Marjoribanks, K. (1979). Family environments. In H.J. Walberg (Ed.), *Educational environments and effects* (pp. 15–37). Berkeley, CA: McCutchan.

Mason, J.M., & Allen, J. (1986). A review of emergent literacy with implications for research in reading. In E.Z. Rothkopf (Ed.), *Review of research in education* (Vol. 13, pp. 3–47). Washington, DC: American Educational Research Association.

McCormick, C.E., & Mason, J.M. (1986). Intervention procedures for increasing preschool children's interest in and knowledge about reading. In W.H. Teale & E. Sulzby (Eds.), *Emergent literacy: Writing and reading* (pp. 90–115). Norwood, NJ: Ablex.

Neuman, S.B. (1986). The home environment and fifth-grade students' leisure reading. *Elementary School Journal, 86*, 333–343.

Plessas, G.P., & Oakes, C.R. (1964). Prereading experiences of selected early readers. *The Reading Teacher, 17,* 241–250.

Resnick, L. (1987). Learning in school and out. *Educational Researcher, 16,* 13–20.

Rossman, J.F. (1974). Remedial readers: Did parents read to them at home? *Journal of Reading, 17,* 622–625.

Ryan, J. (1977). Family patterns of reading problems: The family that reads together. *Claremont College Reading Conference Yearbook, 41,* 159–163.

Sakamoto, T. (1976). Writing systems in Japan. In J. Merrit (Ed.), *New horizons in reading* (pp. 244–249). Newark, DE: International Reading Association.

Sauls, C.W. (1971). The relationship of selected factors to the recreational reading of sixth grade students. *Dissertation Abstracts International, 32,* 2558-A (University Microfilms no. 7129390).

Scott-Jones, D. (1984). Family influences on cognitive development and school achievement. In E.W. Gordon (Ed.), *Review of research in education (Vol. 11,* pp. 259–304). Washington, DC: American Educational Research Association.

Snow, C. (1983). Literacy and language: Relationships during the preschool years. *Harvard Educational Review, 53,* 165–189.

Southgate, V., Arnold, H., & Johnson, S. (1981). *Extending beginning reading.* Portsmouth, NH: Heinemann.

Sulzby, E., & Teale, W. (1991). Emergent literacy. In R. Barr, M.L. Kamil, P.B. Mosenthal, & P.D. Pearson (Eds.), *Handbook of reading research: Volume II* (pp. 727–757). White Plains, NY: Longman.

Sutton, M.J. (1964). Readiness for reading at the kindergarten level. *The Reading Teacher, 17,* 234–240.

Teale, W.H. (1978). Positive environments for learning to read: What studies of early readers tell us. *Language Arts, 55,* 921–932.

Teale, W.H. (1982). Toward a theory of how children learn to read and write naturally. *Language Arts, 59,* 555–570.

Teale, W.H. (1984). Reading to young children: Its significance for literacy development. In H. Goelman, A. Oberg, & F. Smith (Eds.), *Awakening to literacy* (pp. 110–121). Portsmouth, NH: Heinemann.

Teale, W.H. (1986). Home background and young children's literacy development. In W.H. Teale & E. Sulzby (Eds.), *Emergent literacy: Writing and reading* (pp. 173–206). Norwood, NJ: Ablex.

Teale, W.H., & Sulzby, E. (1989). Emergent literacy: New perspectives. In D.S. Strickland & L.M. Morrow (Eds.), *Emergent literacy: Young children learn to read and write* (pp. 1–15). Newark, DE: International Reading Association.

Thomas, K.F. (1985). Early reading as a social interaction process. *Language Arts, 62,* 469–475.

Thorndike, R. (1976). Reading comprehension in fifteen countries. In J. Merrit (Ed.), *New horizons in reading* (pp. 500–507). Newark, DE: International Reading Association.

Torrey, J.W. (1979). Reading that comes naturally: The early reader. In T.G. Waller & G.E. MacKinnon (Eds.), *Reading research: Advances in theory and practice* (Vol. I, pp. 115–144). New York: Academic.

Walberg, H.J., & Tsai, S. (1984). Reading achievement and diminishing returns to time. *Journal of Educational Psychology, 76,* 442–451.

White, K. (1982). The relation between socioeconomic status and academic achievement. *Psychological Bulletin, 91*, 461–481.

Wigfield, A., & Asher, S.R. (1984). Social and motivational influences on reading. In P.D. Pearson (Ed.), *Handbook of reading research* (pp. 423–452). White Plains, NY: Longman.

Williams, D., & Stallworth, J. (1983–1984). *Parent involvement in education project: Executive summary of the final report.* Austin, TX: Southwest Educational Development Laboratory.

PART THREE

Motivating Readers

Teach students a desire to read;
then, when they desire skills,
teach them.

U. Price

Chapter 7

Promoting the Reading Habit: Considerations and Strategies

Jerry L. Johns
Peggy VanLeirsburg

●◆ A lifelong love of reading is a highly desired outcome of reading instruction. As documented in previous chapters, however, evidence shows that the reading habit is not being acquired or practiced by large segments of the population; other evidence from U.S. national assessments and researchers (Telfer & Kann, 1984) validates the claim that students' voluntary reading and enjoyment of reading decline with age.

Harris and Sipay (1990) believe it is unrealistic to expect that we can turn every student (or even a vast majority of students) into avid readers. Although we agree in principle with Harris and Sipay, we think a large part of the problem is *how* students have been turned or directed toward reading. Certain conditions may make it more likely that students' attention, interests, and thoughts will lead to reading.

Problems with Past Practices

Over the years, parents and teachers have engaged in many practices to encourage reading. For example, a student reads a book and gets to add a segment to the bookworm begun on a bulletin board that is now winding its way around the classroom. In another class, tokens are given for each book read, and students can exchange their tokens for toys or other items. Another teacher implements a pizza reward system: students who achieve reading goals each month for several months are rewarded with certificates for free pizzas. These and other related plans to motivate students to read led Berglund (1991) to ask whether we are taking the "most prudent path" (p. 4) to helping students become lifelong readers.

Incentive systems such as these frequently ignore student differences in performance, ability, and interest. Such systems also rely largely

91

on extrinsic motivation: it is often the teacher who initiates reading, maintains it, and ultimately rewards students. Some students may read enough to receive the reward; others may choose not to participate because the goal is perceived as unattainable. Quantity of books or minutes of reading often become the criterion for success. The potential long-term implications or limitations of such programs may be ignored to focus on short-term results.

A Perspective on Extrinsic Motivation

In schools, three common extrinsic motivation strategies for activities are rewards, competition, and emphasis on the instrumental value of the task (Good & Brophy, 1987). A basic problem is that "extrinsic strategies do not attempt to increase the value that students place on the task itself, but instead link task performance to delivery of consequences that the students do value" (p. 319).

Adding a segment to the bookworm and winning a coupon for a free pizza are examples of rewards, as are grades, recognition (for example, placing good papers on a bulletin board), and special attention or personalized interaction with the teacher. Good and Brophy (1987) note that "rewards are more effective for stimulating *level of effort* than *quality of performance* [italics added]" and "are better used with boring or unpleasant tasks than with attractive or interesting ones" (p. 319). In addition, students must believe they have a genuine chance to receive the reward; otherwise, they may become depressed, resentful, and unwilling to participate. Rewards, if used, must make provision for individual differences.

Competition, another common motivation strategy, is so widespread in schools (for example, grading systems, fund-raising efforts, sports, music) that we question whether it is appropriate and desirable to deliberately introduce additional competitive elements into reading programs. In creating a framework to promote reading, we want all participants to be winners. Competition creates losers as well as winners. The possible losses in a student's self-confidence and self-concept as a reader and as a member of the classroom community raise serious questions about competition as a long-term motivation strategy.

The third common form of extrinsic motivation is calling attention to how an ability such as reading can help students meet current needs and help them in future occupations or throughout life. The use of concrete examples that apply reading to real-life situations that are "credible and memorable" and the use of role models who demonstrate the real-life applications are especially helpful (Good & Brophy, 1987, p. 320).

Extrinsic motivation as found in these three forms has some genuine limitations. What follows is an effort to unify and present an overall framework within which the conditions for promoting the reading habit may be achieved. Specific strategies and ideas are presented so teachers can implement the framework.

Foundations for Promoting and Encouraging Reading

Any framework to motivate readers must involve at least four essential preconditions (Good and Brophy, 1987). First, the classroom environment must be supportive: "The teacher should be a patient, encouraging person who supports students' learning efforts. Students should feel comfortable taking intellectual risks because they know that they will not be embarrassed or criticized if they make a mistake" (p. 310). Second, activities and books should be at an appropriate level of difficulty for students. According to Adams (1990), "There is evidence that achievement in reading is improved by placement in materials that a student can read with a low error rate (2 percent to 5 percent), and that students placed in materials that they read with greater than 5 percent errors tend to be off-task during instruction" (p. 113). Third, meaningful learning objectives should guide the selection of activities. The teacher's basic objective to promote reading must focus on making reading a useful, valuable, and desirable activity. Skill and strategy instruction should be richly infused with many opportunities for students to read to fulfill their purposes. Fourth, extrinsic motivation strategies require moderation and variation. When students are eager to learn, no special motivation strategies may be needed. When needed, the overuse or routine use of a particular strategy may lose its effectiveness.

Recently, Marzano (1992) reviewed more than 30 years of research on the learning process and developed an instructional model. The first and perhaps most basic dimension of that model includes positive attitudes and perceptions about learning. The classroom climate is composed of factors external to the students (for instance, the quality and quantity of reading materials and the physical arrangement of the classroom) as well as the students' attitudes and perceptions. Marzano notes that student's attitudes and perceptions affect their mental climate for learning; moreover, a sense of comfort and order are critical aspects in this environment.

A Framework for Promoting and Motivating Reading

Cambourne (1991) has presented several conditions of learning and has applied them to learning to talk. He has also challenged educators to apply these conditions to other kinds of learning.

The model shown in the figure was developed by Cambourne (1991). Among the conditions of learning, two are seen as vital if students are to be engaged in reading: immersion and demonstration. The other conditions—expectations, responsibility, use, approximations, and response—if present, enhance the students' engagement in learning. The proposed benefits include learning that is much more durable and students who are much more empowered because of intrinsic motivation. The ultimate result could be students who have such positive attitudes toward reading and themselves as readers that they will continue to read long after formal instruction ceases.

How can teachers apply these conditions of learning to help promote the reading habit? We will provide examples and stress strategies that promote the important conditions that will stimulate students to read because *they* value it. Cambourne's conditions thus provide the guiding framework for designing, organizing, and presenting strategies. Additional ways to transfer these conditions certainly exist, and we encourage readers to use their experiences to enhance and expand the ideas we present.

Immersion

A literacy-centered classroom provides the basis for immersing students in reading. In such classrooms, a wide variety of printed materials is made available, a classroom library exists, and students are given regularly scheduled opportunities to interact with print. Students are immersed in the medium in which they are expected to learn. Print activities considered important and useful are made salient for students. The reading material in which students "are immersed, is always whole, always meaningful, in a context that is meaningful or from which meaning can be construed" (Cambourne, 1991, p. 17).

Students may interact with print by reading silently. Activities that encourage individual study and immersion in print include whole-class silent reading times, typically designated by acronyms such as SSR (Sustained Silent Reading) or DEAR (Drop Everything and Read). The entire class and the teacher read self-selected materials for a set amount of time. Silent reading may also be an unscheduled, free-time activity for individual students. Classroom libraries encourage and support reading at multiple levels and of various topics. Research by Bissett (1969) revealed that stu-

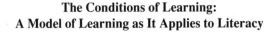

The Conditions of Learning:
A Model of Learning as It Applies to Literacy

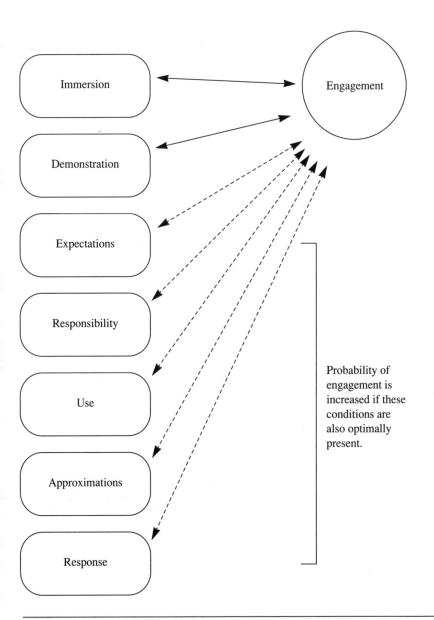

From B. Cambourne, "Breaking the Lore: An Alternate View of Learning," in *Frameworks: An Holistic Staff Development Program in Literacy Education*, Wayne-Finger Lakes Board of Cooperative Educational Services, Stanley, NY, 1993. Reprinted by permission.

dents who had literature collections in their classrooms read 50 percent more books than did students without such collections.

Anderson and others in *Becoming a Nation of Readers* (1985), encouraged educators to increase the amount of time students spend in individual reading. The researchers felt that if students simply read more, their skills and strategies would improve. However, this may not be entirely true, especially when students who are "at risk" are involved. Such students typically do not choose reading as a pleasurable activity; they are not good at it. Simply making them spend more time reading without teacher guidance and follow-up may ensure silent reading time spent in daydreaming and other off-task behaviors (Pinnell, 1988).

In order that independent reading time may be spent more productively, effective teachers will use sensitivity in guiding students and providing activities that stimulate interest and are at appropriate levels. Helping students locate materials of interest and at desired levels of difficulty is a key aspect to improving their level of immersion in available printed materials.

Demonstration

Demonstrations provide raw materials and examples for all learning (Cambourne, 1991). For example, young children learn to speak by hearing speech and language from parents and siblings. The same is true of literacy activities. The importance and function of print, as well as the pleasure gained by reading, are demonstrated first by family members and later by teachers and other members of society. Preschoolers will hold storybooks, turn pages, and "read" the text as they have seen parents and others do. Modeling literacy activities is a powerful force, as Spiegel stressed in Chapter 6. Students will strive to emulate the attitudes and activities of those people who are significant in their lives. They wish to copy the behavior of others who are admired and respected—parents, teachers, peers, television personalities, or sports figures. Role models from many occupations, ages, and ethnic groups may affect positive attitudes about reading.

Within the classroom, there is no more effective model than a teacher who genuinely loves books and reading. The spark of enjoyment will be caught by students who are fortunate enough to have such a role model. Teachers are in a position to read orally to their classes every day no matter what the age or grade level of their students (see also Chapters 10 and 15). Carefully chosen material, whether picture books or chapter books, read with enthusiasm and expression will motivate even the most reticent of readers to continue listening to find out what happens.

Oral reading, then, is a form of demonstration that instructs students about literacy activities and enjoyment. Although the classroom teacher is usually the person to carry out this modeling, other people may be helpful in such a role. School personnel, such as the principal, gym teacher, or secretary, could be invited to read a favorite book or poem to the class. Parents also may be willing to model the enjoyment of reading to the class. Students from other grades, community members, sports heroes, and television personalities could also be effective role models as readers. Some significant role models may be difficult to schedule and impossible to afford. However, many sports personalities and television stars have done promotional spots and posters in support of reading and school attendance.

Teachers need to encourage parents to read to their children of all ages on a daily basis and to applaud those who do. If begun at an early age, daily book reading and discussion in the family promote positive attitudes toward reading and improve school achievement. Many parents are aware that reading to their children, having various printed materials in the home, and reading themselves are important for their children's future reading attitudes and school success (see Spiegel's discussion in Chapter 6). However, there are some parents who would welcome sensitive suggestions from the classroom teacher (*Reading Today*, 1992; Trelease, 1989). Teachers have sometimes helped parents to establish the FRED (Family Reading Every Day) program to help promote reading.

Demonstrations in the classroom may take many forms. A teacher may read various genres, pointing out the differences and purposes of writing types. Author studies, in which more than one book by the same author is read aloud and discussed, may encourage students to read further works by that author. Book talks are a popular and interest-catching form of demonstration. A reader talks about the first part of a work of fiction that was particularly interesting. Next, a thought-provoking section is read aloud, but the reader stops at a pivotal point; students who want to find out more must then read the book. (See also Chapter 10 for more demonstration ideas.)

Expectations

As a condition of learning, expectations can be viewed from several different perspectives. First, students have expectations about themselves as learners. There are also the expectations, direct or subtle, that family members, teachers, or friends have of students.

Students see themselves as able to learn to read until events or people prove otherwise (Cambourne, 1991). Children, when they begin school, firmly believe that they will learn to read; their expectations are high. It is at this young age that permanent attitudes begin to take shape; positive experiences with print may start a lifelong reading habit. To ensure the development of positive attitudes toward reading, students must believe that the challenges they face are within their abilities. They must believe that what they are setting out to learn is actually learnable by them.

Whether at a conscious level or not, individuals set goals for themselves. These goals must be attainable. Teachers who have knowledge of their students' abilities can enable this personal goal-setting process by showing them that they *can* accomplish reading-related tasks. Focusing on reachable goals and avoiding situations that may lead to repeated failures will produce readers with positive attitudes. The perception, then, is that reading is not a task but a pleasure, and pleasurable activities will likely be repeated.

Parents also have high expectations about students. They naturally expect that their children will learn to walk and talk. They communicate such ideals on a daily basis and help young children toward these goals, snapping pictures and shooting videotape along the way. Parents also expect that their children will learn to read—an ideal that may be less clearly articulated or celebrated. Children who understand that reading and learning are valued by their family are more likely to become readers. Families who emphasize reading choose to spend time reading; they have printed material in the home and visit the library. Children who grow up in this atmosphere are likely to see learning to read as an attainable goal.

Teachers' expectations for student achievement also influence students' belief systems. Teachers who hold their expectations high and communicate in word and deed that students *can* read are conveying to students both that they are capable of reading and that it is not negotiable (see also Chapter 5). Teachers understand that reading must be learned; however, the path and the length of time spent on that path may be very different for individuals. Together, teachers and students determine goals that are reasonable and attainable.

Expectations that friends and other community members may have of students can also be powerful and coercive. If the neighborhood and the peer group value reading, the subtle effect is felt, and the student often continues to like and choose reading. Unfortunately, all too often the opposite is true.

Responsibility

Over half a century ago, Olson (1940) proposed the principles of seeking, self-selection, and self-pacing. He believed that students, motivated by internal needs, could take responsibility for much of their learning. Based on their needs and interests, students seek out, self-select, and read printed materials at their own pace.

Cambourne (1991) links much of his discussion of responsibility to demonstration. Students are encouraged to make decisions about and take responsibility for their literacy learning. Responsibility is likely to help foster ownership and actively engage students in learning. Ownership can become a reality for students when teachers invite and encourage active student participation in the literacy-centered classroom.

Earlier in this chapter, we discussed the need to establish classroom libraries containing reading materials about various topics and at multiple reading levels. While the initial holdings may be acquired by the teacher, there are many opportunities for students to be involved. The way in which library materials are displayed and arranged, the procedure for checking out materials, ways to secure new materials, and the proper care of the library holdings represent several areas in which students can take responsibility (Hepler, 1992). As students assume and share duties, establish policies, and develop strategies for enlarging the library, they can take pleasure in their contributions and realize that they play an important role in all aspects of the library. Some teachers have also been successful in promoting paperback book exchanges in their classroom in which students establish and monitor the entire process (Barchers, 1992).

Responsibility can also be stressed during silent reading programs. Students read self-selected materials at their own pace. Because there is no systematic plan to discuss or monitor what is read, students read to achieve their own purposes. They assume responsibility for making sense of the material, and inter-student competition is diminished with greater emphasis on each individual reading to fulfill his or her own purposes.

Use and Approximation

Approximation, as a condition of learning, represents the practice students are engaged in while trying to reach their goals. Just as we accept approximation in spelling while children are becoming writers, we also accept and expect inaccurate pronunciations while students are learning to read. Use, another of Cambourne's conditions for learning, represents the time and effort required to learn complex tasks such as reading. Time and opportunity are needed for students to use or employ reading skills and strategies to gain increasing control over printed materials. We combined these two conditions of learning because we view reading as a process—an individual continuum of development as a student becomes a reader.

Approximation and use are apparent in literacy activities for individuals, groups, and classrooms as students read for information and for pleasure. The basis for the following strategies is the activation of prior knowledge. This precept can be applied across age groups and content areas. It is not enough to assume that students have knowledge of concepts; such information should be experienced and discussed (Pinnell & Matlin, 1989; Samuels & Farstrup, 1992).

Of course, the best means of gaining knowledge is firsthand experience, which might include field trips or classroom demonstrations. Teachers can build on these experiences with discussions that include vocabulary and extend to synthesis and personal opinion. Vocabulary and concepts can be developed with the use of various types of webbing and Venn diagrams, which require students to think about how terms relate. Graphic representations of experiences tend to be enjoyable for students at all grade levels as they interact and develop a web of terms. Discussions might extend to a synthesis of concepts: How did this happen? Why might the character act in that way?

Once students' prior knowledge is activated and they demonstrate an understanding of concepts, class members might break into discussion groups. Carefully determined questions can guide discussion groups toward approximations, modeling discussion done as a whole group. These practice sessions enable students to test their comprehension and learn from one another while offering, supporting, and refuting ideas. Approximation can also be experienced as partners read and talk about factual or fictional material. Although the teacher is a source for helping students refine their approximations, classmates and parents can also be supportive and encouraging.

Students use their developing reading skills in many ways and need to be given a variety of opportunities. Choral reading is a wonderful opportunity for entire classes or small groups to read aloud with much support. As the material is practiced over and over again, familiarity overtakes shyness so that even reluctant readers enjoy the success of participating. Students can suggest expressions and hand motions appropriate to the text. Also in the oral reading mode are plays and Readers Theatre. Participants love to "ham it up" for their classmates while reading their parts. We have found it beneficial to audiotape or videotape student plays after several practice sessions. Students who see and hear themselves reading well will volunteer to repeat those experiences.

Choral readings, plays, and Readers Theatre are experiences that encourage students of all abilities to enjoy reading in their classroom. These activities can also be presented to other audiences. Parents, school staff, and other grades (both younger and older) enjoy such shows and are generally sensitive audiences. Success in reading in front of a group can significantly help develop confidence and improve attitudes toward reading.

Use can also include silent reading. However, whole class silent reading should be monitored. It is not enough that a book is open and eyes appear to be on the page. The teacher should guide silent reading. Berglund and Johns (1983) suggest that the teacher be patient but persistent in expecting success in silent reading programs. For students who can not or will not choose suitable material, the teacher can provide several types of reading material, and the student can make a decision. The teacher can also begin with short periods of silent reading and increase the time as students demonstrate greater engagement.

Silent reading can be used to help students achieve their purposes, as mentioned earlier. For example, Sonya, who is very curious about the rings around Saturn, may find her answers by reading. She needs to use her reading skill to achieve a purpose, one for which she is highly motivated. Students who have been motivated to read books because they enjoy a certain author or have heard a stimulating book talk will use reading to satisfy their goals. Other purposes may include the more functional aspects of school, such as the desire to do well, which might be gained through reading classroom assignments. If students understand or are shown a reason to read and are engaged or motivated, then they will choose to read.

Response

Another condition of learning—response—involves teachers, parents, or others sharing information with learners as they gain control over the reading process. It offers a scaffold for further learning and is specific to the context and situation requiring comprehension and application. Responses vary in detail but appear to have some things in common: they are readily available, unlimited, and nonthreatening, with no penalty for approximations (Cambourne, 1991).

As students interact with teachers and parents, responses help shape desired reading progress. Exchanges need to be accepting, caring, and patient while students are learning the complexities of reading. Students become empowered as they grow in ability and exercise their beliefs about printed materials. Teachers and parents offer support and facilitate independence in growth when they respond to learners.

Students practice their own response to reading when they form literature groups. They discuss selections, form opinions, and debate conclusions. Students in literature groups may choose to respond to text in other ways by writing to an author, presenting a skit, or rewriting the ending of a story. Journals are also forms of student response to reading. Journal writing may be a free response or an answer to a question or an issue. Response journals may take the form of a dialogue between student and teacher or classmate.

Artistic responses to reading are highly acceptable means of organizing and expressing ideas. Students could make a diorama of the time period represented in literature or design a book jacket complete with title and appropriate illustration. Many students have strengths in this area and should be encouraged to integrate creative expression as a response. The days of the book report as the only way to "prove" a book has been read are over. (See also Sinatra's following chapter.)

Creating classroom books is also an effective response. Each student may write a review of a literary selection or an advertisement for its sale. These could be collected and fashioned into a class book, which is shared with each student. Responses to the class book are considered, created, and shared, thereby furthering reading and enjoyment.

Some Parting Words

Promoting interest in reading may be encouraged through the knowledge and application of Cambourne's conditions of learning. Two conditions—demonstration and immersion—are considered essential. Without effective modeling and opportunities to enjoy readily available printed materials, the love of reading may not occur spontaneously. Other conditions for learning (expectation, responsibility, use, approximation, and response) are important to enhance engagement in learning and improve the quality of literacy experiences.

Good teachers are examples for their classes as they model the enjoyment of reading. They guide students toward materials matched specifically for individual level and interest. Good teachers create a learning environment where students actively choose reading as a means to gain both pleasure and information.

The task of directing students toward reading is an enormous responsibility. Effective teaching in the primary grades may persuade more students to share an interest in reading. As students mature, their interests and attitudes are more difficult to modify. If a disinterest in reading has been developed throughout the elementary years, it may be hard to change. The possibility of improving interests and attitudes toward reading are increased when teachers share their love of reading and provide students with the opportunity to enjoy print within a broader context that considers the essential conditions for learning.

References

Adams, M.J. (1990). *Beginning to read: Thinking and learning about print.* Boston, MA: MIT.

Anderson, R.C., Hiebert, E.H., Scott, J.A., & Wilkinson, I.A.G. (1985). *Becoming a nation of readers: The report of the Commission on Reading.* Washington, DC: U.S. Department of Education.

Barchers, S.I. (1992). Creating a classroom library: Book bargains. *Learning, 21*(2), 104, 106.

Berglund, R.L. (1991). Reading motivation: Are we creating intrinsically-motivated readers or fat kids who don't like to read? (commentary). *Illinois Reading Council Journal, 19*(4), 4–5.

Berglund, R.L., & Johns, J.L. (1983). A primer on uninterrupted sustained silent reading. *The Reading Teacher, 36*, 534–539.

Bissett, D. (1969). *The amount and effect of recreational reading in selected fifth grade classes.* Unpublished doctoral dissertation, Syracuse University, Syracuse, NY.

Cambourne, B. (1991). Breaking the lore: An alternate view of learning. In J. Turbill, A. Butler, & B. Cambourne, *Theory of others* (pp. 12–25). Stanley, NY: Wayne–Finger Lakes Board of Cooperative Educational Services.

Good, T.L., & Brophy, J.E. (1987). *Looking in classrooms.* New York: HarperCollins.

Harris, A.J., & Sipay, E.R. (1990). *How to increase reading ability* (9th ed.). White Plains, NY: Longman.

Hepler, S. (1992). Creating a classroom library: Getting started. *Learning, 21*(2), 96, 100, 102.

Marzano, R.J. (1992). *A different kind of classroom: Teaching with dimensions of thinking.* Alexandria, VA: Association for Supervision and Curriculum Development.

Olson, W.C. (1940). Reading as a function of total growth of the child. In W.S. Gray (Ed.), *Reading and pupil development* (Supplementary Educational Monograph No. 51, pp. 233–237). Chicago, IL: University of Chicago.

Pinnell, G.S. (1988). Positive and negative choices: Impact on curricula. In J.L. Davidson (Ed.), *Counterpoint and beyond* (pp. 87–104). Urbana, IL: National Council of Teachers of English.

Pinnell, G.S., & Matlin, M.L. (Eds.). (1989). *Teachers and research: Language learning in the classroom.* Newark, DE: International Reading Association.

Samuels, S.J., & Farstrup, A.E. (Eds.). (1992). *What research has to say about reading instruction* (2nd ed.). Newark, DE: International Reading Association.

Telfer, R.J., & Kann, R.S. (1984). Reading achievement, free reading, watching TV, and listening to music. *Journal of Reading, 27*(6), 536–539.

Those who read more read better, says NAEP. (1992, August/September). *Reading Today*, p. 32.

Trelease, J. (1989). *The new read-aloud handbook.* New York: Penguin.

Chapter 8

Literature and the Visual Arts: Natural Motivations for Literacy

Richard Sinatra

●◆ Many have acknowledged the importance of literature in providing a sound basis for humanistic education. Literature along with music and art contains the best evidence of the unity and continuity of the human condition reflected from past to present (Postman, 1980). By studying classic works, students also discover visions of wholeness and the greater worlds created by humanity's most profound imagination (College Board, 1985). The National Endowment for the Arts (1988) believes that basic arts education comprised of the four major disciplines of literature, visual art and design, performing art, and media art gives students tools for creating, communicating, and making informed and critical choices.

Immersion in literature, as both art form and reading content, can accomplish five goals for developing readers. First, literature generally shows humans at their best. They strive for something against adversity. These strivings are often called "conflicts," such as the pitting of humans against nature, humans against humans, or a human against himself or herself. As young people read and sense their own struggle to overcome, they can learn to emulate and appreciate the human condition. The College Board (1985, p. 15) states:

> By becoming immersed in the works of other periods and cultures, students have a chance to discover the universal human interest in going beyond what is necessary for bare survival by capturing or creating qualities that are pleasing, beautiful, monumental, or extraordinary.

Second, literature as a discourse mode is readily comprehensible to young readers. Its written style complements how they think. Apart from poetry, literature is generally distinguished as the discourse mode of fiction, and its style is narrative. The literary genre of narrative includes picture storybooks, tales, myths and folklore, fantasy, science fiction, and realistic and historical fiction. Possibly the reason children watch hours of TV cartoons is that they are engaged in experiencing the classical narrative elements of plot and style. They are captivated by the struggles of their heroes and heroines to overcome insurmountable difficulties as the continuous and rising story action unfolds on the screen.

Moffett (1983) notes that children use and depend on narrative for their primary mode of thinking, and Higgins (1981) reminds us that story making was one of the first methods that humans used to explain baffling experiences and phenomena not explainable through natural observations of the world. Van Dongen and Westby (1986) point out that while children's development of narrative discourse initiates from their daily lives as they tell stories about themselves and others, their understanding of the human experience grows as they learn the folk and cultural narratives that are passed on through generations. Moreover, when young children place themselves in roles as observers in the narrative, they are assisted in acquiring literacy (Scollon & Scollon, 1981).

Third, through literature, readers learn that language is used in rich and creative ways. The ways words are used and sentences are arranged are perceived in the imagination of the storyteller. Readers, on the other hand, image the juxtaposition of vocabulary and sentences as they attempt to re-create the essence of the storyteller's vision. The more the vocabulary paints the way to richness and texture, the more the reader achieves aesthetically appealing visions of meaning while learning new words. In the classic *The Legend of Sleepy Hollow*, Washington Irving might have written, after Ichabod Crane was rebuffed by Katrina Van Tassel, "Ichabod went to the stable, obtained his horse, and began his sad trip homeward." Instead, he wrote three sentences to capture the same denotative meaning:

> Without looking to the right or left to notice the scene of rural wealth on which he had so often gloated, he went straight to the stable, and with several hearty cuffs and kicks, roused his steed most uncourteously from the comfortable quarters in which he was soundly sleeping, dreaming of mountains of corn and oats, and whole valleys of timothy and clover.
>
> It was the very witching time of night that Ichabod, heavy-hearted and crestfallen, pursued his travel homewards, along the sides of the lofty hills which rise above Tarry Town, and which he had traversed so cheerily in the afternoon. The house was as dismal as himself.

Notice how the comic picture of rousing the borrowed steed is contrasted soon after with the image of the dismal Ichabod, disconsolate as he travels homeward. Both excerpts have the same literal meaning, but Irving's choice of words and syntax is far more connotatively rich, appealing to our sense and our vision. Purves (1985) suggests that the specific language of literary works produces images based on the experience of the reader. Further, emotions accompany such images. (See also Chapter 9 about instilling the love of words in children.)

Fourth, literature provides access to aesthetic experience. Aesthetic experiences are both pleasant and engaging (Miller, 1980): they make one happy or fulfilled, and they dominate one's focus during reading. Miller portrays the aesthetic state in this way:

> The person who reads literature successfully will have a highly conscious and thoroughly pleasant experience, independent of any personal need, in which the particular work that is being read arrests the reader's attention, fixes it, controls it, and concludes it (p. 9).

Smith (1985) adds that during aesthetic reading, the reader is not seeking to acquire information but to explore worlds of sensations and ideas. Readers, therefore, are reluctant to have the experience end and are annoyed when interruption or interpretation by others occurs during the reading experience. During aesthetic reading, the reader experiences and enjoys the ideas, situations, scenes, personalities, and emotions that are evoked and participates in the tensions, conflicts, and resolutions as they unfold (Rosenblatt, 1989). Aesthetic reading helps people become motivated, lifelong readers (Winograd & Smith, 1987).

Finally, the wonder and enjoyment of literature can be easily integrated with and translated to other art forms. Often children reveal the majesty of their imaginations as they interpret stories through visual art, drama, and music. Their drawings, for example, reflect their understanding of text, not only literally but also expressively and aesthetically.

The Arts Connection to Literacy Development

The arts are critical for literacy and thinking development for all people. The arts engage students in unique ways to communicate across language and cultural barriers and to foster discipline, concentration, and self-esteem (Martorelli, 1992). Arts education improves cognition, promotes social relations, stimulates personal development, helps retain students in school, promotes achievement in challenging subject matter, and fosters productive citizenry (Hanna, 1992). Hanna adds that involvement in the arts can engage and empower other domains of knowledge, such as from the fields of nonverbal communication, socio- and psycholinguistics, cognition, and the transfer of learning from one domain to another.

How can arts engagement accomplish such lofty educational and lifelong goals? The arts provide many forms of representation, languages necessary to understand and express these forms, and sensory experiences that stimulate the mind to form new ideas, perspectives, and language combinations. Boyer expresses this expansive concept of arts education:

> Art education, then, is basic because it extends our language. It enlarges the story of the images we use. It makes our understanding discriminating and comprehensive. Music, dance, and the visual arts are languages that reach all people at their deepest and most essential human level (1985, p. 8).

Involvement in the arts stimulates representational thinking. During representational thought, one aspect of reality takes on another aspect, as happens, for example, when a wooden block becomes a train in the hands of a young child. Representational thought, which is highly nonverbal and imaginative in nature, is the basis of the thinking of analogy, metaphor, and symbol substitution. For young children, representational thought can be expressed through different ways, such as gesture and body language, play, modeling, construction tasks, and drawing and coloring. For older learners, the craft and technique of each art form can be expanded to include all the various ways that imagination can create. Thus, the arts provide a means for the mind to reach creative heights and to approach and solve problems in alternative ways. Moreover, through art study, students can gain insight into the interaction between a creator's feelings and techniques used, such as the interplay in a poem between the words chosen and the poet's feelings or the interplay in a painting of the techniques of brush, color, and canvas and the artist's feelings (Rowell, 1983).

Torrance (1979) believes that power resides in creativity exciting more creativity and occurs when children's production of art leads to another form of expression. Creative poetry can stimulate the scientist, and the discoveries of the scientist can stimulate the imagination of the poet. Torrance explains that the more creative acts a person experiences, whether they be those of another or her or his own, the more richly the person lives. Anything that makes such a person more alive is likely to facilitate and produce creative achievement.

The creative act is often energized by imagery or the re-creation of images (Gowan, Khatena, & Torrance, 1979). Where does imagery come from and how does it propel intellectual and emotional forces to capture the creative act? Each literacy we participate in contributes receptive and expressive symbol systems to allow us to turn raw experiences into thought-provoking and emotionally energized images. For instance, during receptive listening in the oral communication system, the learner connects word and sentence structure to mental pictures in the brain; whereas, during the composing and creative acts of using art forms or writing, the learner uses expressive symbol systems to engage meaning. Broudy (1983) considers the broad purpose of arts education to be grounded in the use of the imagination—to provide the power to create and construe images as vehicles of human thought.

I have had the dual benefits of being a reading educator for most of my professional life and of serving a six-year term as facilitator of the Arts in Education Network of the Association for Supervision and Curriculum Development/ As a reading specialist, I have experienced the value of engaging emergent and disabled readers in arts activities to stimulate their oral language. And, as the ASCD Arts in Education facilitator, I was able to learn about many excellent arts in education programs that have emerged during the 1980s. These programs attempt to overcome the United States' loss of "cultural literacy" and were spurred by such national endeavors as the 1977 "Coming to Our Senses" report of the Arts, Education and Americans panel; the College Board's Green and Red Book reports of 1983 and 1985; the 1983 National Commission on Excellence in Education report *A Nation at Risk*; the 1986 National Survey of Arts Education conducted by the National Art Education Association; the Council of Chief State School Officers report of 1985, entitled *Arts, Education and the States*; and the 1988 landmark report *Toward Civilization* issued by the National Endowment for the Arts.

Arts in education approaches today are viewed in more expansive terms than merely using an arts experience to generate or motivate a reading lesson. Many modern arts in education programs take whole literacy approaches that provide students access to their culture's highest levels of thinking and achievement while providing continuing access to print literacy in natural, meaningful, and affective ways.

Art in Education Projects and Programs

A National Arts Research Center located at New York University, conducts staff research and curriculum development in arts education and encourages teacher-assisted projects in arts education across the United States. The projects are concerned with four rather broad themes: how students respond aesthetically to the arts; how students develop their artistic skills; how students acquire knowledge of the historical contexts of art in diverse cultures; and how the interrelationship of the arts and humanities can be enhanced.

The Learning to Read Through the Arts Program, also located in New York City, presents an interdisciplinary, team-teaching approach to improving the reading ability of at-risk students. Classroom teachers, reading teachers, and art teachers participate in the interdisciplinary process of a thematic approach, using the arts as the core for learning. A theme is developed by beginning with one or several activities to stimulate students' interest. For instance, in the theme of Asian art and literature, art projects may begin with any one of the following: Asian scrolls, fans, dragons, kimonos, fish prints, or kites. If the production of a Chinese scroll initiated the project, students discuss the difference between a Western-style painting and an Asian scroll. They are asked to identify significant elements or topics in scroll paintings, with an emphasis placed on the significance of nature, symbolized by the earth, water, and sky. Symbolic meanings of particular items such as dragons, horses, and fish are discussed because they are important in both Chinese visual art and literature. The use of Chinese characters and the placement of objects in a scroll are discussed in terms of how the artist presented a unique viewpoint. Students are taught watercolor techniques and practice the use of specific types of brush strokes, bleedings, and blottings. Students then conceptualize themes for their own individual scrolls and select symbols and colors to reinforce their themes.

Teachers then integrate the language arts and present literature and poetry to correspond with the thematic unit. Students are asked to write a paragraph about their scrolls, read the stories that are exemplified by their scrolls, and give the scrolls titles that are relevant to main ideas of their stories. Students read children's literature and poetry relating to the theme and use writing to express their ideas and findings. For instance, when students read *Learning and the Magic Paintbrush*, they relate the story line to their own scrolls. They are asked to write about such concerns as "If the objects in the story or painting become alive, what would happen?" and "If you could step into your scroll, what would you see, where would you go?" By using such art forms to teach basic skills in reading, the students get hooked on art, especially if they begin at their knowledge and interest levels (Rowell, 1983).

Arts Propel is a collaborative project sponsored by the Rockefeller Foundation and involves Harvard Project Zero, Educational Testing Service, and the Pittsburgh (Pennsylvania) Public Schools. The project integrates the visual arts, music, imaginative writing, and use of portfolios for middle school and high school students. Arts Propel has a particular orientation to arts education that focuses on the processes of production, perception, and reflection (Gitomer, Grosh, & Price, 1992). Production is the key among the three processes in that the arts of perception and reflection are engaged in and around the primary activity of making art. In such a studio orientation, the "doing" sets the stage for the engagement of perceptions and reflection. Producing art introduces students to concepts, processes, attitudes, and emotions that foster the integration of other materials in the curriculum. Perception involves those mental processes in which one sees and understands images, either produced by oneself or others. Reflection occurs when students think and discuss some aspect of the artistic process, such as when a work is revised.

The notion of a "portfolio culture" is central in the Arts Propel studio orientation. This approach offers an environment that recognizes fundamental principles of student learning. It is a constructive, motivated, and integrated process. The Propel portfolio does not include just final, polished pieces; it includes the drafts, sketches, and attempts not followed by a student (Wolf, 1989). With these pieces, students can discuss artistic and creative development with teachers. The portfolio also includes written journal entries, written reflections regarding a piece, and materials related to a topic or theme drawn from other sources. With reference materials, drafts, sketches, fully developed works, and written reflections included in the portfolio culture, interaction occurs between teachers and students, and students and their peers. These interactions promote understanding while facilitating the development of student artistry.

The Discipline-Based Art Education (DBAE) approach in the visual arts is an attempt to raise the status and quality of art education in the traditional classroom by combining content from four foundational disciplines of art—studio or expressive art, art history, art criticism, and aesthetics. To state its philosophical and conceptual approach, the Getty Center for Education in the Arts has published *Beyond Creating: The Place for Art in America's Schools* (1985), *Discipline-Based Art Education: What Forms Will It Take?* (1987), *The Role of Discipline-Based Art Education in America's Schools* (Eisner, 1987a), and *The Role of Imagery in Learning* (Broudy, 1987). Because a balanced emphasis is given to the four disciplines mentioned, a natural, whole learning, whole language environment is achieved through the DBAE approach. What occurs is much oral discussion and analysis of art works. Students also learn expressive techniques and how to use genre forms to transmit messages. For example, because the Arizona Department of Education (1985) followed a DBAE approach in its visual arts program for the elementary grades, teachers from grades one through six were charged with curriculum tasks for creative arts expression, aesthetic assessment, and the study of past and present art and artists. First and second graders were involved in an arts expression task to help them observe and represent their environment. They either made a painting of handmade or manufactured objects commonly found in the house or made a sculpture from such materials as egg cartons, string, cardboard cylinders, and any other throw-away, mass-produced items. The same curriculum goal—to produce art as a representation of one's environment—was adapted for fifth and sixth graders. Curriculum goals included having them choose such activities as clothing design, decor design for a room in their home, or photographing common objects from an artistic viewpoint. Students were asked to discuss or write about their nonverbal representations for which they had to use language in meaningful ways to communicate their experiences. One fifth grader put it this way: "Art is important for me. It fills my mind with ideas" (Taylor, 1989).

In a multicultural school in a Los Angeles, California, suburb, I observed fifth graders successfully transferring ideas as their teacher led them through the disciplines of the DBAE approach. After the students had learned to use a particular painting technique during art production time, the teacher focused their attention on artworks of the same style from a famous period of art history. As students scanned large, projected images of well-known paintings from the 17th-century Dutch landscape masters, the teacher read about each painter and what he attempted to capture in his painting. The students learned that the painters revealed their pride in their country by showing its land and waterways.

During scanning, students were visually engaged while the teacher asked specific questions that tapped students' perceptual, intellectual, linguistic, and aesthetic skills. Students analyzed a painting's *sensory properties*, which called for the ability to see and discuss such elements as line, shape, color, and proportion; they studied its *formal properties*, which required the ability to sense how a work is put together to form its particular character with such elements as unity, balance, movement, and contrast; they analyzed its *technical properties*, which called for a knowledge of how techniques in making art may have contributed to the painting's overall character; and they discussed its *expressive properties*, by considering what the work had to say by focusing on its mood, dynamic state, ideas, and ideals.

The students then discussed what they saw and heard, revealing their vocabulary and concept knowledge. Afterward, the students worked in cooperative groups of four and continued to sort through and analyze art-works now in poster size. Here they were comparing and contrasting art-work from all the periods they had studied. Such an approach aims to increase students' store of images, which Broudy (1987) calls the allusion-ary base. This base comprises concepts, images, and memories and pro-vides underlying meaning to a reader or listener. If this base is impover-ished, the reader or listener may fail to comprehend fully and richly.

Broudy (1983, 1985) has argued that the skills of aesthetic scan-ning are more important than those of art expression or art production in the elementary grades. He feels that such perceptual training "can be regarded as a general approach to aesthetic education, for it is directed toward the perception of the properties that all aesthetic objects exhibit in one medium or another without fusing or confusing the media" (1983, p. 233). The strength of this focus in the early grades is that aesthetic scanning can be taught through the use of any media, requires little creative arts tal-ent on the part of the regular classroom teacher, and provides for concept and vocabulary expansion.

The criteria used in aesthetic scanning are not far removed from the criteria often used in holistic scoring of students' written compositions. Such criteria as unity, theme focus, organization, coherent and smooth movement, use of vocabulary and sentences to achieve an imaginative approach, and technical correctness are the basis for such writing scales.

Through the whole learning approach of DBAE, work in one disci-pline area can be easily integrated with other aspects of the curriculum. This would occur, for instance, when painters and their genres are included in a social studies unit that covers the same period of history. A strong visu-al connection would occur as students see how the times and people of a particular culture are portrayed. "It's like a history class and an art class combined," reported a fifth grader (Taylor, 1989). Children are not only examining art and gaining a source of its history, but also they are continu-ing to develop their creative skills (Greer & Silverman, 1987–1988).

Work in art production techniques can be recaptured in the lan-guage arts setting. Because students experience the actual "doing" in which most of their physical senses are engaged, they have the raw material to re-create the experiences in their compositions, essays, and reports. Further, these re-creations can be expressed through differing written styles. Biogra-phy would naturally follow from the study of an artist while descriptive reports could be written to elucidate art expression techniques. Wilson (1987, p. 75) has noted that important artworks can be revealed to students through three processes:

1. through the "re-creation" of the themes, the subject matter, and the expressive content of the works;

2. through the "co-creation" of critical writing, especially writing that is expressive and metaphorical; and

3. through "contextual re-presentation," with students rewriting or reinterpreting "the historical, cultural, social, and other contextual antecedents and consequences of important works of art."

One student involved in the DBAE approach expressed the close connectedness of art and writing in the following way:

> What I like about art is first we look at art and talk about it. I get ideas about what I want to draw. When I first came to this school I thought I was a bad writer and drawer. But when we started to talk, it made me get ideas on what to write or draw.

The arts in education approach presents a holistic way of providing content, ideas, technique, vocabulary, and history to use language meaningfully and productively in many contexts across the curriculum. Further, when students get involved with talking about art, they become involved with skills that have a direct relationship to reading (Rowell, 1983).

Implications for Reading

Some general points regarding the importance of literature and visual arts as natural motivations for literacy can be made. The first is that imagery and imagination connect both disciplines. The ability of the mind to create mental pictures and to generate imaginative thought permeates such thinking as predicting, remembering, understanding, composing, and creating. Imagery is considered to be a symbolic system specialized for parallel processing of information in which nonverbal memory representations of concrete phenomena are recalled or visual representations are actively manipulated by an individual (Paivio, 1979). Imagination arises out of construction of novel images that may not resemble actual concrete phenomena but produces such endeavors as new symphonies, paintings, poetry, literature, and scientific breakthroughs (Eisner, 1987b).

In Paivio's dual-coding model (1979, 1986), affective and emotional reactions are also nonverbal in nature and would appear to complement the cognitive thinking of imagery. As discussed earlier, the language of literature gives rise to imagery, and such imaginative thought generates feelings, possibly very strong emotional connections during moments of intense aesthetic engagement. Likewise, through such techniques as scanning or perception noted in arts in education programs, students' use of imagery and imagination is piqued as they sense the connections between an artist's feelings and the technique used to express his or her artistry. Purves (1985) noted that, when reading a literary work, the collection of images and emotions evoked leads to a central imagistic and emotional meaning that subordinates the minor feelings and mental pictures produced.

Sadoski alone (1984, 1985) and with others (Sadoski & Goetz, 1985; Sadoski, Goetz, & Kangiser, 1988) has shown that strong relationships exist between emotions, imagery, and plot comprehension for the narrative. In the 1988 study which used three stories, literate readers reported experiencing similar degrees of imagery and emotions as well as sensing similar degrees of plot importance. Further, students offered explicit text information 55 percent of the time and made inferences based on text information 45 percent of the time to support the emotions they described. It is interesting to note that students sometimes reported imagery evidence in lieu of emotional reactions and at other times used emotional reactions to describe their mental images.

Other reading and writing educators have noted that using imagery positively influences reading comprehension (Irwin, 1991; McNeil, 1987) and writing productivity and quality (Jampole et al., 1991; Sinatra, 1986). Chunking or organizing information to assist long-term memory during the reading process can be enhanced by using imagery (Smith, 1982). Paivio (1979) suggests that when imagery is aroused and associated with verbal information, comprehension, retention, and production of verbal language are strengthened. Because the verbal and imaginative systems have rich neural interconnections, learners can use words to describe pictures and use imagery to assist in the choice of words (Bower, 1972).

Imagery production and emotional responding can occur before, during, and after reading and writing and would appear to be involved in the use of such strategies as making predictions, unlocking elements of story structure (grammar), summarizing, appreciating, valuing, brainstorming, and revising. Techniques of how to intentionally stimulate imagery and affective interaction to assist written literacy proficiency can be found in particular sources for the reader (Irwin, 1991; McNeil, 1987; Sinatra, 1986). In their taxonomy of reading comprehension, Smith and Barrett (1979) include such affective factors as responding emotionally to the plot or theme, identifying with characters and incidents, and reacting to the author's use of language.

I would be remiss if I did not conclude with a "thank you" note to today's many whole language and integrated language arts educators. When I visit their schools and classrooms and look at children's writing folders, I see that children's art is a mainstay of the whole literacy process. Teachers use such strategies in picture story maps, big books, flip books, accordion books, and pop-up books to help children learn *how* to read and write while integrating mental visions of their art. While the arts in education programs discussed earlier stress particular disciplines of art as especially important for students to learn, whole language classrooms use the vision of art to help propel and provide greater depth to developing writing and reading skills. Because narrative is the underlying discourse style of literature, children can visualize episodes of time and place or cause and effect relationships in distinct frames of a story map or other retelling activity. These frames become their interpretations of the story's meaning and can reveal deep comprehension of plot and character interactions.

Thus art, particularly visual art, can be a strong force for either the production of the narrative or the interpretation of literature. A student could draw the frames of an imaginative story first and then write of its interpretation. Or a child could read first, then be asked to visualize, draw, or act out the story grammar—the episodes that provide the story's dimensions of time, setting, and action. Finally, the teacher could integrate some arts in education techniques through the sharing of great works that are related to a topic or theme and introduce students to the great cultures of which they are a part.

References

Arizona Department of Education. (1985). *Visual arts sequenced curriculum guide: Grades 1–6*. Phoenix, AZ: Author.

Bower, G. (1972). Mental imagery and associative learning. In L. Gregg (Ed.), *Cognition in learning and memory*. New York: Wiley.

Boyer, E.L. (1985). Art as language: Its place in the schools. In Getty Center for Education in the Arts (Ed.), *Beyond creating: The place for art in America's schools* (pp. 8–9). Los Angeles, CA: The J. Paul Getty Trust.

Broudy, H.S. (1983). A common curriculum in aesthetics and fine arts. In G.D. Fenstermacher & J.I. Goodlad (Eds.), *Individual differences and the common curriculum* (Eighty-second Yearbook of the National Society for the Study of Education, pp. 219–247). Chicago, IL: University of Chicago Press.

Broudy, H.S. (1985). Curriculum validity in art education. *Studies in Art Education, 26*, 212–215.

Broudy, H.S. (1987). *The role of imagery in learning* (Occasional Paper 1, The Getty Center for Education in the Arts). Los Angeles, CA: The J. Paul Getty Trust.

College Board. (1983). *Academic preparation for college: What students need to know and be able to do*. New York: College Board.

College Board. (1985). *Academic preparation in the arts.* New York: College Board.

Council of Chief State School Officers. (1985). *Arts, education and the states: A survey of state education policies.* Washington, DC: Author.

Eisner, E. (1987a). *The role of discipline-based art education in America's schools.* Los Angeles, CA: The J. Paul Getty Trust.

Eisner, E. (1987b). The celebration of thinking. *Educational Horizons, 66,* 24–29.

Getty Center for Education in the Arts. (1985). *Beyond creating: The place for art in America's schools.* Los Angeles, CA: The J. Paul Getty Trust.

Getty Center for Education in the Arts. (1987). *Discipline-based art education: What forms will it take?* Los Angeles, CA: The J. Paul Getty Trust.

Gitomer, D., Grosh, S., & Price, K. (1992). Portfolio culture in arts education. *Art Education, 45,* 7–15.

Gowan, J.C., Khatena, J., & Torrance, E.P. (1979). *Educating the ablest: On the education of gifted children.* Itasca, IL: Peacock.

Greer, D., & Silverman, R.H. (1987–1988). Making art important for every child. *Educational Leadership, 45,* 10–14.

Hanna, J.L. (1992). Connections: Arts, academics, and productive citizens. *Phi Delta Kappan, 73,* 601–607.

Higgins, J.E. (1981). Forum: The primary purpose of fiction. *Children's Literature in Education, 12*(2), 113–116.

Hodsoll, F. (1988). *Toward civilization: A report on arts education.* Washington, DC: National Endowment for the Arts.

Irwin, J.W. (1991). *Teaching reading comprehension processes* (2nd ed.). Boston, MA: Allyn & Bacon.

Jampole, E., Konopak, B., Readence, J., & Moser, E.B. (1991). Using mental imagery to enhance gifted elementary students' creative writing. *Reading Psychology, 12,* 183–197.

Martorelli, D. (1992). The arts take center stage. *Instructor, 132,* 38–39.

McNeil, J.D. (1987). *Reading comprehension* (2nd ed.). Glenview, IL: Scott, Foresman.

Miller, B.E. (1980). *Teaching the art of literature.* Urbana, IL: NCTE.

Mills, E., & Thomson, D.R. (1986). *A national survey of art(s) education, 1984–1985: A national report of the state of the arts in the states.* Reston, VA: National Art Education Association.

Moffett, J. (1983). *Teaching the universe of discourse.* Boston, MA: Houghton Mifflin.

National Commission on Excellence in Education. (1983). *A nation at risk.* Washington, DC: U.S. Government Printing Office.

National Endowment for the Arts. (1988). *Toward civilization: A report on arts education.* Washington, DC: Author.

Paivio, A. (1979). *Imagery and verbal processes.* Hillsdale, NJ: Erlbaum.

Paivio, A. (1986). *Mental representations: A dual coding approach.* New York: Oxford University Press.

Postman, N. (1980). The ascent of humanity: A coherent curriculum. *Educational Leadership, 37,* 300–303.

Purves, A.C. (1985). That sunny dome, those caves of ice. In C. Cooper (Ed.), *Researching response to literature and the teaching of literature: Points of departure* (pp. 54–69). Norwood, NJ: Ablex.

Rockefeller, D., Jr. (1977). *Coming to our senses: The significance of the arts in American education.* New York: McGraw-Hill.

Rosenblatt, L.M. (1989). Writing and reading: The transactional theory. In J. Mason (Ed.), *Reading and writing connections* (pp. 153–176). Boston, MA: Allyn & Bacon.

Rowell, E.H. (1983). Developing reading skills through the study of great art. In J.E. Cowen (Ed.), *Teaching reading through the arts* (pp. 55–67). Newark, DE: IRA.

Sadoski, M. (1984). Text structure, imagery, and affect in the recall of a story by children. In J.A. Niles & L.A. Harris (Eds.), *Changing perspectives in research in reading/language processing and instruction* (Thirty-third yearbook of the National Reading Conference, pp. 48–53). Washington, DC: National Reading Conference.

Sadoski, M. (1985). The natural use of imagery in story comprehension and recall: Replication and extension. *Reading Research Quarterly, 20,* 658–667.

Sadoski, M., & Goetz, E.T. (1985). Relationships between affect, imagery, and importance ratings for segments of a story. In J.A. Niles & R. Lalik (Eds.), *Issues in literacy: A research perspective* (Thirty-fourth yearbook of the National Reading Conference, pp. 180–185). Washington, DC: National Reading Conference.

Sadoski, M., Goetz, E., & Kangiser, S. (1988). Imagination in story response: Relationship between imagery, affect, and structural importance. *Reading Research Quarterly, 23,* 320–336.

Scollon, R., & Scollon, S.B. (1981). *Narrative, literacy, and race in interethnic communication.* Norwood, NJ: Ablex.

Sinatra, R. (1986). *Visual literacy connections to thinking, reading, and writing.* Springfield, IL: Charles Thomas.

Smith, F. (1982). *Understanding reading* (3rd ed.). New York: Holt, Rinehart.

Smith, F. (1985). A metaphor for literacy: Creating worlds of shunting information. In D. Olsen, N. Torrance, & A. Hildyard (Eds.), *Literacy, language, and learning: The nature and consequences of reading and writing* (pp. 195–213). New York: Cambridge University Press.

Smith, R.J., & Barrett, T.C. (1979). *Teaching reading in the middle grades.* Reading, MA: Addison-Wesley.

Taylor, D.C. (1989, February). *District panel presentation: What form is art education taking?* Panel Ten Paper presented at the second national invitational conference, "Education in Art: Future Building," sponsored by the Getty Center for Education in the Arts, Los Angeles, CA.

Torrance, E.P. (1979). Creativity and its educational implications. In J. Gowan, J. Khatena, & E. Torrance (Eds.), *Educating the ablest.* Itasca, IL: Peacock.

Van Dongen, R., & Westby, C.E. (1986). Building the narrative mode of thought through children's literature. *Topics in Language Disorders, 7*(1), 70–83.

Wilson, B. (1987). Implementing and maintaining a district art program. In Getty Center for Education in the Arts, *Discipline-based art education: What forms will it take?* (pp. 74–75). Los Angeles, CA: The J. Paul Getty Trust.

Winograd, P., & Smith, L.A. (1987). Improving the climate for reading comprehension instruction. *The Reading Teacher, 41,* 304–310.

Wolf, D.P. (1989). Portfolio assessment: Sampling student work. *Educational Leadership, 47,* 35–39.

Chapter 9

Instilling a Love of Words in Children

Nancy Lee Cecil

●◆ For most elementary teachers, regardless of their approach to the teaching of literacy, one common thread remains: they introduce new vocabulary to their classes before reading a new story or expository piece. Of course, there is good reason for this continuing practice. Good teachers are aware that knowledge of word meanings is essential for reading comprehension; children simply cannot deeply process text unless they know the correct meanings of most of the words to be read. In fact, some researchers contend that knowledge of word meanings is *the* most important component in the comprehension process (Davis, 1972).

The implementation of such an accepted and significant facet of literacy instruction, however, has often been lamentably dull. Vocabulary has too often been "taught" by asking children to write sentences for new words that they will confront in their reading. Resisting looking the words up in the dictionary, bored students sometimes respond with vacuous sentences such as "I had a *responsibility*," "That was *exhausting*," or "It was *mellow*." Worse yet, in many cases children are asked to memorize vocabulary definitions taken from commercial lists of words that they may not encounter again in their reading for months or even years!

There are many ways teachers can avoid this type of dull instruction and instill a genuine love of words in children by weaving vocabulary development throughout the whole language curriculum.

Talking About Words

A teacher who truly finds the English language fascinating can pass this excitement on to learners by directing the students' attention to words or phrases that she or he finds particularly effective in literature. For example, a sixth grade teacher, reading aloud a description of Niagara Falls in the wintertime, was taken with the way the author depicted "the frigid columns of bluish-white icicles suspended in time, surrounded on all sides by the eerie mist." The teacher exclaimed, "That passage just sends a shiver down my spine and makes me want to curl up in front of a blazing fire!" As she read the description a second time, the children shared their own reactions, many of them accompanied by involuntary shivers.

On another occasion, while reading a poem from an anthology, the same teacher stopped when she read "a plethora of pink poppies" and had the children say it with her. She pointed out the alliteration, letting the children gleefully observe how the quadruple "p" exploded on their tongues. Although the teacher did not require it, the next week the students began using alliteration in their written work.

Another, more direct way of encouraging a discussion about words is through the use of a semantic gradient. With this device, two opposite words such as "good" and "bad" are presented to a group of children. The children must decide what words might go between the opposites and beyond them and where on the gradient they should go. For example, one group of second graders came up with this list:

      perfect
      excellent
      good
      okay
      mischievous
      awful
      bad
      evil

With this device, it is important to help children realize that there are no absolute right or wrong answers. Indeed, from a learning viewpoint, the process and ensuing discussion is more critical than the product. In the scenario using "good" and "bad," for example, there was much discussion about which word was more "bad": "mischievous" or "awful." When the dictionary was consulted (this is fair game), it offered no conclusive answer, so the children had to build a case for their word's placement by offering reasons why they felt one word was "more bad" than the other. One second grader argued, "Well, a little kid can be mischievous by playing a harmless joke on someone, but if someone is awful, they have done something that everyone thinks is very, very bad." Another second grader contended, "But mischievous sounds like that person is always that way. If something is 'awful,' though, it's just once like when you tell somebody, 'That's an awful thing to do.' Mischievous lasts longer, so it must be worse."

Collecting Words

A more direct way of talking about words is to have children collect words and then write them on cards that can be stored in personal word banks. As a precursor to reading a Halloween story, for example, children could participate in a brainstorming session to generate "scary" words. They then file away their collection of scary words. Similarly, children can be encouraged to amass "pretty words," "people words," "Arabic words," and so forth (Frank, 1979). At appropriate intervals, words can be shared; for example, the teacher could ask, "Does anyone have a favorite 'loud' word?" Words can also be referred to for use in individual writing activities.

An activity that can help children begin to focus on their favorite words is called "20 Words." For this activity, the teacher first asks children to make a list of their 20 favorite words, using their word banks, the dictionary, or sharing with each other. They can choose words for any reason: because of the word's emotional appeal (for example, "mother"), because they like the sound ("pumpernickel"), or perhaps because they feel the word is one of the most sophisticated words they know ("gregarious"). Then the teacher allows the children to walk around the room, discuss other students' word choices and borrow from one another. Next, the teacher asks them to cross out the five words they like least. Finally, the teacher asks the children to fill in the following blanks, using their favorite words:

$$\begin{array}{lll} \underline{\hspace{2cm}} & \underline{\hspace{2cm}} & \\ \underline{\hspace{2cm}} & \underline{\hspace{2cm}} & \underline{\hspace{2cm}} \\ \underline{\hspace{2cm}} & \underline{\hspace{2cm}} & \\ \underline{\hspace{2cm}} & & \\ \underline{\hspace{2cm}} & \underline{\hspace{2cm}} & \underline{\hspace{2cm}} & \underline{\hspace{2cm}} \\ \underline{\hspace{2cm}} & & \\ \underline{\hspace{2cm}} & \underline{\hspace{2cm}} & \end{array}$$

The teacher encourages students to experiment with different combinations of their words until they find a pattern that most pleases them. Depending on the group and their wishes, the teacher may then have children share their pieces with one another, read their own and others' aloud, or let the teacher read the final combinations to the group.

One fifth grader wrote the following 15-word free verse poem from this activity:

Cities   roar,
Sunset   valley   flowers,
Marshmallows   toasty.
Brilliant!

Wild	burgundy	chrysanthemums	crash.
Weird!			
Sleek	jitters.		

With this poem, as with others, many interesting comments about possible meanings and interpretations ensue as children intensely experience the power of words.

Exploring the Structure of Words

Coining and defining new words can be an excellent way to show children the structure of words in the English language. This knowledge can further appreciation of existing words and help children begin to learn the meanings of unfamiliar words.

An engaging activity for exploring the structure of words is to have students construct a class dictionary of their own "invented" words. To do this, the children must first be introduced to roots and affixes that have fairly consistent meanings, such as the prefix "auto" (self), the root "vert" (turn), and the suffix "phobia" (fear of). Next, choosing combinations of prefixes, roots, and suffixes that have been studied, children can create new words much the same as they are found in the classroom dictionary. Children then take turns presenting their lexical creations to others who try to guess what the word means from their knowledge of roots and affixes. For example, one fourth grade child offered the word "retroceleride" which, from his understanding of the root "celer" meaning "quickly," the prefix "retro" meaning "backwards," and the suffix, "ide" meaning "the art of or condition of being," he decided meant "the art of walking backwards quickly." He stumped the class. When each child has presented his or her entries to the class, the words are then alphabetized, illustrated, and compiled into an original classroom dictionary.

Encouraging Elaboration

Good writers use words to paint visual pictures of their ideas, feelings, and thoughts. They make characters seem real through descriptions of their physical appearances and idiosyncratic behavior. To underscore the importance of using fresh descriptive words, children can be taught from the earliest grade levels to do "Writing Aerobics." With this activity, children are asked to read a very basic sentence, such as "The canary sang" or "The man laughed," and to use words to make the canary or the man come to life. Children are asked, "What is the canary like? Why is she singing?"

or, for the second sentence, "Who is the man? What does he look like? What does he think is funny?"

Initiating this activity orally in the primary grades allows children as young as kindergarten age to begin to craft revised sentences that help them understand and appreciate descriptive writing, as evidenced by the following, which were written by kindergartners:

> The orange canary sang a sweet song because he just took a bubble bath.
>
> The little old man laughed loudly when he saw his wife put on a funny hat.

"Writing Aerobics" can be expanded to allow children to write stronger, more descriptive paragraphs. Using a technique known as "Magnify the Moment," pairs or small groups of students are assigned one sentence from a paragraph that has been chosen for its "tired" words and general lack of description. Each pair or group is then asked to make the sentence come to life, using "Writing Aerobics" techniques while maintaining the factual content and meaning of the original paragraph. In "Magnify the Moment," however, each sentence may be expanded into two or three sentences to add more information and description to the paragraph. For example, one third grade class read the following basic paragraph:

> One day my dog, Puppy, ran away. I went outside to look for her, but she wasn't there. I asked my neighbors if they had seen her, but they said no. I looked everywhere. Then I went into my house. Puppy was under my bed. She had been there all the time.

Working in small groups, the children then considered their assigned sentences and attempted to make them more interesting and vivid. Their revised paragraph follows:

> One frosty Winter day my black Labrador retriever, Puppy, ran away, so I thought. I couldn't believe it because she had never done anything like that before. I went quickly out in my snow-covered backyard to search for her, whistling and calling her name, but she seemed to have disappeared. So I knocked on the door of my neighbors, the Greens, and asked them if they had seen Puppy. "Gosh, no, I haven't seen her today," exclaimed Mrs. Green, "but I saw her chewing on a bone yesterday!" I left the Greens' house sadly and continued looking around the neighborhood. I went up to the school, but she wasn't there. I searched the churchyard, but she wasn't there either. Finally, I returned to my house, fighting back the tears. There was my terrific dog, Puppy, lying under my bed, sound asleep. She

had been there the whole time! I was so glad to see her that I hugged her. She licked my face happily. "Puppy, you're a good dog after all," I told my friend.

Word games have long been considered a "fringe" of a sound language arts program and have too often been limited to word searches or crossword puzzles, neither of which encourage much active critical thinking or substantive prolonged engagement with words. By contrast, "Camouflage" (Cecil, 1994) requires children to consider a word and its meaning, as well as how that word could be "smuggled" into an original verbal response to a question. To introduce the game, the teacher tells children the object is to decide how best to "camouflage," or hide, a word so that the other students cannot guess it. Then, the teacher gives each child a slip of paper with a written word that is a little more advanced than children's speaking vocabularies. The teacher warns them not to show their words to other children but to consult a dictionary to understand the word's meaning(s).

Next, the teacher either demonstrates or asks a comfortably verbal child to initiate the game. Another member of the class asks a general question such as, "What is your favorite thing to do?" The initiator must consider the question for a few seconds and then decide how to "sneak" the word he or she was given into the response. An obvious strategy—and one that leads to rapid leaps in vocabulary development—is to employ all the "big" words that the initiator can think of to try and throw the other children off the trail. When the initiator finishes answering the question, classmates must then attempt to guess exactly which word was being "camouflaged." The initiator wins if the number of children who guess the hidden word is fewer than the total of incorrect guesses.

Following is an example of how a fifth grader camouflaged the word "resumed" in response to his classmate's question, "What is your favorite season of the year?"

> My favorite season has always been summer because there is no school and I can spend all day doing whatever I want. I like to swim and go to summer camp. I always decide to start some terrific project like making a clubhouse or building a go-cart. Family vacations to unfamiliar places are something to look forward to, also. As strange as it may seem, though, I'm always delighted when school *resumes* again in September.

Hinky Pinkys is an additional activity that can provide motivational discussions about words, a desire to use the dictionary, and a better understanding of synonyms and their use. A "Hinky Pinky" consists of two rhyming words that are discovered by figuring out the meaning of a cryptic, two-word clue. For example, the clue "a fatter arachnid" would also be a "wider spider." Children enjoy doing this activity, especially in groups of three or four or as an overnight assignment in which parents, older brothers or sisters, or others may be invited to join. To expand the level of thinking involved in this task, the teacher can encourage the children to create their own Hinky Pinkys to share with the rest of the class. A sixth grade class presented their classmates with the following five posers:

> Uncomplicated acne: simple pimple
> A flannel waistband: felt belt
> A weird musical instrument: bizarre guitar
> A mellow youngster: mild child
> A narrower meal: thinner dinner

Motivating with Words

These suggestions are by no means intended to exhaust the possible strategies that could be used to turn children on to words, but they are a field-tested beginning. (In Chapter 10 Cramer also gives helpful suggestions for ways teachers can foster a love of words and reading in their classrooms.) For a teacher enchanted with words and word play, these ideas can provide a key to a more exciting literacy program. In a classroom where words are exciting for both the teacher and the children, wonderful things often occur. Soon, just the right word is eagerly sought to express a feeling or describe an event; sentences and paragraphs, too, are expanded to create precise messages or visions. It is a welcome revelation to children who discover that they have at their command the perfect tools to communicate more clearly what is in their hearts and minds.

References
Cecil, N.L. (1994). The wonder of words. In *Freedom fighters: An affective approach to language arts* (2nd ed., pp. 83–94). Salem, WI: Sheffield.

Davis, F.B. (1972). Psychometric research on comprehension in reading. *Reading Research Quarterly, 7,* 628–678.

Frank, M. (1979). *If you're trying to teach kids how to write, you've gotta have this book!* Nashville, TN: Incentive.

Chapter 10

Connecting in the Classroom: Ideas from Teachers

Eugene H. Cramer

●◆ Classroom teachers are a valuable source of ideas for developing positive reading attitudes in their students. However, it is difficult to tap into this vital source of ideas for several reasons. Too often teachers regard their own ideas lightly and hesitate to share them in journals or other educational publications. Also, teachers are usually too busy with classroom activities to take time to write down their ideas.

Accordingly, as a culminating activity for a workshop on affective reading methods, I asked participating teachers to brainstorm ideas they believed would help increase positive reading attitudes in their students. All 30 teachers in the workshop were from the Chicago, Illinois, public schools; they represented all levels from kindergarten to 12th grade, with the majority assigned to elementary school classrooms. Most were teaching in self-contained graded or content classrooms. Some were special education teachers, Chapter 1, or bilingual teachers. I challenged them to recollect affective teaching strategies they had used or to devise methods and situations they believed would actually induce their own students to read with pleasure and satisfaction. The results were overwhelming. A wealth of affective ideas and teaching strategies flowed from the minds of the teachers.

Following the brainstorming session we discussed the teachers' ideas, and several points about affective teaching ideas emerged. First, all participants thought that it had been a very stimulating exercise, so worthwhile that several of them intended to introduce the activity at their schools to involve their colleagues in planning and implementing affective reading activities. Another point was that teaching in the affective domain is more of a state of mind than a set of given activities. That is, affective teaching of reading depends most heavily on a teacher who is enthusiastic about reading, one who wishes to transmit his or her own love of reading to the students, as stressed throughout this work. Also, the discussion brought out the important idea that not all of the activities would be successful in every classroom; the participants emphasized the need to adapt any affective teaching idea to a specific group of students. The teachers concluded that the brainstorming session had been very productive, with ideas flowing quickly and generating still other ideas. That part was relatively easy. The challenging part lay ahead: putting affective teaching ideas into operation would require planning and energy.

Following are the affective strategies suggested by the classroom teachers who participated in the workshop. These ideas are presented in a straightforward way, yet they transcend and are intertwined with many current ideas about reading instruction. Some of the ideas suggested by the teachers rely heavily on extrinsic motivation. Clearly, our long-range goal is to have students at all levels find inherent pleasure through reading. For some students, however, immediate extrinsic rewards in the form of small toys, candy, stickers, or pizza parties seem to be a strong first step toward eventual intrinsic motivation.

Ideas for the Classroom

Classroom Environments

Each of the brainstorming groups stressed the importance of the classroom environment in building positive reading attitudes, as did Johns and VanLeirsburg in Chapter 7. Teachers should do whatever possible to make classrooms "reader friendly." Most participants expressed the hope that more money could be made available in their schools for this purpose. However, they agreed that much can be done even with limited funds. Here are their ideas.

- Surround children with books. Develop a classroom library in which a variety of books are easily accessible. The library should invite browsing and selecting books to take home.

- Have a simple checkout system for children to take books home from the classroom library. Do not get bogged down in management details.

- Make the reading environment attractive. An inexpensive carpet, some colorful posters, a couple of bean-bag chairs, and possibly a floor lamp or two can do much to enhance a reading corner in the classroom.

- Attend to students' physical comfort during reading sessions: adequate light, heat, ventilation, comfortable seating, and space.

- Offer healthful foods as "treats" during reading and listening times, such as raisins or crackers. By linking a basic human need with reading, a pleasurable association with reading may be established.

- Arrange seasonal and topical displays of books in the classroom and discuss them with your students. Read sample passages and then leave the books prominently displayed. Children will pick them up to take home.

- Plan bulletin boards that reflect the joys of reading. Themes might include adventures, seasonal sports, animals, dinosaurs, holidays, other countries and customs, and so on. Illustrate the bulletin boards with book jackets, titles, pictures, and comments from authors.

- Display photographs of all students with lists of books each has read underneath their pictures.

Modeling, Scaffolding, and Praising

To help children grow toward independence in their reading and learning, teachers must model and scaffold the behaviors they wish their students to acquire. If teachers want students to become avid readers, teaches must become avid readers. Scaffolding is a step in this process; students do not become avid readers all at once. When they make positive steps toward desired behaviors teachers must be ready to support these efforts. Further, teachers can create classroom situations that promot satisfying literate behaviors. Participants in the brainstorming groups were adamant about this message.

- Read to your class the children's books, poems, and stories that you most enjoy. Discuss with the class why you especially like these texts.

- Let a child become the "teacher" who reads to the class and instructs them.

- Let students take turns putting the "morning story" on the board. In lower primary grades the morning story consists of a few short sentences that describe the day. It might include such things as the day, the date, a weather statement, or a reference to some special event that is happening in the school or community. In upper grades, the morning story should be longer and more complex, dealing with current or historical events in the community, nation, or world. Morning story content depends on current topics under consideration in the classroom. These stories can be dictated by the class or written in advance by the teacher. Students copy the morning story and use it as a basis for discussion.

- Establish "DEAR" to model your valuing of reading. For example, after lunch every day, teacher and students just drop everything and read books of their choosing. Start with short time periods and gradually increase.

Personalized Reading and Interesting Introductions

Teachers in the workshop indicated that the more they "personalized" reading for their students, the deeper was the students' involvement with books. To illustrate what they mean, here are some of their suggestions for personalizing recreational reading assignments.

- Always emphasize *reading for fun.* Share your own recreational reading with your students. Let them see you enjoying a book or a magazine article. Discuss with them what you have been reading. Children seem to be endlessly fascinated with what teachers are really like.

- Introduce materials that cover a wide range of interests. As you get to know your class, you will be able to select books from the school or public library that will appeal to them. Librarians are usually a good source of ideas about what children at various age levels are most interested in.

- Get input from children and consider their choices when selecting books to read aloud or to add to the classroom library.

- Look for a book to satisfy a particular child's interest, and try to personalize introductions: "Here's a book you'd love, Leslie."

- Locate books on topics of class interest; for example, "bullying," "death in a family," or others. Read and discuss these topical books. Again, librarians can help you to find books on specific themes.

- Introduce two or three books briefly each week to pique children's interest. Then leave the books on a special table or bookshelf.

Not Just Books

One of the brainstorming groups suggested that students may be attracted to reading by things other than books. They believed that if teachers introduce items and materials related to books, children may be enticed to follow up these opening discussions by reading to find more knowledge. Here are some of their ideas.

- Bring in a concrete object from a story. Have a class discussion about it and then read the story. An umbrella said to possess "magical qualities" could set the stage for reading aloud Pamela L. Travers's *Mary Poppins*. A plastic toy Indian placed on the teacher's desk during the reading of Lynne R. Banks's *The Indian in the Cupboard* could stimulate imaginations. Here are just a few more ideas: a spider in a terrarium for *Charlotte's Web* by E.B. White; a world globe to illustrate the location of Australia for students reading or listening to Judith Viorst's *Alexander and the Terrible, Horrible, No Good, Very Bad Day*; some unpopped corn and a corn popper to bring to life Tomie dePaola's *The Popcorn Book*; a cooking pot and a stone to illustrate *Stone Soup* as retold by Ann McGovern; an old pair of boy's sneakers to lead into Jerry Spinelli's *Maniac Magee*; a ripe peach to imagine growing to a tremendous size in *James and the Giant Peach* by Roald Dahl; any of the items confused by Peggy Parish's Amelia in *Teach Us, Amelia Bedelia* such as a roll for calling, an onion and a light bulb for planting, apples for taking away in arithmetic, and so on. The possibilities are endless.

- Discuss interesting pictures. Use descriptive words for colors, shapes, actions, and emotions. Depending on the level of the class, find relevant pictures, paintings, and photographs to lead into discussions of a story's content. Vibrant colors can lead to new vocabulary words: red can be expanded to pink, magenta, crimson, rust, and so on. Common shapes can also be described: square, rectangle, triangle, pentagon, polygon. Physical actions and facial expressions can be introduced and discussed through pictures, then related to upcoming stories. Students should be encouraged to find examples of these colors, shapes, actions, and emotions in pictures they examine. Helping children to build a storehouse of sensory impressions linked with descriptive words provides a vital support system for their later reading.

- Start a classroom picture file. Magazine advertisements are a wonderful source of exciting, vivid pictures. Reproductions of paintings and drawings from the "old masters" are another. Cut out pictures and mount them on cardboard so they can be used for sequencing activities. Teachers can devise their own system of filing pictures so they are able to find what is needed when it is needed. Seasonal pictures, depictions of historic events, scenes from stories, mythology, fairy tales, current films, and TV programs—everything you can think of can be useful for this file.

• Encourage children to draw illustrations of a story or poem while the teacher or a classmate reads. A follow-up session in which the artists share their creations can lead to a discussion of mental imagery or how each person visualizes events of a story in slightly different ways.

• To reinforce the importance of literacy, have students bring in reading materials other than books. As students bring in items, have them discuss where they found each item and why people read it. These materials could be placed in a large cardboard box labeled "What People Read." Sample items might include calendars, record jackets, printed T-shirts, posters, placards, campaign ribbons, buttons, postcards, maps, stamps, insurance policies, drivers' licenses, or cereal boxes. The possibilities are huge.

• Use the telephone directory to look up the address and phone number of a pizza parlor, a pharmacy, a dentist, or other company. What you look up will depend on topics of current interest. This activity teaches alphabet skills and "creative" searching and provides a valuable introduction to using the telephone.

• Teachers and parents can help students practice reading by posting notes addressed to each child on the chalkboard, bulletin board, or refrigerator.

• Practice reading with product labels—children identify what is in the product.

• Clip articles from newspapers and magazines on subjects of interest to children and share them with students.

• Use videotape of public television specials to enhance students' background knowledge and interest in social studies. Be alert for special programs dealing with current and historical events, election campaigns, environmental policy issues, hearings conducted by government agencies, and any other current societal issues. Students' participation in social studies depends greatly on the amount of background information they possess. If possible, try to involve parents by having them do the videotaping and by having them discuss these issues with their children at home.

- Use comic books. If you have not looked at any comic books lately, we suggest you buy some samples and review them. Ask students for input as to their current favorites. We have found that the vocabulary used in many comic books is quite sophisticated and that some students are not certain of many of the words they encounter in them. Numerous vocabulary lessons can be generated from such materials. Comic books also provide an excellent means for discussing the differences between fantasy and fact, right and wrong, and heroes and villains.

Oral Reading Activities

Several of the brainstorming groups emphasized the importance of reading aloud, whether by the teacher or by the students, as a powerful motivating tool in reading. Many of their ideas overlapped from group to group, indicating that teachers hold these ideas as primary, as mentioned by others in this work. The most prominent activity suggested is that teachers should read to children every day. Establish a regularly scheduled read-aloud time and present books and stories that are as "magical" as you can find, books that stimulate curiosity and imagination. Teachers should choose books they enjoy personally, practice before reading to the class, and perform with enthusiasm. There are many ways to vary oral reading activities, as the following ideas demonstrate.

- Read aloud, leaving out a crucial part of the story, and ask students to make predictions about what will happen. Then children read for themselves to confirm their predictions.
- Invite other adults to your classroom to read aloud their favorite childhood books, as Chapter 8 suggested.
- Call the read-aloud session "Let's Make a Deal": when children deserve a reward, read them a favorite story. This can be effective two or three extra times a week.
- Tape-record favorite stories. (This can be done during regular read-aloud sessions; just have the tape recorder set up and ready.) This is a good way to build a collection of read-along tapes to add to your classroom library. Store the tape with the book in a plastic zip-top bag and display it prominently.

Every student should be given many opportunities to read aloud. The teachers who participated in the workshop agreed that children need a lot of oral reading practice to develop fluency. It is important, however, that students be given a chance to rehearse privately before they are asked to "perform" publicly. Here are some of the ideas from the brainstorming groups for encouraging children to read aloud.

- The teacher models and the whole class echo-reads, sentence by sentence, through a new story or passage. Then the entire class "choral" reads the passage. Next, small groups read the passage aloud. Finally, solo readers take turns reading the passage.

- Send passages home with each child to announce that he or she needs to "rehearse" reading with family members.

- Have a "Joke of the Day" read aloud by students on a rotating basis. Children bring in favorite jokes written on 3- x 5-inch cards, place them in a box, draw one, and read it aloud. This is a good "sponge" activity for just before lunchtime or end of the school day.

- Let a child practice at home and then read a fable or fairy story to the class.

- Have the class make read-along tapes, with music and sound effects.

- Encourage children to read aloud a sentence or a paragraph to "prove" a disputed point.

- Have storytelling sessions in which both teacher and students take part.

- Try a language experience activity. The class dictates a story to the teacher, who writes it on the chalkboard or on a transparency. Children read it aloud as a group, in pairs, and singly. Children may copy the story to take home to read aloud to parents and siblings.

- As a reward for the class, read comics from daily and Sunday newspapers. Have class members take turns on successive days.

- Have small groups do choral reading activities. They select a favorite poem or short story, rehearse, and present it to an audience—either their classmates or several other classes, perhaps in the lower grade levels.

Plays and Dramatization

Using classroom drama activities to motivate young readers is closely related to using oral reading activities for the same purpose. Many ideas about plays and dramatization came from the teachers' brainstorming groups. Because there are numerous publications available that give detailed information about dramatization, the following ideas are suggested as reminders of the many possible activities.

- Dramatize or use improvisation of books, characters, or plots. Have children pretend to be characters in a story they have just read or heard. Dialogue may be improvised in the children's own words, or it may be the exact words from the original text. An alternative is to have the teacher or a student read the text while the others pantomime the action.

- Dramatize a story or play as Readers Theatre. Rehearse several times. Encourage students to match their voices to the meanings of words and change their voices to fit the characters they are portraying. Present the polished production to another class.

- Have children make up their own play around a theme for a school assembly—for example, Thanksgiving, safety rules, meeting a new friend, or caring for pets. Decide on a theme, then discuss sources of information, devise a story, write the dialogue, and select music, costumes, and sound effects. Then rehearse and produce the play.

- Put on a puppet play. Design cloth puppets from socks or stick puppets from paper plates fastened to ice cream sticks to be characters from a story. The "stage" could be as simple as a large table or the teacher's desk, or it could be a more elaborately designed puppet theater. This is a good project for involving parents who have building skills.

Vocabulary Games

Vocabulary development should be exciting, as Cecil stressed in the previous chapter. Teachers were emphatic about the importance of helping children expand their store of words. Here are some of their suggestions.

- Do rhyming activities. Ask children to provide rhyming words to selected cue words from a story.

- Play "My Neighbor's Cat Is...." For the first round, students take turns completing the sentence with words beginning with "A." Anyone who cannot add a word is eliminated. Next round is "B" words, and so on. Children may (or may not) use dictionaries.

- Try word hunts: students in small groups use magazines or newspapers to locate specific types of words, such as math words, science words, words beginning with specific letters, animal words, flower words, food words, and so on. Younger students may cut out the words and paste them on posters for display. Older students may simply circle the words with markers, seeing who can find the most within a specified time limit.

• Introduce anagrams, crossword puzzles, and word-search puzzles.

• Post a "Riddle of the Day" on the classroom door or bulletin board for children to solve. The first child with the correct answer gets a prize. Encourage students to locate riddles of their own for possible use in this game.

Before Reading

Preparing students for an upcoming reading experience is an important step in leading them to reach a deeper level of understanding and enjoyment of a new story. There are many ways this might be done. Here are a few that were suggested by the workshop teachers.

• Have the children discuss the title and illustrations before they read the story. Let them make guesses (predictions) as to what it may be about and what might happen. For this activity there are no wrong answers.

• If possible, locate appropriate music that fits the tone or mood of the new story. Ask the children to listen to the music and try to imagine what the story will be about.

• Sometimes you may be able to bring in an object that has significance in a new story. Let children examine the object and talk about it. Tell them to watch for this thing as they read the story and figure out why it is important.

• Lead your class through a mental imagery experience that relates to the story they will read. Select ideas from the story's setting that appeal to different senses, and have children imagine they are visiting this new place. For example, what does the barn look like in *Charlotte's Web*? What sounds would you expect to hear in that barn? Have students demonstrate the sounds they think of either individually or as a whole class. What do you think Wilbur's breakfast tastes like? How does it compare with your own? Imagine touching a spider's web: What does it feel like? What does hay smell like? Suggest they use their images as they read the story.

After Reading

After students have read a story or a passage, the teacher's discussion becomes a critical issue. Teachers in the workshop believed that it is important to get students simply to talk about the experience—to share their ideas, images, and memories. The key is to help students make connections between what they have just read and their prior experiences. Discussing reading is vital: there are many ways to do this, and each teacher must find a personal way to excite children about their reading. Most important is not to make this an "inquisition" in which children get the mistaken idea that there is always a right and a wrong answer to the teacher's questions. Teachers should try to lead but not dominate the discussion by asking open-ended questions such as "What would you have done when...?" or "How did this story remind you of...?" or "How would you feel if...?"

Nearly every story lends itself to some sort of follow-up activities after reading. Planning and involving the whole class in these activities is another way to help students connect reading to real experiences in their lives. One after-reading activity that can stimulate much thinking and discussion is to have students compare different versions of the same story as told by different authors. Many versions of familiar children's stories are available for such comparisons. For example, there are many small variations in the text versions of *The Three Little Pigs* as retold by Galdone (1970) and by Marshall (1989). Galdone's version follows traditional storytelling language with few linguistic embellishments, whereas Marshall's uses a more modern conversational style, employing such sentences as "You can say that again!" Students can enjoy both versions while picking out the differences in storytelling technique.

Older students enjoy comparing any modern version of *Cinderella* first with John Steptoe's *Mufaro's Beautiful Daughters: An African Tale* and then with its original, harsher version "Ashputtel" as originally related by the brothers Grimm. Our suggestion is to reserve these classic stories for older students who should be better able to separate fantasy from fact.

The important point is that students can begin to compare texts at an early age while learning that there is not a single "right" or "wrong" way to tell a story, that word choices do make differences in our enjoyment of stories, and that stories may vary with time and custom.

Book Reports

The topic of book reports aroused strong responses among the brainstorming groups. The traditional book report format, they believed, causes too many children to avoid reading simply because they strongly dislike writing the report. Therefore, they suggested that book reports be done in a variety of formats.

- Read favorite parts aloud.
- Draw a picture of a favorite character.
- Make up a song.
- Dress up as a book character.
- Make a minibook using empty kitchen matchboxes.
- Create "show and tell" dioramas from shoeboxes of scenes from a book.
- Modernize an old story.
- Use the classroom computer as a book report database. Students enter bibliographic information and a brief comment about each book they have read.

For those teachers who feel that they must assign traditional book reports, the teachers in the brainstorming groups offered the following ways in which the task might become more palatable.

- Organize a book report club. Award stars on a wall chart for book reports.
- Place all book reports in a box and have a weekly drawing for the book report of the week. Call it the "Book Report Lottery." The author of the book report drawn is given a prize.
- Have each student create a personal figure of himself or herself to be placed on the bulletin board. When a student completes a book report, a mark is placed by the student's name. The student can then choose any picture of food he or she wants to go on the figure. The picture of food is used to reflect the caption, "Reading Is Mind Food."
- Take pictures of all students who turn in a book report for the week. The pictures go on a bulletin board labeled "Reading Is Mind Food" or "Happy Readers' Book Club."

Reading, Writing, and Publishing

Teachers in the workshop came up with many ways to have students become involved in writing activities. These teachers believe that when students become "authors" themselves they grow increasingly sensitive to text and are more likely to become lifelong readers. In each of the writing activities suggested, the teachers stressed the importance of audience—that is, after writing, children expect their works to be read. Sometimes an "author" may read his or her own work aloud. Other times, the work may be printed and read silently by classmates and then discussed.

- Select a famous or a favorite author as "Author of the Month." Compose letters and send them to authors of favorite books.
- Have children write their own books on the classroom computer.
- Write and send letters to pen pals, for example, a child who has transferred to another school, a soldier posted, or other person. Read aloud letters received in response.
- Publish a classroom newspaper.
- Rewrite a story as told from the viewpoint of another character in that story.
- Have children first discuss and then write alternate endings for stories.

Investigative Methods

Some of the teachers suggested that children may be motivated to read when they become "investigative reporters." For example, members of small groups investigate a topic of interest to present to the whole class. One member may be the "designated writer." All should participate in the final editing.

Another possibility is to arrange to take the class on a fieldtrip to a museum. Help students generate questions they would like answered, or assign a few questions to the small groups to search out answers to be discussed after returning to the classroom.

A special type of research involves interview activities. Students select persons they would like to learn more about. They prepare questions in advance, conduct the interview, analyze the answers, and write down their findings. Information obtained is shared with the class, either orally or in writing.

Games and Contests

Many children respond to "friendly" competition, but as Johns and VanLeirsburg mentioned earlier, the overuse of such methods may be detrimental. One strategy is to devise contests that all students can "win." Sometimes it is a good idea to pair students and have them share the work and the prize.

- Encourage students to earn "raffle tickets" for each book or specified number of pages read (as appropriate per child). Raffle tickets may be exchanged for a desired item.

- Hold reading contests with everyone having a chance to win by reading a specific number of books or pages on a specific topic chosen through class discussion.

- Set up month-long reading contests. Make a chart on which children can fill in titles of books they have read.

- Have children choose their own books and give short oral accounts of their reading to the class for small prizes.

- Organize a treasure hunt. For the first rounds, the teacher writes clues for finding objects in the room. Later, the children can write clues for one another.

Rewards and Other Incentives

Some of the teachers suggested that some children are motivated by small rewards for reading. The rewards need not be elaborate: pencils, stickers, or bookmarks are frequently used. Also effective are wall charts that honor, highlight, and award readers. The teachers believe that giving extrinsic rewards for reading to children who are especially "turned off" can lead them eventually to finding the intrinsic pleasures of getting "lost in a book."

Libraries—Classroom, Home, and Public

According to the teachers in the workshop, some children simply do not know very much about libraries. They suggest that teachers should discuss libraries with their classes, probing to find out the extent of the children's knowledge. They suggested the following activities.

- Take a fieldtrip to the public library to get a library card for each member of the class. Arrange with the librarian a convenient time to walk through the library to examine the resources available.

- Following the visit to the library, collect books and magazines for a classroom library. Allow materials to circulate. Gather ideas from class members on how their library should be arranged.

- Join a book club (such as Troll Books, Trumpet, or Scholastic) so that children can start their own personal libraries.

- Visit a library book fair.

Ideas for Preschool and Kindergarten

"Catch them early" was the advice from the kindergarten teachers in the workshop. The following are ideas for very young children.

- Read to children daily—several times a day, if possible.
- Reread favorite stories.
- Label character dolls (Curious George, Babar, Paddington) and display them as you read the story.
- Make a book. Students dictate books to the teacher who writes them down. Then children draw illustrations for the books to display in the classroom.
- Obtain some big books and read from them frequently.
- Have children retell stories in their own words after listening to the teacher read them.
- Have available many "easy" books—picture books, alphabet books, fairy tales, and nursery rhymes.
- Be aware of developmental reading differences.
- Label objects in the classroom with a label maker.

Ideas for Home

Teachers were especially adamant about the importance of reading at home. They encourage all teachers to prepare brief handouts to send home with ideas for parents to use with their children. Here are a few ideas for families, which have been mentioned in earlier chapters.

- Encourage parents to read aloud regularly to their children. Parents should establish regular read-aloud times and stick to them. Try to let nothing interfere with these sessions to reinforce the message that parents believe reading is valuable and fun.
- Parents can help young children practice reading by leaving short notes on the family bulletin board or refrigerator.
- Send suggestions home to parents of younger students for appropriate bedtime stories to read aloud.
- Encourage parents of older students to supply dictionaries and encyclopedias at home.
- Have children borrow books from the classroom library and take them home to read aloud to parents. Parents sign a paper to estab-

lish that they enjoyed the child's reading. Do not label this as homework; try homeplay!

Ideas for Family Trips

- Family members take turns being the "designated reader" of a favorite book to help pass the time on a long journey.

- Play the "alphabet game" in which family members watch for letters of the alphabet in sequence from the many signs along the roadside. When a letter is spotted, the player must read the word in which the letter was found. The first player to reach the end of the alphabet is the winner. Variations include using signs on just one side of the road, using printed words beginning with the target letters, or arranging teams by reading ability.

- On longer trips, give children a road map and ask them to find the road being traveled, next towns, number of miles to the next city, and so on.

- Stop and read historical markers. Discuss the significance of the events described. Calculate the years since the events occurred.

Ideas for Leisure Hours

- Select an Author of the Month. For example, with young children, read all the books written by a favorite author: Norman Bridwell, Peggy Parish, Jack Prelutsky, H.A. Rey, Maurice Sendak, Shel Silverstein, and Judith Viorst were a few of the authors mentioned as possibilities.

- With older children, select a theme or a genre to pursue in depth. Possibilities include sports, adventure, classic fairy tales, fables, historic periods, countries, multicultural similarities and differences, and so on.

- Have children listen to or view the news at home and discuss it in class.

- Read the comics together.

- Memorize poems, and recite them on trips.

- Find easy recipes, and help children read and follow the directions for concocting delicious treats for the family.

- Visit a bookstore to explore the wide variety of children's books available. Help a child begin collecting a personal library.

A Final Word

For all these affective reading activities, no claim to originality is made. Ideas abound for helping children discover the pleasures of reading. What is significant is that this list has been compiled by practicing teachers: they know what works, and they offer these ideas as springboards for others who wish to join them in their quest to have every child become a lifelong reader.

It is interesting to note that none of the teachers' comments included a reference to using technology as a means of motivating students' reading interests. One can only speculate that technological resources are either not available or are not being used as a means of motivating students in reading. Whether this is a widespread phenomenon would make an interesting topic for further research. How might computers, CD-ROMs, electronic books, and telecommunications be used as motivational tools in classrooms?

My thanks go to the following teachers who participated in the affective reading education workshop and who enthusiastically gave their permission to use their ideas: Willie Baldwin, Dora Burns, June Congious, Charles Davis, Ethel Doogan, Nancy Feldman, Rosa Green, Sarah F. Hawthorne, Bertha Kokuma, Veronica Levine, Judith L. Monroe, Mercedes Moreno, Kristin Pfeiffer, Neva Piepho, Kathleen Rademacher, Bartolo Rivera, Jean L. Sachs, Donna M. Soukup, Rita Stasi, Gail Tibensky, Karen Tiersky, Susie B. Travis, Ann Tuohy, Yvonne Vaccarella, Sally Weiner, and Alice Wood.

Children's Books

Dahl, R. (1961). *James and the giant peach*. New York: Puffin.
dePaola, T. (1978). *The popcorn book*. New York: Scholastic,
Galdone, P. (1970). *The three little pigs*. New York: Scholastic.
Grimm, J. & Grimm, W.K. (1985). *Grimm's fairy tales*. New York: Puffin.
Marshall, J. (1989). *The three little pigs*. New York: Scholastic.
McGovern, A. (1968). *Stone soup*. New York: Scholastic.
Parish, P. (1977). *Teach us, Amelia Bedelia*. New York: Scholastic.
Spinelli, J. (1990). *Maniac Magee*. New York: Scholastic.
Steptoe, J. (1987). *Mufaro's beautiful daughters*. New York: Lothrop, Lee, & Shepard.
Viorst, J. (1972). *Alexander and the terrible, horrible, no good, very bad day*. New York: Macmillan.
White, E.B. (1952). *Charlotte's web*. New York: HarperCollins.

PART FOUR

Responding to Reading

What is read with delight is commonly retained, because pleasure always secures attention, but the books which are consulted by...necessity and perused with impatience seldom leave any traces on the mind.

S. Johnson

Chapter 11

Helping Children Choose Books

Marrietta Castle

●◆ I cannot remember learning to read. I can only remember being able to in first grade. I also remember liking *the idea* of being able to read; however, I did not particularly like to read. Dick, Jane, and Sally were the only characters in literature I encountered in those early elementary years, and all they seemed to do every day was look, see, and go, declaring mindlessly when the going got rough, "Oh, oh, oh." Those were *Happy Days* (the title of the book by Montgomery, Bauer, & Gray, 1948) for them, but hardly for me. I passed from teacher to teacher, encountering only text-books and workbooks. I do not even remember seeing many trade books at school, and there were few in my home.

Things changed in the sixth grade: Mrs. O'Neil turned me on to books. She did not do it in any formal or forced way. For instance, on the first day of school she began to read to the class. Initially I thought it was a strange and terribly childish thing for her to do, but I came to look forward to those quiet moments when I could savor the story as it filtered through her familiar voice. She read softly but with feeling, and sometimes she stopped to share a personal anecdote, pose a question, or mention how this story was like others she had read. She always had a book in her hand or on her desk, and she seemed to know everything about every one of them. She obviously loved books.

Even Mrs. O'Neil's classroom was different from others. I recall that the entire back wall was covered with bookshelves from which she was constantly pulling books and recommending them to students. Every topic of study stimulated the use of a book, and social studies and science time was filled with projects that required serious investigation into many of the volumes on those shelves. I remember a particular study about Mexico when we composed plays in small groups, made costumes and props, learned to sing Spanish songs, and wrote invitations to our parents to attend our special performances. Textbooks and workbooks were seldom used, and I cannot remember a time when we were not involved in plays, poetry recitals, choral readings, and creative writing. Literature of our own making merged with that of other authors, and all flowed freely around the classroom, to our homes, and back. I began to read voraciously.

Whether I was a Type A ludic reader, as Nell (1988) explains, who used reading to escape, or a Type B ludic reader who used reading to heighten experience, choosing books became a valued and enjoyable part of my life. It is that same constant and insatiable choosing that I would like to see in our classrooms and homes today.

The phrase "helping children choose books" touches on important aspects relating to creating lifelong readers. One concern, of course, is getting children to choose reading over other possibilities—or at least along with other possibilities—as a tool for self-directed learning or as a leisurely pursuit both in and out of school. *Who Reads Best* (Applebee, Langer, & Mullis, 1988), a report of the U.S. National Assessment of Reading Progress, cited evidence that indicates students focus more on the pragmatic aspects of reading in school: "It appears that as students go through school, those in both the upper and lower quartiles increasingly read to answer particular questions rather than for more general learning or relaxation" (p. 32). Although this report showed that purposes for reading out of school were more likely to be to relax or pass the time, only 20 percent of the students at grade 3 and 55 percent of those at grade 11 claimed they used reading for those purposes. Even the percentage of students who reported that they did out-of-school reading primarily to learn something new decreased from 40 percent at grade 3 to 20 percent at grade 11. And, as would be expected, poorer readers at all grade levels reported much less out-of-school reading.

Helping children choose to read for various purposes in different settings appears tantamount to creating a truly literate citizenry. Moreover, helping children select books that satisfy their personal, social, and academic needs is critical for ensuring that children do indeed choose to read. As the authors in this work agree, for educators to tackle the challenge of helping children choose books they need to (1) model that they are readers; (2) provide ready access to a wide range of interesting materials; and (3) set up incentives for reluctant readers. Although these are three distinct goals, critical elements for developing lifelong readers must be practiced together, not separately. For example, teachers cannot serve as reading models without providing access to a wide variety of reading materials; as students have access to materials and use them for real purposes following the teacher's example, they will serve as models and create incentives for reluctant readers. Each practice contributes to and is interrelated with the other, and affective classrooms serve student needs because they possess a critical mass of these practices.

Teachers as Models

I can think of no more powerful way for teachers to foster a love of reading than to read to, with, about, and in front of children. Mrs. O'Neil understood that in 1954. Every day she demonstrated that reading served both pleasurable and functional purposes through her conversations and actions. Her enthusiasm, her insights, and her expectations created an environment that literally enticed children from diverse backgrounds into literacy and learning. As Donald Graves (1990) aptly stated, we become "literacy apprentices," discovering how to make our own decisions while observing closely the teacher's reading and writing behaviors.

By their example, teachers strongly influence students' definition of reading, how they view its purposes, their literary choices, and their commitment to its inclusion in their lives (Cullinan, 1992a; Otto 1992–1993; Spiegel, 1981). Teachers must be aware of the verbal and nonverbal ways they communicate their feelings about reading to students, because it is through interaction and emulation that students come to accept the value each teacher places on reading and to view the medium as the message. Melvin (1986) discussed the impact of this message in her article, "First Moments in Reading," in which she stressed making reading an important component of the first day of school, the first minutes of every day following, and the first minutes of every reading class. Including time for teacher or student read-alouds, silent reading, and book discussions in these first moments ensures that real reading takes precedence over other instructional practices. "If we want students to value reading as a personal tool for learning and for pleasure, we must schedule class time to reflect this sense of values" (Melvin, 1986, p. 634).

Reading to Students

Reading aloud by teachers is recalled time and again by adults as of one of their earliest pleasant associations with reading (Carlsen & Sherrill, 1988), as Fisher mentioned in Chapter 4. But, even so, do teacher read-alouds merit inclusion in the school curriculum? The evidence is overwhelming: reading to students is one of the most effective methods for creating capable readers who continue to choose reading for a lifetime (Anderson et al., 1985; Clay, 1979; Cullinan, 1992b; Kimmel & Segal, 1983; Trelease, 1989; see also Chapters 5 and 15 and Part Three in this work.) Teachers who take the time to read to students convey the clear message that reading is important and deserves equal placement along with other important instructional events in the school day. Reading aloud to students is also one of the most effective ways to introduce new books and quality literature to them.

If improved attitudes toward reading were the only advantage for children who are read to, I believe that would be enough to justify its inclusion in the daily curriculum. However, not only have studies documented the motivational benefits of reading aloud to students, but they have also shown other direct benefits, including growth in understanding of language patterns, text structure, vocabulary, fluent oral reading, others' experiences, multicultural concepts, the authoring role, imaging, and so on. Children who are read to, especially from an early age, are introduced to significant ideas and literary forms that they might otherwise miss. In fact, even if students can already read, read-alouds should continue, with material slightly above students' reading level to stretch their ideas and interests.

Often teachers ask whether students should be allowed to do other things while being read to. I often answer with another question: would you allow students to clean their desks, sharpen pencils, do paperwork, or carry on side conversations when someone is speaking to them? Although attention can clearly be feigned, inattention can be reduced by setting clear goals that include good listening posture and elimination of distractions. The question becomes moot when teachers choose stimulating books and position themselves close to students during read-aloud time. Also, by being prepared students both physically and mentally for active listening, students are primed to construct meaning as they listen. Once they feel an attachment to the characters, setting, or problem, they will become totally absorbed in a story, much like falling under the spell of a storyteller. Nell (1988) referred to this spell as "the witchery of a story" (see Chapter 3) when the reader becomes unconscious to self and drifts into the world of words and images.

Absorbed readers are a consequence of planning and preparation. Setting the stage for read-alouds through brief discussions will give students time, reason, and means to focus on what is being shared. I particularly like Schmidt's (1986) simple but effective suggestions to teachers or others preparing to read aloud:

1. Use the title or picture to elicit possibilities about what students might expect to hear in the story.

2. Ask a question that helps students link their own personal experiences to the story content.

3. Share a personal experience of your own related to story content
(p. 2).

As the story or information is clearly and enthusiastically presented, readers should maintain good eye contact, inviting each listener personally to connect with the content through individual glances and dramatic
phrasing (Dwyer & Isbell, 1989). When the material concludes, the reader
should be sensitive to student reactions to the ideas just expressed. If the
material is particularly captivating, students will need time to drift back to
reality. A few moments of silence may be called for. Asking a question or
making a comment immediately after reading *A Bridge to Terabithia* by
Katherine Paterson or Sharon B. Mathis's *The Hundred Penny Box*, for
instance, would be unconscionable because they are such powerful books.

Reading to students need not be limited to preschool or the early
elementary years when children are developing basic speaking, listening,
reading, and writing skills. Many teachers discovered that students of all
ages love being read to long before *Becoming a Nation of Readers* recommended this as "a practice that should continue throughout the grades" (p.
51). Middle school and high school teachers, including those working with
gifted students, have realized unexpected enjoyment and excitement in
classrooms as they shared read-alouds (Ecroyd, 1991; Matthews, 1987).
Although sophisticated young adolescents can be tough audiences, few can
resist stories, poems, or informational articles that relate to current movies,
rock videos, newspaper headlines, or popular TV programs. Humor, fear,
gore, or romance usually elicit responses, whether negative or positive, and
risk-free discussions can lead to insights about universal themes of love,
hate, war, life, death, and family relationships (see Richardson's Chapter 15
on reading aloud in secondary classrooms).

Content area teachers at middle school and high school levels
should share with students the literature of their fields, material that they
enjoy reading, informational as well as inspirational works, and especially
biographies about individuals and events that have inspired them to enter
their areas of study. Short picture books are no less enticing than those that
appear more age appropriate. All or portions of wonderful books such as
Children of the Dust Bowl by Jerry Stanley, Russell Freedman's *Lincoln: A
Photobiography*, *Encounter* by Jane Yolen, Glennette Turner's *Lewis
Howard Latimer*, and Philip Johnson's *The Great Canadian Alphabet Book*
can build insights into fields of study and capture the imagination of future
mathematicians, scientists, and social leaders.

When selecting books for read-alouds, teachers must be wary of the subtle messages their choices are conveying. In one study analyzing the books 254 elementary teachers most often chose for reading aloud to children, researchers found that preferences included twice as many books with male protagonists as female (Smith, Greenlaw, & Scott, 1987). In books that did have female protagonists, the females appeared to be narrowly defined and negative while the male characters were positive but stereotypical. The situation became worse in higher grades. In addition, groups such as minorities, the elderly, and the mentally and physically challenged were rarely represented. The researchers concluded that teachers were probably "unaware of the degree of sex bias in their read-aloud preferences, but they were contributing to the perpetuation of sex role stereotyping that has been part of the socialization process for all of us for too long" (p. 407).

Reading with Students

Reading to students leads naturally to another important modeling activity for teachers—providing for and participating in sustained silent reading, as described in Chapter 7. Because students are not likely to include recreational reading in their out-of-school agenda (Anderson et al., 1985; Valencia, Hiebert, & Kapinus, 1992), it is critical to include it at school. Even if students read silently for a minimum of only ten minutes a day or an hour a week, reading skills will improve (Center for the Study of Reading, 1986; Morrow, 1985). Setting up a consistent structure, starting with shorter periods and gradually moving to sustained blocks of time, and providing options for locating and becoming absorbed in interesting material are basics for a profitable SSR time.

It is also important to make sure that the teacher and other adults present during SSR time read along with students (Fielding & Roller, 1992; Sanacore, 1992). Teachers should resist the urge to plan lessons, correct papers, or even confer with students about their reading during this time. When the entire class participates as readers, sharing occasional book talks before and after sessions, reading aloud interesting passages, and assisting less able readers with selections, all become immersed in the pleasures of reading. I have noted, too, that teachers who accompany students to the school library each week, select their own books to read as students make their selections, and take time to sit in the library or the classroom to read books immediately after choosing are more likely to develop voluntary readers. In such environments, reading is contagious.

As teacher read-alouds and SSR take their rightful places in the classroom, many teachers have discovered that their own independent reading agendas need strengthening. Research on both preservice and inservice, teachers' reading habits shows some appalling statistics (Mour, 1977; Searls, 1985). For example, Gray and Troy (1986) found that only 29 of 80 elementary education students surveyed were reading a book at the time of the survey, and only half indicated that reading was an enjoyable pastime. However, because teachers are aware that children's literature, along with journals and professional books, can play a prominent role in professional growth, "Teachers under Cover" (Cardarelli, 1992) and "Teachers as Readers" groups (Hansen, 1993; Micklos, 1992) have been formed. Through shared book talks and in-depth discussions in these groups, teachers have rediscovered the joys of reading for pleasure, and their enthusiasm has served as a catalyst for dynamic discussions in their classrooms. (See also Chapter 13 in this work.)

In the final analysis, modeling comes down to trusting yourself and trusting books to carry the message that reading is a worthwhile pursuit. If teachers do not read independently and use reading to fulfill personal needs, then why should students? Ultimately, teacher learning succeeds under the same conditions that student learning thrives: models, mentors, and time to participate in shared activities revolving around literature.

Books Within Arms' Reach

In her book *Lyddie*, Katherine Paterson describes her main character as a girl who keeps a page from *Oliver Twist* at arms' reach daily as she works in the mills during the early 1900s. Lyddie used this particular book, a favorite that had first been read to her, to read and reread on her own to gain reading competency. That strategy is as applicable today as it was in Lyddie's time. Reading material must be easily accessible and relevant to entice children to read.

One of the best ways to help children become fluent readers and choose reading as a leisure activity is to make sure that books are nearby at all times. Just as research into how some children become readers at very early ages has shown the influence of immediate accessibility to books in the home (Greaney, 1986; Taylor & Dorsey-Gaines, 1988), that same accessibility appears paramount in literacy development at school. "Children in classrooms with libraries read more, express better attitudes toward reading, and make greater gains in reading comprehension than children who do not have such ready access to books" (Anderson et al., 1985). Perhaps this is because, when books are close at hand, students can locate them and get involved in reading quickly, with minimum effort and loss of learning time. Other students and teachers are also nearby to assist in choosing books and in sharing their many pleasures.

Setting Up a Classroom Library

I once taught in a second grade classroom in an older, inner-city building, which had no reading center and no reading materials beyond some old basals. I quickly learned that there are many ways to create a library center with little effort and money if parents and students are involved. Even window ledges with sturdy cardboard boxes tipped on their sides can serve as bookshelves. The most important criteria for an inviting library is that books are visually and physically accessible to children and easily checked out and in. Poorly designed reading centers in which books are disorganized, fall easily, or make browsing difficult will simply not be used by children.

The following suggestions can help in setting up effective in-class libraries (Castle, 1987; Fractor et al., 1993; Hickman, 1983; Routman, 1991; see also the chapters in Part Three of this work):

1. Create highly visible centers. Students will be drawn to areas that look attractive and important. Use shelving, posters, bulletin boards, stuffed animals, props, puppets, or even ceiling displays to entice readers to the area. Display some books with their covers out (and other with their spines facing) to provide visual incentives to read.

2. Keep it quiet. Use partitions, tables, or shelves to set boundaries and shut out distractions. Provide comfortable seating, such as carpeting, pillows, or a couch; usually room for only five or six students is best. Set and enforce expectations for quiet reading and conversation.

3. Provide a variety of materials: picture books, storybooks, paperbacks, basal readers, student-authored books, maps, newspapers, phone books, dictionaries, encyclopedias, and brochures are all possibilities. Commercial, student-, or teacher-prepared audiotapes can also be available to encourage students whose second language is English or who learn differently to read. Props such as flannel boards can also promote rereading and language development with books. Large poster boards or sheets of art paper can serve as "graffiti walls" for students to write comments about reading and books.

4. Organize the books. Categorizing by genre, theme, topic, author, reading level, content area, or combinations of these features can help students recommend books to one another and locate books quickly. Color or letter codes on books can help in reshelving and identifying books that come from the classroom library.

5. Give students ownership. Allow them to name the area, help decorate it, develop rules for its use, and assist in securing and organizing materials. Let them maintain the library's day-to-day checkins and checkouts and the periodic promotion of new books. Maintain an attitude of responsible use within a risk-free environment, helping students cooperatively establish and maintain clear policies regarding damaged and lost books.

Creating Collections for Classroom Libraries

Of course, the first place to start in creating or enlarging classroom collections is to contact school or public librarians. As some of the most bookwise people in schools, these experts can suggest titles, ways to organize collections, possible funding sources, or even agree to provide sets of books on a rotating basis for classrooms. In addition, these specialists have access to book-selection tools such as *The Bookfinder* (Dreyer, 1992) to facilitate locating books on special topics. Using school or library budgets to purchase different collections for several teachers and then rotating these collections among classrooms may solve the difficulty of obtaining a wide variety of books for each classroom. While any quantity of books is better than none, the best classroom libraries usually have a minimum of 8 to 10 books per child (Fractor et al., 1993).

Never underestimate the power of students and parents to help create valuable classroom collections. When I inherited the classroom without books in my first year of teaching, I simply told students that we had an important mission ahead of us, and we went to homes, bookstores, libraries, and businesses in search of books for our classroom. We also published our own books and invited other classes to do the same.

I have always found parents eager to help, regardless of their socioeconomic status. If they have no books to donate, they can visit garage sales, hold book fairs, create lists of good books to acquire, staff writing centers where children create their own contributions to classroom libraries, and make phone calls or send requests to clubs, churches, and service organizations. Some businesses such as banks, newspapers, and real estate firms that are made aware of literacy needs in a community may be willing to sponsor small grants for book buying. In addition, community clubs, professional organizations, and educational institutions, including those involved in teacher education, look for projects and worthwhile service opportunities. These groups are often eager to form partnerships with schools on behalf of literacy. Even placing containers in public libraries, stores, or restaurants can promote book donations for nearby schools.

Enterprising teachers have long used commercial school book clubs to build classroom libraries and promote recreational reading. The inexpensive paperbacks these clubs provide not only allow children to buy books, but also give bonus points for free classroom orders when students make purchases. I know of a teacher in an economically depressed community who gained sponsorship from a local bank, which provided every child in her classroom with up to US$8.00 monthly to purchase books from a book club. As a teacher educator, I have also found it beneficial to introduce undergraduate students to these book clubs and to allow them to order books voluntarily just as children would do. Students also manage the process entirely on their own, and, like the children they will someday teach, they become aware of the types of reading material available, begin building their personal collections, and learn how the clubs operate.

I have seldom been disappointed in the quality of books offered through the clubs. An interesting U.S. study by Strickland and Walmsley (Sandmann, 1993) entitled "School Book Clubs and Literacy Development" reassures me and other educators that although some "junk" buying can be a part of student purchases, most clubs present a wide variety of culturally diverse books, ranging from easy-reading to challenging levels and including classics, contemporary stories about sports, books about family and school life, informational books, biographies, mysteries, adventures, and folk tales. "The range of offerings contradicts the impressions among some teachers that club lists lack breadth" (p. 6). In fact, these same researchers reported that 90 percent of the teachers they interviewed in kindergarten through fifth grade used book clubs.

Choosing the "Right" Book

Just because students make use of well-stocked classroom libraries does not mean that they no longer need materials from the school or public library. Children must be taught how these libraries differ and how all three can support their interests and needs. Most of all, new or experienced readers should find it easy to choose the right book at the right time from all these libraries. No one deserves getting caught up in the "too game"—finding books that are too easy, too hard, too long, too short, or too boring. Reluctant readers especially are those most penalized by these frustrations, as they often confront mismatches between reader and text. If the mismatches are frequent and persistent and make choosing too time consuming, too much work, and, most important, too damaging to feelings of self-worth, they may simply give up reading altogether. For these reasons, children need to be assisted with their choices to ensure that reading becomes too enjoyable to pass up.

I have discussed reading aloud to students and providing time for leisure reading as ways to expose students to a wide variety of books, but how can students and teachers make their selections for these activities? How can they know what types of books are best for inclusion in classroom libraries? Interviews and observations in one study showed that the top five criteria students in grades one through four used for book selection were structure, content, familiarity, genre, and series (Carter, 1988). If structure is indeed the primary criterion, it appears that children do judge a book by its cover. Structural elements include such visual factors as cover design, illustrations, length, and size of print. Whether selections based on this single criterion are good or bad, it may reflect how many students, especially younger readers or less experienced older readers, choose books. Teachers who are aware that these factors are influencing student choices can help students become more thoughtful about their selections and develop alternative strategies as well. For example, a student who selects a book about turtles based on its colorful cover design and illustrations may be encouraged to read a short passage from the book to see if it is at the appropriate difficulty level before making a final selection. Whatever the decision, students must be allowed to check out more than one book per visit and to return to the library when necessary. A week without access to a good book to read could be the very week a child decides books are simply not worth the effort.

Series, the fifth criteria Carter (1988) found to be important to children when choosing books, reflects a marketing strategy that publishers discovered long ago. When children become interested in a book by a particular author or with particular characters, they readily seek out other books by that author or with the same characters. When children have savored a good story, they want more; when they become acquainted with certain characters, they are comfortable with keeping them nearby, at least in their imaginations. Freedman and Frost (1993) report that many bookstores devote about half their shelf space in children's areas to series books. They found as many as 18 different series in one bookstore, written mostly for middle and upper elementary students. Their analysis of series books, however, showed them lacking in many qualities apparent in good literature:

> The characters are often flat and undeveloped. Major characters in these books seldom represent any minority group or diverse lifestyle. They are usually set in suburban communities or picturesque small towns.... These books often lack rich language, and the writing is formulaic (p. 43).

Freedman and Frost (1993) continue to explain that often these books have secondary authors who operate on the framework established by the primary author. For example, Ann M. Martin, primary author for The Babysitters series, admits that she writes only the outline for the books; others fill in the details. This explains the phenomenal number of books published in any given series on a yearly basis.

In spite of this, Freedman and Frost are not suggesting that teachers discourage children from reading these "lighter" series books. They are suggesting, however, that teachers also recommend and expose students to other kinds of "connected" literature of high quality—multiple works by the same author but with characters, plots, and language that are stronger and more richly developed. Books such as those by Mildred Taylor, which tell the continuing tale of the Logan Family (*Roll of Thunder, Hear My Cry*, *Let the Circle Be Unbroken*, and *The Road to Memphis*), and those by Cynthia Voigt about the Tillermans (*The Homecoming* and *Dicey's Song*) are excellent. Those by Vera B. Williams about Rose and her family (*A Chair for My Mother*, *Something Special for Me*, and *Music, Music for Everyone*) are also high quality. Still others that involve families but have animal characters that young children enjoy are those by Beverly Cleary that feature an adolescent mouse (*The Mouse and the Motorcycle*, *Runaway Ralph*, and *Ralph S. Mouse*), and Mary Calhoun, about a clever Siamese cat (*Cross-Country Cat*, *Hot-Air Henry*, and *High-Wire Henry*).

Other quality books that are seldom classified as series books in bookstores or libraries are the multiple publications of particular authors that can stand alone but can also be read as a group. Once students find that they enjoy a particular genre or style, they can be lead to authors who offer similar books. For younger readers, there are Byrd Baylor, Eric Carle, Eloise Greenfield, Steven Kellogg, Leo Leonni, Cynthia Rylant, Maurice Sendak, Nancy Shaw, and Chris Van Allsburg; older readers will enjoy books by Betsy Byars, Paula Danzinger, Jean Fritz, Jamie Gilson, S.E. Hinton, E.L. Konigsburg, Patricia MacLachlan, Katherine Paterson, and Gary Paulsen. These are only a very small sampling of the writers who can easily hook children on reading and prolong their pleasure through related literature.

However, choosing books only because they contain favorite characters or are written by favorite authors can still be limiting. Making choices based on several features will surely promote more and better choices. By encouraging students to discuss interests and recreational reading habits and by observing students' choice-making behaviors, teachers can plan effective intervention strategies to expand reading repertoires (Fielding & Roller, 1992; McGill-Franzen, 1993). Direct instruction and specific guidance for groups or individuals may be necessary to aid children in internalizing and automatizing better choice making. For example, teaching an explicit plan such as "How to Pick a Book by Hand" described below may help students, especially those who read less well, find books that fit their abilities:

1. Pick a book you think you want to read.
2. Open to a page near the middle.
3. Read it to yourself.
4. Hold up a finger for any word you don't know.
5. If four fingers and a thumb are raised, the book may be too hard.
6. Try the same thing with another page. If it is still too hard, get another book.

Of course, if interest is high in a particular book, it could be read *to* or *along with* a student. Partner reading is commendable (Fielding & Roller, 1992): shared effort means shared rewards. Partner reading implies everything that partners can do together with books. Using multiple copies of some books, particularly for beginning readers, is an excellent way to encourage readers to approach books as a team. Parents can also become a part of this team when two copies are available for checkout. Sometimes when children are given a "running start" in a book by first having a part read to them, they can take off on their own, using the knowledge and word-recognition skills they have accumulated through watching and listening. Other students may be able to read a book only *after* all of it has been read to them, perhaps more than once. They will reread and relisten when interest remains high and they know the payoffs. Even children who are never able to tackle a book at a particular level on their own can expand their ideas through looking at illustrations, reading easier parts, or listening to another read. Either way, they will be nourished in knowing that good "stuff" comes from books.

As adults, surely we recognize the fact that we read books at many levels for different purposes in different ways. So can children. Hansen

(1987) noted that second graders could benefit from reading three types of books: challenge books, ones that can only be read a few minutes at a time before tiring; medium books, those that present some difficulties but not too many to interfere with comprehension; and easy books, ones that can be read smoothly with few word and concept difficulties and may even be reread several times. Ohlhausen and Jepsen (1992), using what they called the "Goldilocks Strategy," have suggested a series of minilessons to acquaint students with the idea that books can be too easy, too hard, or just right; books at each level can serve valuable purposes. They advise teachers to give students frequent opportunities to explain how and why they make the choices they do. "This can happen daily in small group and individual book conferences and in whole class discussions, or quarterly during individual assessment conferences" (pp. 39–40).

The best teachers seldom leave choosing to chance. They not only share good decision-making strategies about books through formal, direct instructional moments such as those recommended by Ohlhausen and Jepsen (1992) and Ollman (1993), but they also promote wiser choosing through informal dialogues and networking. Posting class lists of favorite books, keeping card files of books students have read, using student response journals, maintaining individual reading folders, or scheduling brief sharing sessions weekly can provide students with many options for choosing. Teachers who read a wide variety of children's books can easily participate in such informal dialogues and networks.

Knowing the typical preferences for certain age groups may also be of interest to teachers as they make their own selections for read-alouds and guide student choices. In Chapter 4 of this work "Who Reads What and When?," Fisher discussed children's preferences in detail, including lower and upper grade choices ranked by story type, genre, and specific titles. However, teachers should be aware that student preferences will always be highly individual, and we cannot always know what is the "right" book for a student. What a child selects one day may depend on a momentary feeling or circumstance, one to which we are not privy. I would caution educators to resist the temptation to assume too large a role in measuring the rightness of a book. Only the child knows when it is a perfect fit.

Reading Incentives

One of my favorite books, *Mostly Michael* by Robert Kimmel Smith, tells the story of an 11-year-old boy who does not like to read. When his teacher discovers he has cheated on a book report near the end of the school year, he is assigned to read ten books over the summer. What at first seems like the worst possible punishment turns into a new leisure habit and an attitude adjustment for Michael. When writing in his diary about his first visit to the library, he records his reply to the librarian's question about the books he likes: "Easy ones, I said, because I am a slow reader." As the book continues, an astute friend, the children's librarian, and Michael's parents help him find the incentive to read.

This part of the story reminded me of the many Michaels I encountered as a sixth grade teacher. I was an experienced teacher in a new school, and this time I inherited an impressive classroom library complete with a couch. There were hundreds of paperbacks in an attractive classroom reading center, with a well-stocked school library nearby. What more did I need? Students who chose to read. It became apparent within a short time after school started that about 10 percent of the students were doing 90 percent of the reading. In spite of my reading to and with students and providing in-class reading time, changes in the attitudes of reluctant readers seemed to be progressing much more slowly than I had hoped. I decided to take action.

Contracts

First, I wanted students to become more aware of their own reading habits and motivations as well as those of others, so I helped them develop written questionnaires and oral interview questions for gathering information about what other students and adults read, why they read, and how much they read. My students responded to some of the questionnaires and interviews, too, and were excited about doing real "research." Next, I set up large and small group discussions so we could share what was gleaned from our data gathering; students even created charts and graphs to show information such as hours of reading, time spent reading compared to other leisure activities, types of reading material, or preferred books by subject area. Another project unfolded as the class explored the reading world around them: I asked each student to keep a record of what she or he read, where, and how often. After four weeks students and I discussed individual findings in one-on-one conferences.

Last, I asked all students to make a commitment to work at improving their reading habits over the next three months, either by reading more or by reading a wider variety of literature. In consultation with their parents, students filled in and signed a contract much like the one on the next page. The information gathered from the four-week self-study and the one-on-one conferences helped students determine realistic individual goals. A letter to parents, who had already been involved in the earlier project, informed them about the contracts and enlisted their help. The letter read as follows:

Dear Parent,

This week your son or daughter will be discussing a reading contract with you which will involve the selection and reading of books both in and out of class. The goals for this project are

1. to stimulate the student's interest in reading for enjoyment;
2. to encourage the student to develop the habit of reading;
3. to expand the student's areas of interest;
4. to expose the student to a variety of literature.

Please take time to look over the contract and discuss with your child the best possible choice of goals based on his or her interests and reading ability. Once the contract is finalized, I hope you will continue to encourage your child to select suitable books and to read regularly at home. Trips to the library or bookstore, giving books as gifts for special occasions, and participating in the book clubs by placing monthly orders can help your child find books she or he will enjoy.

To motivate your child to read, you might like to allow an extra 15 minutes just before bedtime for reading. You could encourage your child to read interesting passages to you or another member of the family. You could read the same book and discuss parts together. Your entire family could participate in a quiet reading time nightly or at least several nights a week. By all means, keep reading times enjoyable and relaxing.

As your child finishes reading a book, your signature will be required on a short file form. By briefly discussing the book or asking a few questions about how she or he liked it and why, you and I can help the student keep an accurate record of progress.

Feel free to contact me about particular books your child would like to obtain, and I'll do my best to help her or him find something suitable. You are encouraged to use the public library and any other sources to find books within your child's interest area. There is nothing wrong if easy or short books are selected once in a while. Remember, any reading is better than no reading.

The class decided on the reward for students who met their contracts. In the years I used this program, students settled on ribbons, gift certificates to bookstores, opportunities to read to younger students, and extra credit on grades. Special incentives also marked the halfway point, such as being given in-class time to create special bookmarks and release time to work with younger students in classroom reading and writing activities. As

Reading Contract

Name _____ Date _____

I wish to fulfill the following contract in regard to recreational reading:

_____

_____

_____

_____

_____

_____

_____

_____

_____
Date

I will fulfill this contract by   Student's signature _____

_____   Parent's signature _____

                                         Teacher's signature _____

- -

Evaluation

I   did   did not (circle one)   fulfill this contract because _____

_____

_____

As a result of this contract I have learned _____

_____

_____

_____

explained later in this chapter, these extrinsic rewards were never intended as an end in themselves, but they served well initially to increase the time and effort students spent on reading and to expose them to the literature they had long neglected. My role was to help students monitor progress and find material of interest. For example, students kept their own reading folders that contained booklists, records of completed books (sheets with title, author, date completed, category, and rating), and book club orders. The brief forms they filled out and had parents sign for each book were added to a class shoebox file for others to refer to. Innovative book projects were used from time to time, such as mobiles, posters, and book talks. Sometimes students dressed in costumes representing a character or reflecting a book's theme or topic. However, students did not do traditional written book reports.

Students were also encouraged to visit the classroom and school libraries frequently, as I integrated literature into the reading, English, and social studies areas I taught and maintained in-class reading times. The school librarian, the students, and I also did "book teasers" by reading a particularly interesting part of a book to tantalize would-be readers. Swap days were planned so that students could bring in books they no longer wanted and swap with classmates. Conferences and informal conversations throughout helped me and students focus on reading and learning. Although I did not keep detailed records about the success of the program, feedback from students, parents, and other teachers led me to believe it was successful in many ways, particularly in helping students read more often and more diversely while bolstering their attitudes that reading was a worthwhile activity. In the final analysis, only 4 students out of 68 in both of my sixth grade sections did not meet their contracts in the first year I used the program; only 2 did not in the second year.

Although there is little recent professional literature about contracts (Kassens, 1984; Parkhurst, 1981; Salmon & Laughlin, 1979), my firsthand knowledge of the benefits of using them with poorly motivated readers has been encouraging. I am not advocating their use in all situations, however, and I am certainly not advocating their use in rigid ways. What appears crucial to student success with contracts are ownership, support, and cooperative effort. What began as a teacher idea became a student-controlled program—students had choices and took responsibility for many of the activities incorporated throughout. Perhaps the true measure of the success of using reading contracts with my classroom was when students continued reading at high levels when the contracts were removed. In fact, students seemed not to notice that they no longer needed to keep lists of books and fill out reading forms. They continued to do so for their own uses. It was apparent that they had internalized the value of reading, and it had become its own reward.

Another type of reading contract involves individual or all-school goals to read for a particular number of minutes nightly or over time. One such program called "The Reading Millionaires Project" (O'Masta & Wolf, 1991) challenged students to read a million minutes outside of school. With the strong support and planning of administrators, teachers, and parents, the project was structured around a banking analogy: entries were made in a "Reading Minutes Deposit Savings Book" for time spent reading at home. Special activities, celebrations, charts, newsletters, and book fairs helped generate enthusiasm and maintain momentum for the project, and the overall effect was extremely positive. Evaluations showed that "94 percent of the parents reported that their child enjoyed reading more as a result of the project," and "all teachers participating in the project indicated that the school-wide effort to involve parents in the reading process assisted them in promoting reading in the classroom" (p. 661). This and similar projects appear to be worthwhile.

Extrinsic and Intrinsic Rewards

Michael, the character I spoke of earlier who began to change his reading habits in *Mostly Michael*, illustrated some interesting lessons about intrinsic and extrinsic motivation. Michael was a low-average student with low self-esteem who appeared to know very little about how to improve his own school performance. His realization of the rewards of reading came as the result of punishment. I cannot think of anything that would appear more damaging to positive feelings about reading and self than to force a child who already hates to read (that is why he cheated in the first place) to read ten books and write a formal book report on each...and to do it during his summer vacation. But Michael had other experiences while he was working through his punishment, and, whether by the author's design or by accident, they seem to support many of the elements of good motivational theory. As is often the case, good fiction contains good messages.

In a summary of various viewpoints about "The Complex Art of Motivating Students," Willis (1991) focused on those who believe that school successes and failures would be more motivating if they carried heavier consequences. Paraphrasing a statement by Sandra Graham, associate professor of educational psychology at the University of California–Los Angeles, he writes,

> Teachers who express sympathy for students who fail may be doing them a disservice.... Similarly, praising students must be done with care. Teachers often give low-achieving students a great deal of praise in order to keep them motivated.... However, when students receive praise for performing a simple task, they generally infer that the teacher thinks they are "really stupid" (p. 5).

The art of motivating students is indeed complex and individual, requiring sensitivity to what works in any situation with any student.

Wiesendanger and Bader (1989) assessed 9- to 12-year-olds' perceptions of commonly used rewards and motivational activities related to reading and found that the most popular rewards involved choice and independence: getting extra credit or free time in school, being excused from class work, or getting to go to other classes. Earning grades, names on a bulletin board, or stars on a chart were rated as the least popular rewards. Students thought the best things a teacher could do to encourage them to read were read a few pages of a book and then leave it for them to check out, tell about places where stories take place, or tell about books she or he has read. Least encouraging activities included asking oral questions about a story before starting to read or giving students written questions to answer while reading. After reading, students liked the idea of going to a movie or play about the book or meeting the author; they disliked writing a book report or taking a test about the story. Wiesendanger and Bader concluded that teachers should re-evaluate instructional practices that deal with competition, prequestioning, book reports, and testing.

Other attempts to evaluate the effects of intrinsic and extrinsic motivation in learning (Alderman, 1990; Brophy, 1987; Chance, 1992, 1993; Csikszentmihalyi, 1990; Kohn, 1993) show a mixed bag of opinions (see also Chapter 7). Almost all agree that incentives usually work if they are age and ability appropriate, are used in supportive environments, are used for worthy goals, and are not overused. When extrinsic motivators are used, teachers should keep the focus off the rewards and on the development of knowledge and skills that are of more lasting intrinsic value. Extrinsic motivators also appear most effective when used in situations where more effort or quantity of output is the goal rather than quality of performance. If students understand the value of the goal they are aiming for and believe that reasonable effort will help them achieve that goal, then they are likely to persist.

Most important, extrinsic motivators may be a starting point to capture the attention and energies of reluctant readers, but they cannot be an end in themselves. I agree with Csikszentmihalyi (1990) when he says,

If educators, instead of treating literacy as a tool, focused on the rewards intrinsic to literacy, they might get students interested enough in exploring the various domains of learning for the sake of what they can find there. When that happens, the teacher's task is done (pp. 125, 126).

People as Incentives

. Often the best incentives are other people. Many teachers have discovered the benefits of cross-age tutoring or book sharing programs in which younger and older students work together in small groups or one on one. In addition, peers, parents, and community members can serve as literacy models through shared read-alouds, book talks, and discussions.

Hudley (1992) described an intervention program for at-risk high school African American and Hispanic females called Project Read in which successful minority women brought self-selected materials (for example, magazine articles, biographies, inspirational stories, poetry) to share with students during a lunch period. The goal was to improve the attitudes and recreational reading habits of these students by introducing them to interesting and relevant materials. Although the program provided benefits as expected, it also uncovered dissatisfactions with regular teachers who were unprepared to meet the needs of culturally and linguistically different students. It appears that literacy and literacy models can empower students to examine many aspects of their lives, not just their reading habits.

Reflections

I began this chapter with a story about Mrs. O'Neil. It seems only appropriate that I look once more at her influence. That first book Mrs. O'Neil began reading to us sixth graders was titled *Beautiful Joe*. Although the book had no pictures, I still carry vivid images of the dog who was described so well. Only a few years ago, I found a copy of the book in an old bookstore; when I turned to the copyright page, I discovered to my amazement that it had been published in 1902. Why, I asked myself, would a teacher in 1954 read to students a book that was published over 50 years earlier? Then I remembered that Mrs. O'Neil retired only a few years after I left sixth grade. In 1902 she was just a girl, maybe even a sixth grader. Do you think she chose that book to read because her teacher read it to her?

References

Alderman, M.K. (1990). Motivation for at-risk students. *Educational Leadership*, *48*(1), 27–30.

Anderson, R.C., Hiebert, E.H., Scott, J.A., & Wilkinson, I.A.G. (1985). *Becoming a nation of readers: The Report of the Commission on reading.* Washington, DC: U.S. Department of Education.

Applebee, A.N., Langer, J.A., & Mullis, I.V.S. (1988). *Who reads best?* Princeton, NJ: Educational Testing Service.

Brophy, J. (1987). Synthesis of research on strategies for motivating students to learn. *Educational Leadership, 45*(2), 40–55.

Cardarelli, A.F. (1992). Teachers under cover: Promoting the personal reading of teachers. *The Reading Teacher, 45*(9), 664–668.

Carlsen, G.R., & Sherrill, A. (1988). *Voices of readers: How we come to love books.* Urbana, IL: National Council of Teachers of English.

Carter, M. (1988). How children choose books: Implications for helping develop readers. *Ohio Reading Teacher, 22*(3), 15–21.

Castle, M. (1987). Classroom libraries: Valuable resources for developing readers. *The Delta Kappa Gamma Bulletin, 54*(1), 18–20, 50.

Center for the Study of Reading. (1986). *Suggestions for the classroom: Teachers and independent reading.* Champaign, IL: Author.

Chance, P. (1992). The rewards of learning. *Phi Delta Kappan, 74*(3), 200–207.

Chance, P. (1993). Sticking up for rewards. *Phi Delta Kappan, 74*(10), 787–790.

Clay, M.M. (1979). *Reading: The patterning of complex behavior.* Portsmouth, NH: Heinemann.

Csikszentmihalyi, M. (1990). Literature and intrinsic motivation. DAEDALUS, *Journal of the American Academy of Arts and Sciences, 119*(2), 115–140.

Cullinan, B.E. (1992a). Prologue. In B.E. Cullinan (Ed.), *Invitation to read: More children's literature in the reading program* (pp. x–xxii). Newark, DE: International Reading Association.

Cullinan, B.E. (1992b). *Read to me: Raising kids who love to read.* New York: Scholastic.

Dreyer, S.S. (1992). *The bookfinder.* Circle Pines, MN: American Guidance Service.

Dwyer, E.J., & Isbell, R. (1989). The lively art of reading aloud. *The Clearing House, 63,* 111–113.

Ecroyd, C.A. (1991, October). Motivating students through reading aloud. *English Journal,* 76–78.

Fielding, L., & Roller, C. (1992). Making difficult books accessible and easy books acceptable. *The Reading Teacher, 45*(9), 678–685.

Fractor, J.S., Woodruff, M.C., Martinez, M.G., & Teale, W.H. (1993). Let's not miss opportunities to promote voluntary reading in the elementary school. *The Reading Teacher, 46*(6), 476–484.

Freedman, R., & Frost, S. (1993). Series books: Recreational reading or the core of a literature-based reading program. *Illinois Reading Council Journal, 21*(2), 42–46.

Graves, D. (1990). *Discover your own literacy.* Portsmouth, NH: Heinemann.

Gray, M.J., & Troy, A. (1986). Elementary teachers of reading as models. *Reading Horizons, 31,* 179–184.

Greaney, V. (1986). Parental influences on reading. *The Reading Teacher, 39*(8), 813–838.

Hansen, J. (1987). *When writers read.* Portsmouth, NH: Heinemann.

Hansen, J. (1993, April/May). Discovering books for teachers as readers groups. *Reading Today,* 35.

Hickman, J. (1983). Classrooms that help children like books. In N. Roser & M. Frith (Eds.), *Children's choices: Teaching with books children like* (pp. 1–11). Newark, DE: International Reading Association.

Hudley, C.A. (1992). Using role models to improve the reading attitude of ethnic minority high school girls. *Journal of Reading, 36*(3), 182–188.

Kassens, Z. (1984, September). Give kids reading options. *Instructor, 44*, 46, 51.

Kimmel, M.M., & Segal, E. (1983). *For reading out loud: A guide to sharing books with children.* New York: Delacorte.

Kohn, A. (1993). Rewards versus learning: A response to Paul Chance. *Phi Delta Kappan, 74*(10), 783–787.

Matthews, C.E. (1987). Lap reading for teenagers. *Journal of Reading, 30*(5), 410–413.

McGill-Franzen, A. (1993). "I could read the words!": Selecting good books for inexperienced readers. *The Reading Teacher, 46*(5), 424–426.

Melvin, M.P. (1986). First moments in reading. *The Reading Teacher, 39*(7), 632–634.

Micklos, J. (1992, June/July). Teachers as readers groups: Reviving the love of literature. *Reading Today*, 20.

Montgomery, E., Bauer, W.W., & Gray, W.S. (1948). *Happy days.* Chicago, IL: Scott, Foresman.

Morrow, L.M. (1985). *Promoting volunteer reading in school and home* (Fastback No. 225). Bloomington, IN: Phi Delta Kappa Education Foundation.

Mour, S.I. (1977). Do teachers read? *The Reading Teacher, 30*(4), 397–401.

Nell, V. (1988). *Lost in a book: The psychology of reading for pleasure.* New Haven, CT: Yale University Press.

Ohlhausen, M.M., & Jepsen, M. (1992). Lessons from Goldilocks: "Somebody's been choosing my books but I can make my own choices now!" *The New Advocate, 5*(1), 31–46.

Ollman, H. (1993). How to choose a good book. *Journal of Reading, 36*(7), 565–567.

O'Masta, G., & Wolf, J.M. (1991). Encouraging independent reading through the Millionaires project. *The Reading Teacher, 44*(9), 656–662.

Otto, W. (1992/1993). Readers r us. *Journal of Reading, 36*(4), 318–320.

Parkhurst, R.E. (1981, March). An enrichment system for any classroom. *Arithmetic Teacher, 45*, 46.

Routman, R. (1991). *Invitations.* Portsmouth, NH: Heinemann.

Salmon, V.R., & Laughlin, C. (1979, October). Excellence incentive: An instructional program for the underachiever. *NASSP Bulletin*, 21–23.

Sanacore, J. (1992). Encouraging the lifetime reading habit. *Journal of Reading, 35*(6), 474–477.

Sandmann, A. (1993). Study shows teachers rely on book clubs for most K–5 literature. *The Council Chronicle, 2*(4), 1, 6.

Schmidt, B. (1986). *Invest in read-aloud time and collect the interest* (The Heath Transcripts No. 2). Lexington, MA: Heath.

Searls, E.F. (1985). Do you, like these teachers, value reading? *Reading Horizons, 25*,(3) 233–238.

Smith, N.J., Greenlaw, M.J., & Scott, C.J. (1987). Making a literate environment equitable. *The Reading Teacher, 40*(4), 400–407.

Spiegel, D.L. (1981). *Reading for pleasure: Guidelines.* Newark, DE: International Reading Association.

Taylor, D., & Dorsey-Gaines, C. (1988). *Growing up literate: Learning from inner-city families*. Portsmouth, NH: Heinemann.

Trelease, J. (1989). *The new read-aloud handbook*. New York: Penguin.

Valencia, S.W., Hiebert, E.H., & Kapinus, B. (1992). NAEP: What do we know and what lies ahead? *The Reading Teacher, 45*(2), 730–734.

Wiesendanger, K., & Bader, L. (1989). Children's view of motivation. *The Reading Teacher, 42*(4), 345–347.

Willis, S. (1991). The complex art of motivating students. ASCD *Update, 33*(6), 1, 4, 5.

Children's Books

Calhoun, M. (1979). *Cross-country cat*. New York: Mulberry.

Calhoun, M. (1981). *Hot-air Henry*. New York: Morrow Junior Books.

Calhoun, M. (1991). *High-wire Henry*. New York: Morrow Junior Books.

Cleary, B. (1965). *The mouse and the motorcycle*. New York: Morrow.

Cleary, B. (1970). *Runaway Ralph*. New York: Avon.

Cleary, B. (1980). *Ralph S. Mouse*. New York: Dell.

Clement, R. (1991). *Counting on Frank*. Milwaukee, WI: Gareth Stevens.

Freedman, R. (1987). *Lincoln: A photobiography*. New York: Clarion.

Johnson, P. (1981). *The great Canadian alphabet book*. Willowdale, Ont.: Hounslow.

Mathis, S.B. (1975). *The hundred penny box*. New York: Puffin.

Paterson, K. (1977). *Bridge to Terabithia*. New York: Crowell.

Paterson, K. (1991). *Lyddie*. New York: Puffin.

Smith, R.K. (1987). *Mostly Michael*. New York: Dell.

Stanley, J. (1992). *Children of the dustbowl*. New York: Crown.

Taylor, M. (1976). *Roll of thunder, hear my cry*. New York: Dial.

Taylor, M. (1983). *Let the circle be unbroken*. New York: Bantam.

Taylor, M. (1990). *The road to Memphis*. New York: Dial.

Voigt, C. (1981). *The homecoming*. New York: Atheneum.

Voigt, C. (1982). *Dicey's song*. New York: Macmillan.

Williams, V.B. (1983). *Something special for me*. New York: Greenwillow.

Williams, V.B. (1984). *Music, music for everyone*. New York: Greenwillow.

Williams, V.B. (1988). *A chair for my mother*. New York: Morrow.

Yolen, J. (1992). *Encounter*. San Diego, CA: Harcourt Brace.

Chapter 12

Values, Agendas, and Preferences in Children's and Young Adult Literature

June D. Knafle

●◆ Teachers and parents are generally well aware that children's literature has changed over the years from tales meant to convey moral lessons to pleasant stories and adventures depicting idealized family life to more realistic stories of our times. Although the earlier moral tales, have, with the exception of fables, been mostly ignored, the pleasant stories and adventures are fondly remembered. They portray childhood as a happy time, and assumptions concerning stable family life are implicit in those books. When U.S. society began to changed in the 1960s, children's literature reflected those changes in increasingly realistic and even graphic ways to the extent that by the end of the 1970s, children's and young adult (YA) literature depicting stable family life became the exception, not the norm. Happy endings and protective adults could no longer be taken for granted. Further, children were no longer to be given evasive answers or to have harsh realities hidden from them.

The change in the way society views children and teenagers today is reflected in current books, especially problem or YA novels. These books focus on death, divorce, premarital sex, drugs, alcoholism, contraception, abortion, alienation, sibling rivalry, peer cruelty, homosexuality, racism, hostility, and egocentricity. Current styles of writing emphasize struggle and conflict, and even swearing is no longer uncommon. Many current books, especially paperbacks, have become very popular and are often passed around until they fall apart. Children and teenagers read and respond to these books with an intensity that may be overlooked by adults.

The way we look at books has changed, too. It is often difficult for us to understand how a book like *Harriet the Spy* by Louise Fitzhugh, which we consider amusing and even charming, could have caused so much controversy when it was published in 1964. Harriet's exaggerations and caricatures do not shock us or make us uncomfortable; rather, they make us laugh.

In an insightful book, *Don't Tell the Grown-Ups: Why Kids Love the Books They Do* (1990), Lurie contends that much of children's literature that has stood the test of time was clearly subversive when it was published: it defied society's conventional values, exposed adult pretensions, and mocked adult institutions. For example, Tom Sawyer was decidedly not the sort of boy parents would hold up as a role model for their children, Alice was not the docile and timid girl favored in mid-Victorian times, and *Little Women's* radical tomboy, Jo March, was not what society considered desirable at the time. Books such as *Harriet the Spy*, *The Long Secret* (published in 1965), and *Pippi Longstocking* (published in 1950) were widely criticized and censured when they appeared, becoming popular and widely recommended only after many years.

Many modern books not only contain flawed characters but also have taken on a dark tone. Egoff (1981) writes that despair is the major theme in an increasing number of novels, such as Robert Cormier's *The Chocolate War*. A book with a theme of kidnapping, K.M. Peyton's *Prove Yourself a Hero*, imparts a feeling of the futility and hopelessness of life. Although Paula Fox's *How Many Miles to Babylon?* and *Portrait of Ivan* do not have hostility and alienation as the major themes, the main characters must cope with difficult family situations. Death is also a common theme (for example, Katherine Paterson's *Bridge to Terabithia*). Children and teenagers are often without depicted adult influence and striving to cope with life on their own, sometimes being solely responsible for younger siblings, as in Cynthia Voigt's *Homecoming*, sometimes being responsible only for themselves, as in *Maniac Magee* by Jerry Spinelli, and sometimes struggling to survive without preparation in the face of disaster, as in Gary Paulsen's *Hatchet*. Even in picture books, parents are sometimes portrayed as flawed, as in John Steptoe's *Daddy Is a Monster...Sometimes*. But most picture books remain relatively unaffected by the influences that have changed higher level books.

Religion in the lives of children is conspicuous by its absence in recent novels, except for such portrayals as the caricatured Christian grandmother in Judy Blume's *Are You There God? It's Me, Margaret* and the thoroughly self-serving malevolent Brother Leon in *The Chocolate War* by Robert Cormier; characters with deep religious convictions tend to be depicted as weak or eccentric (for example, Ernestine Blue in *Is That You, Miss Blue?* by M.E. Kerr) and as victims of their peers and charges. These portrayals are a drastic change from earlier blatantly Christian writings for children and adolescents. Fantasy also has taken a complete turn from the viewpoints of C.S. Lewis and J.R.R. Tolkien to a fascination with the supernatural world of the occult. Egoff (1981) believes that existentialism has replaced religion and that sociology and psychology have replaced morality.

But, fortunately, there are many exceptions to the grimness of much of contemporary realistic fiction, especially at the lower levels. Since 1989 *The Reading Teacher* has published a regular and useful section entitled "Children's Books" in which the authors summarize and discuss recent books according to particular topics. Most of the books are appropriate for the primary and intermediate levels. In "Building Relationships" (Galda, 1991a), the relationships in the books reviewed are with families, friends, and pets, and the books go beyond the surface level; for example, they feature loving relationships with grandparents as well as the realities of aging and dying. A number of the books focus on children's peer and sibling interrelationships; conflicts are usually resolved, and acceptance and tolerance of diversity seem to be the norm. Some of the topics in the books reviewed, especially those of cultural pluralism and politics, will not only engage students in reading but also help them respond to and deal with today's individual and societal problems. These books also lend themselves to the incorporation of specific values.

Cultural Pluralism

Understanding and appreciating different cultures as our worldview becomes more global are the focus of several recent articles by Galda, Cox, and Cotter (Cox & Galda, 1990; Galda & Cotter, 1992; Galda & Cox, 1991); suggestions are given for incorporating appropriate books into the curriculum. For example, recent books reflect changes in society such as biracial families (*Wait and See* by Tony Bradman) and do not hesitate to depict settings of poverty (Charlotte Pomerantz's *The Chalk Doll*) and abandonment and poverty (*The Most Beautiful Place in the World* by Ann Cameron). Two charming picture books that show loving family relationships during economic hardship are Barbara S. Hazen's *Tight Times* and Vera B. Williams's *A Chair for My Mother*. Cross-cultural understanding is fostered by books such as *Georgia to Georgia: Making Friends in the U.S.S.R.* by Laurie Dolphin.

African folk tales and stories have become prominent, along with increasing numbers of books featuring Hispanic, Native American, and Asian characters and settings in the United States and other countries.

These books also reflect recent trends of introducing young children to cross-cultural values and beliefs. Some recount creation myths from various countries, the most widely available of which is Virginia Hamilton's *In the Beginning: Creation Stories from Around the World*, a Newbery honor book. *In the Night, Still Dark* by Richard Lewis tells a traditional Hawaiian creation myth; another recent picture book recounts a Mayan creation myth (*Why There Is No Arguing in Heaven* by Deborah N. Lattimore). *Raven's Light* by Susan H. Shetterly tells a U.S. northwest creation myth, and Lynn Moroney's *Elinda Who Danced in the Sky* is an Estonian tale. *Llama and the Great Flood* by Ellen Alexander gives an Incan version of the story of the great flood, and *Beyond the Ridge* by Paul Goble tells the Plains Indians' view of death, including native chants and prayers. *Tower to Heaven* by Ruby Dee is a humorous tale from Ghana, and Richard Lewis's *All of You Was Singing* is an Aztec myth of the origin of music on earth. *Why Rat Comes First* by Clara Yen is one of many stories about the Chinese Zodiac, and *The Dark Way* by Virginia Hamilton is a compilation of tales of the spirit world.

Over the years researchers have analyzed stories from different countries. McClelland (1963) read third and fourth grade stories from 40 countries and reported distinct differences in the values they expressed; for example, stories from Middle Eastern and North African countries stressed the importance of cleverness and the ability to outwit others, while stories from Chile and Japan stressed kindness and obligation to others, and stories from Germany stressed loyalty. However, interpreting values in children's literature is often complex because reading is an interactive process (Langer & Nicolich, 1981; Rosenblatt, 1982). Machet (1992) found that South African adolescents' perceptions of values in stories were influenced by their personal values, which differed according to their sociocultural group. Thus, children sometimes have opposite reactions to characters and events in stories. With this in mind, teachers could quite profitably elicit discussion supporting various viewpoints with the goal of fostering new and broader insights and understanding.

Political Issues

Politics has always been a topic in many children's books. Hurlimann (1967) provides an interesting historical background of trends and events that have influenced the politics in children's books. Many people in the United States remember Munro Leaf's classic picture book about a pacifist bull, *The Story of Ferdinand*, which was surprisingly popular during World War II, but few are aware of the large number of children's books published in other languages that reflect the values of given societies and movements. Russian children's books have been especially used as political tools, and government control has been easily accomplished by centralized government publication and distribution.

Some of the changes in Chinese children's literature, which reflect changes in the values of the society, are profound. While Mitchell (1980), in a survey of Chinese children's books written since 1965, found that almost all books reinforced ideals of group conformity, Zhang and Breedlove (1989) reported that recently writers were using traditional forms such as fairy tales and animal stories to challenge traditional values. They cite a 1980 award-winning short story, "Who Will Be Our Future Monitor," in which a traditionally well-behaved girl is belittled and an aggressive boy is praised, as exemplifying an increasing number of stories in Chinese children's literature.

Some books have a counter-culture political viewpoint. *The Grandchildren of the Incas* by Matti A. Pitkanen shows the difference between current government treatment of the people and their past self-sufficiency, and Thomas Locker's *The Land of Gray Wolf* depicts the destruction of Native Americans' way of life by white settlements. *When Africa Was Home* by Karen L. Williams tells the story of a boy's return to the United States after his parents' sojourn in the Peace Corps, and the United States and its people are seen as lacking warmth and important values of care and compassion.

A number of books deal with war from a child's perspective. In *The House of Sixty Fathers*, Meindert DeJong marvelously portrays the Japanese invasion of China in World War II through the eyes of a small boy who struggles to save himself and his pig. Karl Bruckner's *The Day of the Bomb* recounts a young girl's life and death in Hiroshima. And, of course, Anne Frank's *The Diary of a Young Girl* is a familiar classic. A more recent book about a young girl being hidden from Nazis by Danes is Lois Lowry's *Number the Stars*, the 1990 Newbery award winner. Even a picture book has recently appeared concerning the Holocaust: Roberto Innocenti's *Rose Blanche* depicts stark, compelling images of a German town and the nearby concentration camp as seen through the eyes of a young girl. Thought-provoking stories for older children about the Holocaust are *Upon the Head of a Goat: A Childhood in Hungary 1939–1944*, a 1982 Newbery honor book, and *Grace in the Wilderness: After the Liberation 1945–1948*, both by Aranka Siegel. Bette Greene's *Summer of My German Soldier* shows friendship stretching beyond the confines of nationality and religion. An antiwar picture book is *Hiroshima no Pika* by Toshi Maruki.

Galda (1991b) discusses many books that deal with ecology and the environmental problems civilization has created. Those topics have become very popular within the last 10 to 15 years, but a similar message appeared in Richard Adams's *Watership Down*, published in 1972, when the warren of British rabbits was destroyed by construction. And many people know and love the early book *The Little House* by Virgina Lee Burton, which chronicles the problems of a growing city.

Individualism and Egocentrism

Shannon (1986) analyzed a sample of 30 books from the 1978, 1980, and 1982 Children's Choices lists (which are described by Fisher in Chapter 4) for beginning independent and younger readers according to measures of individualism, collectivism, and balance; he found that in 29 of the 30 books, the authors focused on individualism, including "the propositions that people act in their own best interest, the goal of life is to secure the maximum personal freedom" (p. 659). None of the books focused on collectivism with such concerns as "social development, service to community, cooperation toward shared goals, community, and mutual prosperity" (p. 660), and only one presented a balance between individualism and collectivism. Shannon concluded that "recent books suggest modern world relativism—that the individual is the true arbiter of all values" (p. 657).

Stephens (1989) examined 14 favorite children's books and 30 Newbery award and honor books, 5 from each 10-year period from 1927 to 1987, according to "self-righting" tendencies in the characters. Character resiliency was the focus, and there were 6 categories along with a final category labeled either S (social group goals reached in resolution) or W (character withdrawn or seeking individual goals). The analysis of favorite books shows the presence of all categories in all the books with 12 of the 14 books falling into the S category; the same pattern is shown in the Newbery books from 1928 to 1967, with 19 of the 20 books categorized as S. However, in the 1968 to 1977 period, 3 of the 5 books are categorized as W, and in the 1978 to 1987 period, all the 5 books are categorized as W. Additionally, in the 1978 to 1987 period, the categories are not uniformly present: "character seeks and receives human adult help" is missing from 4 of the 5 books; "character develops special talent or interest" from 3 of the 5; and "character is cheerful, confident, and enthusiastic" from 3 of the 5. The change shows a clear difference between the Newbery books in the later decade and those in the earlier decades. Some might say the later books are more reality based, depicting the problems and ambiguities of real life; others might say the later books reflect a more egocentric life view with little regard for group social goals.

Egoff (1981) believes that the emphasis is clearly on self, selfhood, self-determination, and self-discovery and that existentialism is the core of much modern fiction; personal morality is shaped by the complexities of modern existence. She states, "As modern society espouses the viewpoint, 'if I do it, it must be right,' so with literature, 'if I like it, it must be good'" (p. 302).

However, Caldecott winners seem to be different. Knafle, Wescott, and Pascarella (1988) analyzed Caldecott winners from 1938 to 1986 and found no significant differences in the values presented in the books between each ten-year period. The largest category of values found in the books by far was neutral values, followed by positive behavior, positive feelings, traditional values, negative feelings, negative behavior, Judeo-Christian religious values, and other religious values. Similarly, the values found in the Caldecott books were found in basal readers used in the United States (Knafle, Rodriguez-Brown, & Budinsky, 1991). These researchers also noted distinctive differences in values presented in U.S. and Hispanic children's readers in kindergarten through fourth grade. The U.S. series was much more bland than the Spanish series, which, in addition to including values with religious and traditional moralistic overtones coupled with idealistic family values and roles, also included themes in which such behaviors as fighting, being drunk, and treating others cruelly were presented.

Problem Novels

The problem novel, a subcategory of realistic fiction sometimes difficult to distinguish from the broader category, is extremely popular and influential and portrays specific conflicts and crises. Authors in this genre show children and teenagers beset by such problems as alcohol, drugs, divorce, unwanted pregnancy, incest, peer acceptance, obesity, and physical and mental handicaps. Just as television and movies today deal with all types of struggles, so does the problem novel, and in the same graphic, often superficial, way. Problem novels aim to reflect today's life; the language is often explicit, and violent scenes are frequent and detailed.

Alienation, emotional pain, and hostility toward adults, especially parents, are the main themes, and the characters are uniformly self-centered. The atmosphere is bleak, and adults who are not physically or emotionally absent are often portrayed as uncaring, inept, insensitive, and cynical. Yvette in Paul Zindel's *I Never Loved Your Mind*, when asked why she does not live with her parents, says, "Because they're bastards. My mother's a dumb one. My father's a mean one" (p. 42). Sean's cynical and crude father in *My Darling, My Hamburger*, also by Zindel, is portrayed as being responsible for Sean's deserting his pregnant girlfriend.

Many of the themes of problem novels have filtered down to books for younger children. Two recent picture books are Leslea Newman's *Heather Has Two Mommies*—a story of a lesbian couple, one of whom was artificially inseminated—and Michael Willhoite's *Daddy's Roommate*—a story of a homosexual couple.

The tone of problem novels and the theme of alienation from parents were influenced by J.D. Salinger's groundbreaking *The Catcher in the Rye* published in 1951 and established by Emily Neville's 1964 Newbery award novel *It's Like This, Cat* (Egoff, 1981). Writers such as Judy Blume and Norma Klein enjoy far-reaching popularity and are also among the most frequent targets of censorship attacks, usually because of their treatment of sexuality. Indeed, Judy Blume's name on a book seems to be enough to ensure censorship activities, regardless of the content of the book. Paula Danziger's novels are also very popular and are sometimes regarded as more wholesome alternatives to Blume's.

The fact that children's and YA literature reflect current events is demonstrated by Rosenthal (1988), who discusses the increasing number of child and adolescent suicides in relation to the increasing number of novels dealing with suicide, self-destructive protagonists, and surviving family and peers' attempts to understand suicide and depression (for example, *Tunnel Vision* by Fran Arrick, Eve Bunting's *Face at the Edge of the World*, and *Second Star to the Right*, by Deborah Hautzig).

Children's authors, like other authors, usually write about what they know or wish to understand. Ellen Howard (1988) discusses her reasons for writing *Gillyflower*, a book that deals with incest and a little girl's emotional and psychological reactions to it. She states that children "cannot learn to recognize and rise above evil if they are not taught it exists.... It is knowledge that empowers" (pp. 9, 11).

A more depressing worldview is provided by Robert Cormier, whose YA books are clearly outside the mainstream of what adults have traditionally thought would be suitable reading material for teenagers. His books have been the frequent targets of censorship efforts, but they may not be dismissed the same way as many YA books containing sex and violence are simply because they are so well written. Cormier's characters are fascinating in their malevolence; his characters are the sort that the reader can vividly recall many years after having read about them. The problem that many people, especially adults, have with his books is that his protagonists usually do not triumph in the end but rather are victimized by others—often adults who seem totally lacking in a sense of fair-play or compassion, sometimes even for their own children. An excellent and insightful discussion about the dark side of human nature in Cormier's books may be found in "The Bland Face of Evil in the Novels of Robert Cormier" (Veglahn, 1988). When Cormier was interviewed about his unhappy stories, he said, "As long as what I write is true and believable, why should I have to create happy endings?... Life just isn't like that" (Schwartz, 1979, p. 88). So many teenagers are such avid fans of Cormier that adults need to read and reflect on his characters and stories to understand the motivations and situations young adults find so powerful and compelling. *The Chocolate War* and *I Am the Cheese* are two especially engrossing novels.

Cynicism

Some authors seem deliberately intent on drawing teenagers into, or indoctrinating them into, adult cynicism concerning society's traditions and rituals. Egoff (1981) states that many realistic novels have a sense of the adult author intruding into a child's world and that some books' objectives seem to be "the stripping away of any hopes or illusions the reader may have about life. Stretched to this degree, the desire to 'tell it like it is' comes very near to misanthropy" (p. 44). Because some of those authors are especially skillful writers who also choose topics of intense interest to teenagers, it is not surprising that teenagers devour their seemingly sophisticated works. Whether young adults are truly influenced by such writings or merely interested, fascinated, or intrigued is another question.

Humor has taken on an ironic and satiric tone. (This shift has occurred at all levels; even fundamentalist Christians who grew up enjoying *Mad* magazine surreptitiously can find its Christian counterpart in *The Door*.) And some critics of children's literature bring their biases to their reviews, many probably unknowingly; for example, a reviewer might describe a book as a comedy, whereas a reader might think that only a cynic would find the unfortunate, even tragic, characters or events humorous.

Preferences

Children's and young adults' preferences are often shaped by such simple things as the kind and number of books readily available to them.

Because the publishing of juvenile books increased dramatically in the 1980s, it is possible that this affected children's preferences. Small publishers also proliferated, often vying for a share of the market with increasingly daring, off-beat, and special-interest topics.

Peers' interests and recommendations are, of course, paramount in influencing reading interests, as are the interests and recommendations of favorite teachers, librarians, and parents. Award-winning books often become widely read because of their publicity and the fact that they tend to stay in print longer than other books. Ethnic interests are also a powerful influence, as the increased publishing of African American, Hispanic American, and Native American books for all grade levels confirms.

There may often be an element of vicarious excitement connected with the popularity of some novels. Just as a conservative middle class adult may be intrigued with the world described by John Steinbeck, so may some teenagers enjoy the adventures and experiences of characters in problem novels. Although Dewey, the main character in Paul Zindel's *I Never Loved Your Mind*, would be considered a smart-alecky, sarcastic dropout by many adults, teenagers who would not act in a similar manner enjoy reading about Dewey, sharing vicariously in his adventures.

As mentioned earlier, some problem novels show hostility toward adults and rebellion against values viewed as outdated and oppressive. That hostility and rebellion, often common components of growing up, may partially account for problem novels' popularity among adolescents. L'Engle's (1980) view that children do not like antiheroes or books portraying life as totally unfair is clearly not shared by many of the authors and readers of modern fiction.

There is also the myriad YA books widely available in supermarkets, newsstands, and bookstores that many librarians wish would just go away; those books will never appear on library shelves. Many are poorly and hastily written and contain sensational elements of graphic sex, violence, revenge, exploitation, and the supernatural, perhaps comparable to the supermarket tabloids. Others are merely formula romances. But they do sell.

The powerful influence of television cannot be denied, not only in terms of content, but also in its fast-paced presentation and conclusion. Children who have grown up spending a significant number of hours each week being entertained by such fast-moving action are often unwilling to spend the time necessary to understand complicated plot structures and character development. Many authors seem to tailor their books to fit short attention spans, but whether many of these books will stand the test of time is another question. (See also children's author Irene Shultz's Chapter 16 about writing novels for discouraged readers.)

Outlook

Even victorious Archie in *The Chocolate War*, who proclaims that you are either the victim or the victimizer, is not portrayed as a happy person or as someone to emulate. Cormier presents him in such a way that, although the reader may be fascinated by him, the reader is also repelled by him and his values. In Cormier's other books as well, corruption is presented as just that, and although the reader may find the portrayal especially compelling when it encompasses respectable authority figures, a feeling of revulsion toward those figures and their corruption is the result. We have not yet reached the point where conscienceless and remorseless protagonists are portrayed as heroic role models for children and young adults; I hope we never will. However, as one looks at current media coverage of modern life, it is not pleasant to think about future possibilities for realistic children's books. Perhaps a way to counteract some of the disturbing presentations would be to read and discuss books together as a family, especially controversial children's and YA books; such discussions might be a way to open up new levels of intergenerational interaction and understanding (Knafle, 1989). Additionally, parents, teachers, and librarians could provide more balance to children's and teenager's reading by recommending historical fiction and biographies. Some teachers have found that reluctant readers have had new worlds opened to them through characters and events in these books.

References

Cox, S., & Galda, L. (1990). Multicultural literature: Mirrors and windows on a global community. *The Reading Teacher, 43*(8), 582–589.

Egoff, S.A. (1981). *Thursday's child: Trends and patterns in contemporary children's literature.* Chicago, IL: American Library Association.

Galda, L. (1991a). Building relationships. *The Reading Teacher, 45*(1), 54–61.

Galda, L. (1991b). Saving our planet, saving ourselves. *The Reading Teacher, 45*(4), 310–317.

Galda, L., & Cotter, J. (1992). Exploring cultural diversity. *The Reading Teacher, 45*(6), 452–460.

Galda, L., & Cox, S. (1991). Books for cross-cultural understanding. *The Reading Teacher, 44*(8), 580–587.

Howard, E. (1988). Facing the dark side in children's books. *The Lion and the Unicorn, 12*(1), 7–11.

Hurlimann, B. (1967). *Three centuries of children's books in Europe* (B.W. Alderson, Trans. and Ed.). New York: World. (Originally published 1959)

Knafle, J.D. (1989). Sharing books bolsters family bonds. *PTA Today*, *14*(5), 24–25.

Knafle, J.D., Rodriguez-Brown, F.V., & Budinsky, M. (1991, Spring). Values in American and Hispanic children's readers. *The Journal of Educational Issues of Language Minority Students*, *8*, 53–70.

Knafle, J.D., Wescott, A.L., & Pascarella, E.T. (1988). Assessing values in children's books. *Reading Improvement*, *25*(1), 71–81.

Langer, J.A., & Nicolich, M. (1981). Prior knowledge and its relationship to comprehension. *Journal of Reading Behavior*, *13*(4), 373–379.

L'Engle, M. (1980). *Walking on water: Reflections on faith and art.* Wheaton, IL: Harold Shaw.

Lurie, A. (1990). *Don't tell the grown-ups: Why kids love the books they do.* New York: Avon.

Machet, M.P. (1992). The effect of sociocultural values on adolescents' response to literature. *Journal of Reading*, *35*(5), 356–362.

McClelland, D.C. (1963, November). Values in popular literature for children. *Childhood Education*, *40*, 135–138.

Mitchell, E. (1980). Children's books from the People's Republic of China. *Language Arts*, *57*(1), 30–37.

Rosenblatt, L.M. (1982). The literary transaction: Evocation and response. *Theory into Practice*, *21*(4), 268–277.

Rosenthal, L. (1988). To be or not to be: Suicide in literature for young people. *The Lion and the Unicorn*, *12*(1), 19–27.

Schwartz, T. (1979, July 16). Teen-ager's laureate. *Newsweek*, 87–88, 92.

Shannon, P. (1986). Hidden within the pages: A study of social perspective in young children's favorite books. *The Reading Teacher*, *39*(7), 656–663.

Stephens, B. (1989). Taking the second step in reading. *The Reading Teacher*, *42*(8), 584–590.

Veglahn, N. (1988). The bland face of evil in the novels of Robert Cormier. *The Lion and the Unicorn*, *12*(1), 12–18.

Zhang, M., & Breedlove, W.G. (1989). The changing role of imagination in Chinese children's books. *The Reading Teacher*, *42*(6), 406–412.

Children's Books

Adams, R. (1972). *Watership down.* London: Rex Collins.

Alcott, L.M. (1868). *Little women; or, Meg, Jo, Beth, and Amy.* Boston, MA: Roberts Brothers.

Alexander, E. (1989). *Llama and the great flood.* New York: Crowell.

Arrick, F. (1980). *Tunnel vision.* New York: Dell.

Blume, J. (1970). *Are you there God? It's me, Margaret.* Englewood Cliffs, NJ: Bradbury.

Bradman, T. (1987). *Wait and see.* New York: Oxford.

Bruckner, K. (1963). *The day of the bomb* (F. Lobb, Trans.). Princeton, NJ: Van Nostrand.

Bunting, E. (1985). *Face at the edge of the world.* New York: Ticknor and Fields.

Burton, V.L. (1942). *The little house.* Boston, MA: Houghton Mifflin.

Cameron, A. (1988). *The most beautiful place in the world.* New York: Knopf.

Cormier, R. (1974). *The chocolate war.* New York: Pantheon.

Cormier, R. (1977). *I am the cheese.* New York: Dell.

Dee, R. (1991). *Tower to heaven.* New York: Henry Holt.

DeJong, M. (1956). *The house of sixty fathers.* New York: HarperCollins.

Dolphin, L. (1991). *Georgia to Georgia: Making friends in the U.S.S.R.* New York: Tambourine.

Fitzhugh, L. (1964). *Harriet the spy.* New York: HarperCollins.

Fitzhugh, L. (1965). *The long secret.* New York: HarperCollins.

Fox, P. (1967). *How many miles to Babylon?* New York: David White.

Fox, P. (1969). *Portrait of Ivan.* Englewood Cliffs, NJ: Bradbury.

Frank, A. (1957). *The diary of a young girl.* New York: Norton.

Goble, P. (1989). *Beyond the ridge.* New York: Bradbury.

Greene, B. (1973). *Summer of my German soldier.* New York: Dial.

Hamilton, V. (1988). *In the beginning: Creation stories from around the world.* San Diego, CA: Harcourt Brace.

Hamilton, V. (1990). *The dark way: Stories from the spirit world.* San Diego, CA: Harcourt Brace.

Hautzig, D. (1981). *Second star to the right.* New York: Avon.

Hazen, B.S. (1979). *Tight times.* New York: Viking.

Howard, E. (1986). *Gillyflower.* New York: Atheneum.

Innocenti, R. (1990). *Rose Blanche.* New York: Stewart, Tabori & Chang.

Kerr, M.E. (1975). *Is that you, Miss Blue?* New York: HarperCollins.

Lattimore, D.N. (1989). *Why there is no arguing in heaven.* New York: HarperCollins.

Leaf, M. (1936). *The story of Ferdinand.* New York: Viking.

Lewis, R. (1988). *In the night, still dark.* New York: Atheneum.

Lewis, R. (1991). *All of you was singing.* New York: Atheneum.

Lindgren, A.E. (1950). *Pippi Longstocking* (F. Lamborn, Trans.). New York: Viking.

Locker, T. (1991). *The land of Gray Wolf.* New York: Dial.

Lowry, L. (1989). *Number the stars.* Boston, MA: Houghton Mifflin.

Maruki, T. (1982). *Hiroshima no pika.* New York: Lothrop.

Moroney, L. (1990). *Elinda who danced in the sky: An Estonian folktale.* San Francisco, CA: Children's Book Press.

Neville, E.C. (1963). *It's like this, cat.* New York: HarperCollins.

Newman, L. (1989). *Heather has two mommies.* Boston, MA: Alyson.

Paterson, K. (1977). *Bridge to Terabithia.* New York: Crowell.

Paulsen, G. (1987). *Hatchet.* New York: Viking.

Peyton, K.M. (1977). *Prove yourself a hero.* London: Oxford University Press.

Pitkanen, M.A. (1991). *The grandchildren of the Incas.* Minneapolis, MN: Carolrhoda.

Pomerantz, C. (1989). *The chalk doll.* New York: Lippincott.

Salinger, J.D. (1951). *The catcher in the rye.* Boston, MA: Little, Brown.

Shetterly, S.H. (1991). *Raven's light: A myth from the people of the northwest coast.* New York: Atheneum.

Siegel, A. (1981). *Upon the head of the goat: A childhood in Hungary 1939–1944.* New York: Farrar, Straus & Giroux.

Siegel, A. (1985). *Grace in the wilderness: After the liberation 1945–1948.* New York: Farrar, Straus & Giroux.

Spinelli, J. (1990). *Maniac Magee.* Boston, MA: Little, Brown.

Steptoe, J. (1980). *Daddy is a monster...sometimes.* Philadelphia, PA: Lippincott.

Voigt, C. (1981). *Homecoming.* New York: Random House.

Willhoite, M. (1990). *Daddy's roommate.* Boston, MA: Alyson.

Williams, K.L. (1991). *When Africa was home.* New York: Orchard.

Williams, V.B. (1982). *A chair for my mother*. New York: Greenwillow.

Yen, C. (1991). *Why rat comes first: A story of the Chinese Zodiac*. San Francisco, CA: Children's Book Press.

Zindel, P. (1969). *My darling, my hamburger*. New York: HarperCollins.

Zindel, P. (1970). *I never loved your mind*. New York: HarperCollins.

Chapter 13

Response to Literature:
Models for New Teachers

Camille L.Z. Blachowicz
Cathryn A. Wimett

●◆ Research in literacy instruction has begun to emphasize the importance of expert modeling for those learning a new task. "Doing as I do" has always been a time-honored phrase in any learning situation. How to model literacy instruction, specifically instruction that values affective response to literature, is the subject of this chapter. Background knowledge and experiences are acknowledged as essential to literacy development and are also relevant to the development of instructional skill. For today's teachers in training, this is an especially critical point. Faced with current literacy practices that stress a process orientation, many teachers in training draw mainly on educational backgrounds filled with behavioral objectives, skill packets, and individually prescribed instruction.

In the United States, this phenomenon is further complicated by a change in the teaching force that reflects the increased diversity of the population. While this characteristic represents a potential strength for preservice teachers who will be working with a diverse student population, many first-generation college students who choose a career in teaching cannot draw on childhood familiarity with the classics of children's literature, authors, or the conventions of literature or its study (Rose, 1989). Further, in many U.S. states, courses in children's or young adult literature are not required for teacher certification. Therefore, for this group of young and developing teachers, it seems doubly necessary to model practices in inservice literacy education that develop their own literacy background at the same time that they develop repertoires of instructional routines.

Further, all of us in preservice education are confined by the limited time we have for preparation of today's professionals before they enter their student-teaching situations. How to model effective practices for children while retaining time for dealing with some of the many content issues of literacy instruction, then, is a substantial problem that many teacher educators are beginning to address (Brazee & Kristo, 1986; Henney, 1991). One way we have begun to address the problem is to use processes for the college students' own learning that can be adapted by them for use in practice.

Journals in Preservice Preparation

In a review of some instances of experimentation with journal use in preservice classes, Schell and Danielson (1991) noted that unstructured, semistructured, and highly structured journals each have different goals and stimulate different reading, writing, and thinking processes. In our classes, our primary goal was to provide an experiential base for reflective discussion of writing in journals before their use in practice teaching and to deal with content issues important to literacy instruction. The importance of allowing for and nurturing affective response was a paramount goal, but other, more traditional instructional content was also included. For example, in all the journal experiences, structuring questions to stimulate thinking was an important consideration so that such issues as levels of questioning and question-answer relationships were topics that were naturally addressed in the process. Also, in both narrative and expository reading, text structure and organizational issues related to structure (for example, cause and effect) were natural issues that arose in understanding and responding to what was read.

Dialogue Journals as Response to Literature

We experimented with dialogue journals as vehicles for responding to literature. Three different models were tried: methods students writing in journals on the same novel with the methods instructor; methods students writing in journals with individual children on self-chosen novels; and methods students writing in journals over a ten-week period with an instructor-identified elementary school class, with the instructor also involved in the journal as a "third party." Each of the trials had different learning outcomes.

Writing in journals about the same novel gave the class a shared experience base for later literature response activities and also a firsthand example of how the experience of reading a novel could differ dramatically from person to person. The novel we read was *Roll of Thunder, Hear My Cry* by Mildred Taylor, about a strong African American farm family in the Depression era. Some students were very much taken with the vivid characters and descriptions of early schooling, perhaps because of the context of reading the novel in a teacher preparation class. Others focused on the social issues, not all of which they were entirely comfortable discussing in our heterogeneous class.

For one African American student, the book served as motivation to discuss a novel with her mother—something she had never done before as her mother did not describe herself as a reader. The mother had grown up in a situation much like that described in *Roll of Thunder, Hear My Cry*, and she sent many items of historical interest to the class. The student, who was very shy, became quite open in class discussions because of this. She heightened the sensitivity of the class toward working with students whose parents might not be readers. Her process of discussing with her mother was one that students noted for future use. For another African American student, the process led to an attempt at writing. Declaring that she never wanted to read "one more story of a poor but noble sharecropper family," she shared with the class her desire to read some books about the black middle class of the 1930s. This led to class investigations looking for such books. The student began a personal project to interview her relatives and begin a photo collection on the topic.

For many of the students, the writing process began as a painful one. Just as children do, they began by summarizing what they had read and were drawn into more reflective questioning by our own questions. The journals eventually became vehicles by which we all came to know one another more deeply, especially regarding family-related issues. The group, which was mostly female, focused on three characters: Mrs. Logan (the mother), Big Ma (the grandmother), and Little Man (the youngest child who encounters overt racism for the first time). The students found it interesting that few of them wished to focus on Cassie, the narrator of the story and the person most frequently described as the central character. This led to discussions of various responses to the same book, which we used to critique "teacher-centric" questioning.

The major strengths of this process included the shared base a single novel can present for exploring diversity in response to literature and experiencing more personal interaction between teacher and students. On the negative side, the students did not have much of a feel for how the process would work for "real" children nor for the mechanical difficulties of writing in journals.

The second experiment had each student locate a child with whom to keep a journal on a book that they would choose together. The ages of the children ranged from 9 to 17, and they were often members of the families of the methods students. With this format, discussions focused more on journal-writing mechanics and strategies for getting children to be more elaborate and function on a higher level in their responses. A major outcome for the college students was a richer understanding of the variety of school-age students' responses and also of their reading interests. We began to deal with issues of variety, preference, and limitation that did not emerge with the adults. On the negative side, we could not model good questioning as thoroughly for the college students, though they did begin to develop, as a class, a generic set of elaborating questions to try with their various students.

A third experiment with journals involved having the students write with a fifth grade class for ten weeks. We worked with the classroom teacher who first asked us to find out about the reading interests of our college students. We did this by using the "book stacking" activity which we will discuss later, followed by a written self-evaluation. We then matched students with fifth graders so that there would not be any gross mismatches in either interest or rate of reading, the latter of which turned out to be a very important factor. The methods students then met their partners to get to know one another and choose the first two books to read. We also devised a journal pick-up method in which we would transport the journals to the college class each week.

The class was then "off and running"—an apt phrase because the first thing the methods students learned was how fast some fifth graders can read. In this case, because these fifth graders had already done much journal writing, in many instances they became the ones to model more reflective questions for the college students, though the preservice teachers still encountered challenges with students who wanted to write little beyond summative responses. As the ten weeks progressed, the college students struggled to keep up with their journal partners and asked many questions about managing and undertaking such an activity when they became the sole teacher for an entire class.

This third experiment helped students address management issues of using journals. The cooperating teacher gave suggestions relating to how teachers could skim many books and how being unfamiliar with a book allowed a teacher to ask more authentic questions; she also encouraged the students to define a repertoire of generic questions, which led many of them to read and use Atwell's *In the Middle* (1987). In this experiment, the college students shared more problems with the methods class and offered more ways in which they approached the same issues than had the earlier journal trial groups.

Reviewing the three experiments, we found that each was valuable and each had different outcomes. In discussions about the first experiment, students noted that they thought they could begin with the group process in their own student-teaching and first classrooms as it made using journals seem more manageable than having everyone read a different book. Indeed, of the 22 students who were involved in this process, 17 tried using journals in student-teaching with 9 choosing to keep group journals on the same book. They all felt it had worked. However, several said they had many problems with managing the journal process, which they had not anticipated. Even though we had discussed many of these management issues, they had not had firsthand experience developing and using strategies for coping with them.

Both groups who used journals with school-aged children felt that they had received a more authentic picture of what was required of the teacher and of how much elementary students' literary tasks and response modes vary. Students who were assigned unfamiliar partners felt they had a more realistic experience with the process of coming to know a child and using that knowledge to advance the journal-writing process. Using journals during the whole ten weeks, rather than just over one novel, allowed them to see how student response varied because of what was read and to learn to deal with issues and problems that arose, such as a child not liking a book, the habitual book switcher, children who were "stingy" in responding, those who really did not understand, those who chose books that were much too easy or too difficult, and so forth. Everyone in the third group stated that they had learned more about children's literature from selecting and reading so many books.

Each of these experiments had utility for both the students and for us. We are now trying to combine the first and third models so that we can share a novel together yet work with children. Our idea is to choose a series of two books, fiction and nonfiction, buy multiple copies, and enlist a class of journal partners who would be willing to make those the first two books in the process.

Journals on Course Texts

One aspect of using journals we did not deal with in the earlier experiments was how journals could be used with textual material. To provide students with a structure through which they could regularly reflect on course content, we asked them to write a journal entry for most class sessions. They could choose to respond to any combination of assigned readings, class activities, professional observations, and personal experiences. We read and responded to each journal before returning it to the student at the next class meeting.

Directions to students regarding these journal entries have continued to evolve over three years. Originally, we simply directed students to focus their journal entries on textbook reading assignments. Because we were uncomfortable with both the quality and quantity of the resulting entries, we then asked students to respond to each reading assignment with either a summary or an outline of the content *and* a personal response to the reading. We realized that these entries became very mechanical, with emphasis placed on the formulaic summaries or outlines. Our focus had become form and not content, and students' journals clearly reflected that bias.

In our most recent experiment, in an attempt to validate students' personal reflections, we described the journal content as their reactions to assigned readings, class activities, clinical observations, and personal experiences. However, we stipulated that some references must be made to assigned readings because one of our goals is always to encourage students to keep up with their readings and to integrate those readings with class experiences. Suggestions such as outlines, summaries, responses to text questions, concept maps, audio- or videotapes, and three-dimensional artwork were offered as possible variations on journal entries.

As a result of these directions, students chose a wide variety of journal formats. Many students wrote in a stream-of-consciousness style as they reflected on portions of the readings while weaving in personal experiences and reactions. Some students outlined text content and reflected on that content periodically or at the end of the outline. A few students chose to respond to questions posed at the beginning of each chapter in our textbook. Infrequently, a student created a concept map organizing chapter content with a brief personal reflection. One student audiotaped her responses to reading and class activities, while another painted a T-shirt that dramatically portrayed her answer to the "basals or children's literature" dilemma.

Student Reflection on Journals

To develop the habit of reflective engagement, an important aspect of writing in journals (Bacharach, 1991), we asked students to analyze their own responses to the journal-writing process. We did this by collecting and analyzing open-ended responses after their first student-teaching experiences. Forty-nine of the 62 who responded said they had tried using journals during student-teaching with over half saying that it worked well. Fifty-eight said they intended to try some sort of journal writing in their first classes. It is also interesting to note that all 62 respondents said they had discussed using journals with their cooperating teachers. Not all of the cooperating teachers used journals in their classrooms, but most were receptive to having the student teachers do some adapted form of journal writing with their students; only 6 students reported that their teachers felt it was not appropriate or a waste of time. Further, 13 students noted that their teachers asked for more information about journals and wanted the students to share with them the readings and ideas from the methods class.

Literature Engagement

As noted earlier in this chapter, many student teachers do not come to us with extensive backgrounds in children's literature nor have they experienced, in their own schooling, many ways to respond or relate to literature. With these points in mind, we wanted to stress three issues in our methods classes: (1) valuing and using the backgrounds our students bring to class; (2) responding to the need to read to students of all ages; and (3) giving students alternatives to traditional, teacher-directed novel studies and book reports as a means of response. We approached the first two goals by modeling how to learn about reading interests and reading aloud. Then we described literature circles and a unique alternative to traditional book reports. All four activities were designed to invite students' affective responses.

Book Stacking

We found many of our students reluctant to discuss books or reveal themselves as readers at the beginning of the term. Frequently, in simple discussions, they would fall back on the *"Charlotte's Web* Syndrome," so named because when we surveyed the books they remembered, each class spent much time on *Charlotte's Web*, which they considered a "safe" classic. Many times we felt that this book and other well-regarded classics emerged not only because they were enjoyed by the students, but also because either the students were afraid to reveal the books they really read or they did not have an extensive list of children's books that they had actually read.

We wanted to get to know our students quickly and begin to talk about books and reading. Therefore, we tried starting a few classes with "book stacking." For this activity the instructor collects many books—at least three for each member of the class. These can be children's or adult books, of many types and genres. A varied stack is placed on each chair in the classroom before the group comes into class. When the students enter, they are asked to sit at a place at which there is at least one book they would like to read. (This is also a good technique for getting the students to not sit in preselected places during each class.) A browsing time of 15 to 20 minutes is required, after which students sit and explain why they chose a particular seat with a particular stack of books.

This is a good ice-breaker that gives the teacher an idea of the reading interests of the class and helps the students learn more about one another. Many times two students choose to sit with the same stack. This is not only fun, but it helps them get to know each other and recognize shared interests. Subsequent "stacks" can take many approaches. Sometimes we have students bring in a stack for the next class that contains books they like. It is important that the first, teacher-created stacks contain a wide variety, from Isaac Asimov to Raymond Carver to Danielle Steele, so that students feel liberated to reveal their true interests. It also helps students begin to talk about the various needs that books fulfill. This activity eventually led some to read *Voices of Readers* (Carlsen & Sherrill, 1988), a recommended book that deals with this issue.

Later, when the methods class had begun to work with the fifth graders who used journals, we created stacks for them. Once this was done as part of an interest interview. On another occasion, we tested our developing knowledge of our middle grade students, inviting them to the classroom to see if they would pick the stacks we predicted. Another time the methods students attempted to create stacks for their classmates after having observed their preferences.

Students have begun to report back on the use of book stacking in their own classes. One student teacher has had students respond to books by making "character stacks"—stacks of books that the characters in the book they read would choose to read—and explaining their choices. Others have used the process to get to know their students and help them talk about books.

Reading Aloud

We know that reading to students is one way to stimulate their enjoyment and appreciation of a wide variety of children's literature. Therefore, we read to preservice methods students in an attempt to broaden their awareness of children's literature, model effective teaching, and entice them to read to their classmates, and eventually, to their students.

We begin our reading and language arts methods classes by reading to students for 10 to 15 minutes. A short chapter book, such as *Nightjohn, Sadako and the Thousand Paper Cranes, Stone Fox, A Taste of Blackberries, Sarah, Plain and Tall*, or *The Hundred Dresses*, is read at the beginning of the first few class sessions until the book is completed. Throughout the reading, students are invited to respond. They naturally wonder about characters' motivation, piece clues together, predict future events, and beg us to read more than the planned amount of text for a particular class.

From the first class, students are invited to think about what they might like to read to all of us when the chapter book is finished. Usually, there are more than enough requests to read. Because students are encouraged to borrow children's literature from us and because they are compiling a focused, annotated bibliography of children's literature in the first few weeks of the course, they are anxious to share the discoveries they have made with the class. On the rare occasion when no student volunteers to read, we will again read to them.

Students have chosen a wide variety of literature to read to us. Short, predictable books and poems are favorites with many students. Others have read a chapter from a trade book that has been chosen to whet our appetites and encourage us to read the entire book. Occasionally, a student has read an excerpt from a novel or biography because it holds some special appeal for her or him.

Students have enjoyed being read to even as adults. Often they commented in their journals that listening to a good story helped them relax so that they could concentrate on class activities, rather than being distracted by all the things that were on their minds. They looked forward to the next read-aloud time. While student-teaching, several students asked to borrow specific books to read to their classes. Others spoke of rereading a selection that was read in class or of reading something else by the same author. So, it seems that the goal of modeling a positive response to literature, as well as an effective teaching strategy, has, in the case of reading children's literature to preservice teachers, been reached.

Literature Circles

Literature circles offer another opportunity for students to explore and respond to literature by participating in student-led, heterogeneously formed discussion groups. We hoped to provide students with the shared experience of reading yet another example of good children's literature and discussing their reactions with peers, while at the same time becoming familiar with the complex process of organizing reading instruction through literature circles. In addition, we decided to take this opportunity to focus on the development of pre-, during, and postreading activities in relation to the structure of the literature circle format.

Students first became familiar with the concept of literature circles by reading relevant sections of their textbook (Barr & Johnson, 1991) and *Best Practice 2* (National-Louis University, 1991), a publication that has been developed as a result of reform efforts in the Chicago, Illinois, public schools. Class discussions then focused on techniques for introducing literature to children in order for them to select the literature they want to read. For their first experience, our college students decided that they all wanted to read the same novel. We selected *Tuck Everlasting* by Natalie Babbitt, primarily because of its ability to evoke affective responses.

The next step involved discussing the roles that students can play as members of a literature circle as well as the concept that established roles can be matched to particular examples of literature and new roles can be created as needed. We considered the possibilities of discussion director (question asker), vocabulary enricher (word finder), literary luminary (story highlighter), historian, scientist, predictor, and checker, and the need to prepare for these roles by taking notes during or after reading. Other roles to consider are poet, illustrator, songwriter, and any others that focus on expressive arts. Role assignment should be used selectively and sparingly, and students should always feel free to follow the natural flow of the discussion. Roles are recommended only when they may be helpful.

As a prereading activity, students were asked to respond to an anticipation guide that we had prepared. We asked them to consider statements taken directly from *Tuck Everlasting*, decide whether they agreed or disagreed with those statements, and then discuss their reactions in their literature circles. Then students were asked to predict what this book might be about. We participated only minimally in their discussions, asking a question or two on occasion.

After students had discussed their reactions to the anticipation guide, we explained that the roles of discussion director, vocabulary enricher, and literary luminary were appropriate for *Tuck Everlasting*, with literary luminaries focusing on the development of three specific symbols. These symbols were identified and students chose their roles. Then students were given some time to read in class, prepare for their roles, and discuss their responses to *Tuck* through the structure provided by the roles. Together we decided to divide the book into two more sections, read outside of class, and then discuss reactions during the class-time literature circles. Students tried out a different role with each section of reading so that they could sample as wide a variety of experiences as possible.

After students finished reading *Tuck*, we asked them to participate in a postreading activity by responding in their literature circles to statements presented on a reaction guide. After discussing their responses to the five statements, they wrote an essay focusing on one of the statements.

We plan to continue to provide methods students with literature circle experiences, "collect" multiple copies of several novels to provide choices, and help students develop a pre-, during-, and postreading framework for two or three novels that they might be able to use with their own students. Recently, we have established classroom sites in which students form literature circles with children while they are enrolled in methods classes. These concrete experiences have enabled the college students to tailor the use of literature circles to meet the needs and interests of children.

Book Report in a Box

We have tried numerous other ways of combining high–affect-producing activities with the development of instructional techniques. One of the most enjoyable is "book report in a box" (BRIAB). The goal is to model an activity that is engaging and allows students to respond in a way that integrates reading, writing, speaking, and listening and provides for dramatic and artistic expression. We also try to suggest that there are many ways for students to report on a book besides the traditional book report form that so many students dislike, as has been suggested in earlier chapters in this work.

In BRIAB, students fill a box, shopping bag, or other suitable container with artifacts that reflect what was most interesting and affecting to them about a piece of literature they read. For example, for *Roll of Thunder, Hear My Cry* students chose to focus on characters with whom they felt a special affinity. Students filled their boxes with articles evocative of their characters; one box, for example, had a piece of chalk, an apron, a stick of glue, some work gloves, a piece of lace, and a ruler—items that represented Mrs. Logan.

The students brought their boxes, exchanged them with others, and attempted to figure out who the character was and why the items were chosen. Sometimes this was done orally, sometimes in writing, sometimes through drawing, with the character shown with the objects in some sort of meaningful situation. For the box described in the previous paragraph, Mrs. Logan was shown using the ruler and chalk in her teaching, using the glue to block out an offensive phrase in the class books, and wearing work gloves in the fields and lace in church. Another time, students chose to present dramatic monologues on the artifacts, with Mrs. Logan describing what meaning each item had to her life. Because the artifacts can have multiple meanings, discussion naturally occurs as the box creator and the box interpreter compare and contrast their responses.

Currently we are experimenting with "chapter in a box" with students assembling boxes of artifacts to respond to content issues in their textbooks. For example, a collection of writing from children of different ages relates to developmental spelling. While a more content-focused response results from these efforts, we are still attempting to help students express affective responses to these issues. In the developmental spelling box, for instance, one student produced a saved essay from fifth grade with many red marks, along with a reflection on how this made her feel about something important she was trying to say. The discussion from the group about this artifact was rich, reflective, and meaningful for instruction.

Preparation Through Collaboration

We have shared in this chapter the results of our experimentation with developing preservice teachers' own literacy by modeling strategies they could use in the classroom. Encouraging affective response to literature is an important component of building a literate community in the classroom, and this does not have to be done at the expense of dealing with important instructional strategies and content. It is important to note that we participated with the students as we tried these investigations so that we were partners in the research; our refinements and changes were a direct result of the feedback we received. We hope that this process of being collaborators also presented models to the students, in much the same way that our literacy activities served as examples that could be extended to elementary classrooms.

The notion of learning as a problem-solving, reflective, communal activity is one we hoped to foster as well. As one student noted when she wrote about a debriefing in her journal, "I was glad to see that you didn't have everything figured out all the time. It made me feel more confident that I could face problems and work them out."

References

Atwell, N. (1987). *In the middle: Writing and learning with adolescents.* Portsmouth, NH: Heinemann.

Bacharach, N. (1991, May). *Facilitating emerging theories of reading in preservice students.* Paper presented at the annual meeting of the International Reading Association, Las Vegas, NV.

Barr, R., & Johnson, B. (1991). *Teaching reading in elementary classrooms: Developing independent readers.* White Plains, NY: Longman.

Brazee, P.E., & Kristo, J.V. (1986). *Evaluation: Whole language, whole child.* New York: Scholastic.

Carlsen, G.R., & Sherrill, A. (1988). *Voices of readers: How we come to love books.* Urbana, IL: National Council of Teachers of English.

Henney, M. (1991, May). *Can a whole language approach be effectively implemented in a university level course?* Paper presented at the annual meeting of the International Reading Association, Las Vegas, NV.

National-Louis University. (1991). *Best practice 2: Teaching and learning in Chicago.* Chicago, IL: Chicago Project on Learning and Teaching.

Rose, M. (1989). *Lives on the boundary.* New York: Penguin.

Schell, L.M., & Danielson, K.E. (1991). Dialogue journals in reading education classes. *Journal of Reading Education, 16*(3), 20–26.

Children's Books

Babbitt, N. (1975). *Tuck everlasting.* New York: Farrar, Straus & Giroux.

Coerr, E. (1977). *Sadako and the thousand paper cranes.* New York: Scholastic.

Estes, E. (1944). *The hundred dresses.* San Diego, CA: Harcourt Brace.

Gardiner, J.R. (1980). *Stone fox.* New York: HarperCollins.

MacLachlan, P. (1985). *Sarah, plain and tall.* New York: HarperCollins.

Paulsen, G. (1993). *Nightjohn.* New York: Delacorte.

Smith, D.B. (1973). *A taste of blackberries.* New York: Scholastic.

PART FIVE

Developing Affective Reading Programs

It should be the teacher's aim to give every child a love for reading, a hunger for it that will stay with him through all the years of his life. If a child has that, he will acquire the mechanical part without difficulty.

E. Mayne

Chapter 14

Affect Versus Skills: Choices for Teachers

Betty S. Heathington

●◆ The role of teachers in developing and maintaining positive attitudes as well as changing the negative attitudes of their students regarding literacy is a crucial one in today's schools. Many teachers seem to agree with this statement, yet they report that they do not give top priority to fostering positive attitudes toward literacy in their classroom activities (Heathington & Alexander, 1984). When forced to make a choice between promoting positive attitudes or emphasizing skill development, teachers seem to choose skill development. Their practices indicate they believe that skills are more essential for their students than the attitudes their students have toward literacy.

Some argue that attitudes toward literacy should be the center of teachers' instructional planning and activities, as Huck (1973) urges:

> If we teach a child to read, yet develop not the taste for reading, all our teaching is for naught. We shall have produced a nation of "illiterate literates"—those who know how to read, but do not read (p. 203).

Likewise, the words of Smith (1983) remind us where our first priorities should be as we teach students to read and write:

> Literacy is like boats and telescopes, useful but not restricted to utilitarian ends. To teach reading and writing as if their most important uses were for completing tax returns and job applications is like using a telescope as a doorstop (p. viii).

He states further,

> The real tragedy is that competent readers and writers as well as the less able leave school with a lifelong aversion to reading and writing, which they regard as purely school activities, as trivial and tedious "work" (p. 115).

These statements reveal the futility of teachers' instructional efforts unless they give first consideration to students' attitudes toward literacy. As stressed by the authors in this work, students will not be lifelong readers and writers unless teachers instill a joy for learning in their activities. To view literacy as joyous, students must be surrounded every day with rewarding experiences in reading and writing. Forcing students to engage in activities they see as meaningless only drives them to adopt an attitude of hating those engagements and avoiding literacy activities once they leave school. This is not to suggest that a focus on affect will impede skill development. In fact, the opposite result should be achieved with students whose teachers hold affect as the top priority: higher student achievement will result as students' involvement with literacy activities increases.

Teachers should examine their beliefs about literacy instruction on a continuous basis. These beliefs have come from many past events and sources: how they were taught as children in school; how they were educated to teach by their professors in their teacher education institution; how they were trained by their cooperating teachers in public schools during their student-teaching or internship; how their colleagues teach; and how they have learned to teach on their own. These beliefs form the basis of the role they will play in fostering attitudes toward literacy. If teachers have not seen the affective domain as the central or guiding focus in literacy activities, they likely will not believe that such a focus is necessary. Beliefs, derived from experiences, are reflected in behaviors. Therefore, teachers also need to examine their behaviors and classroom practices to determine if the role they play is one that fosters positive attitudes toward literacy. (See also Chapter 17, which describes staff development as a way to help teachers change their attitudes.)

Following are eight scenarios to help teachers examine their beliefs and behaviors in literacy instruction. Two opposing beliefs and behaviors are examined in regard to each scenario: in one, attitudes are considered as foremost, and in the other, skills are considered as the top priority. Teachers can then determine which belief and behavior is more typical of their role in the classroom. Some teachers may think that they believe their primary goal is developing positive attitudes; however, when they examine their behavior in similar scenarios in their classroom, they may have to reassess their beliefs.

Scenario One

Mr. Adams, a fifth grade teacher, must make a decision in his planning for the first six weeks of school. He has a small block of time he can devote either to reading a library book to his class or reviewing reading skills. He read a short passage from a library book to the students the first day of school, and they loved it, making positive comments and discussing the book among themselves. However, as Mr. Adams looks over his students' achievement scores in reading from the previous spring, he notes numerous students with low scores in comprehension. Should he read to his students or schedule time to give them practice in finding the main idea in written paragraphs by choosing from among multiple-choice answers to select the best titles for the paragraphs?

In this scenario, the teacher must choose between two behaviors: reading to his students, emphasizing the enjoyment of this activity, or having students work on main ideas, emphasizing skills and achievement development.

Because of the national attention in the United States regarding the literacy levels of students in current classrooms and the stress such attention has focused on monitoring and testing of literacy skills, teachers often respond by concentrating on activities that emphasize skills. Teachers realize their accountability is usually based on the skill development of their students and, in some schools, teachers' success is based on this achievement, rather than on any measure of their students' love of reading and writing. It is not surprising that teachers do not concentrate on students' attitudes toward literacy activities but instead give their first attention to the skill needs of their students.

Teachers should remember that continual routine work on skills can be a boring activity for students. Instead, students could be reading and writing about topics that are important to them. They could be talking and listening to others about their reading and writing. They could be engaging in the varied, interesting activities that Cramer suggests in Chapter 10.

Scenario Two

Ms. Rodriguez teaches second grade in a school system that has a policy that teachers must group students by ability for reading instruction and spend 30 minutes per group each day using basal readers. Ms. Rodriguez has heard about a whole language program in a nearby school system that does not use a basal reading series. The students in that system are allowed to select their own library books to read during reading time. Ms. Rodriguez has read some articles on whole language and wonders if it would work in her classroom. She is concerned that if she does the basal lessons and the accompanying workbook and skill pages as mandated by her system, there will not be enough time to use literature and cover her other subject areas during the day. Should she teach the three basal groups or approach the reading supervisor in her system about using whole language, combining all of the subject areas together for reading, writing, and discussion? She questions whether it is a wise decision to ask the reading supervisor about a change because she thinks that the supervisor must have more knowledge than she of what is best for her students.

In this scenario, not only does the teacher have to make a choice between the current skills-based program and a program emphasizing students' selection of their own materials that promotes an affective literacy environment, but she must also deal with her own decision-making ability. The public outcry and concentration on the unacceptable reading achievement test scores of many students in U.S. public schools may have convinced teachers that the public knows which literacy activities are best for students. Hall (1986) has described the situation:

> Just as the arts are not as highly valued in our society as technology, the view of teaching as an art is not as widely accepted as is the perspective that teaching effectiveness can be measured objectively through test results and other quantitative measures (p. 34).

Explaining further, Hall states that teachers are treated "as assembly line workers with a quota to attain in a certain time period" (pg. 34). They teach students literacy skills, then they measure whether such skills have "taken."

The decision making that must go into each teacher's day is far more intricate than this "instruct skills–measure skills" process. Teachers must realize that they are capable decision makers. To do this, they must be well read and knowledgeable about their roles as educators. Assured of their expert knowledge, teachers should voice their professional opinions about what is best for the students in their classrooms. They should become vocal advocates for proven state-of-the-art strategies that can help their students enjoy and succeed in life. There should be no question in their minds as to whether they are decision makers.

Scenario Three

Ms. Powell, a seventh grade teacher, notices that for several days, a student, Mary, has been reading a library book instead of answering the assigned questions at the end of the chapter in her reading textbook. The teacher is fearful that unless Mary answers these comprehension questions, her comprehension will be diminished, and she will score poorly on the achievement tests. Should Ms. Powell demand that Mary finish the basal reading questions or allow her to read the library book in which she is interested?

This scenario examines two aspects of teaching: the choice between an affective reading encounter versus a skills-oriented one and a teacher's need to structure all aspects of students' literacy activities. Is the teacher the sole planner for what is best for students, or should the teacher share that role with students and parents? If teachers continually decide on all reading materials for students, will students be able to make independent decisions once they graduate from school? In Scenario Three, the teacher could let Mary read her own book and then ask Mary to describe the main ideas from that book instead of doing the structured textbook exercise.

Strickler (1977) describes children who complete their formal education knowing how to read but not knowing "why to read, when to read, and what to read" (p. 3). If teachers do not allow students to make these decisions as they progress through school, students will not have that ability once they graduate. Self-selection of materials and of times to read must become part of students' literacy activities from their first days in school.

Scenario Four

Ms. Norman is a fourth grade teacher with 25 students in her class. She feels very responsible for teaching these students to write correctly; she believes that she can correct all the errors these children make in writing by marking the grammatical and spelling mistakes on their written stories. Ms. Norman is a busy teacher both during the day and at night. She simply cannot get all the students' papers corrected. The children often want to talk to her about their stories, but she does not have time due to her involvement in correcting the papers. Should she give fewer writing activities to her students? Or should she find alternative ways to teach students how to write correctly?

This scenario illustrates a belief and behavior about an aspect of literacy that has serious implications for affect—correcting students' mistakes. Many teachers believe that they must correct their students' promptly so that mistakes are not reinforced. Often teachers will return every creative writing endeavor to students with numerous red marks to indicate grammatical errors. They will interrupt a student's oral reading to correct a word the student has mispronounced. Teachers must be careful when and how they correct students' mistakes. Through excessive corrections and criticisms, teachers may make students anxious about reading. Wigfield and Asher (1984) discuss studies that show most successful teachers of low–socioeconomic status children use praise and encouragement as motivators. A private explanation from the teacher or from another student is usually a better way to handle the situation.

Scenario Five

Mr. Cohen, a third grade teacher, has read that he should provide positive reinforcement to his students concerning the books they are reading in their free time. However, he figures that even if he spends only 15 minutes with each student per week, for his 25 students, that would consume over 6 hours of his basal reading time per week. He questions whether he will have enough time to provide positive reinforcement for his students' free-time reading and still be able to conduct his regular reading activities with his three reading groups. Should he forget about reinforcing free-time reading, should he cut his regular basal reading activities short by an hour a day, or should he find some other solution?

In this situation, the teacher is assuming that the total responsibility for providing positive reinforcement for literacy activities rests with him. He must recognize that many others can help him provide positive reinforcement. A teacher must collaborate with many groups including parents, volunteers, and other students to help students be positive about literacy. It is often peers serving as mentors who can best reach and encourage certain students. Sometimes teachers are trying so hard to keep their students working independently that they fail to see the significant value of their working together, encouraging and promoting one another. When teachers help their students become "positive reinforcers" for other students, it takes the burden of all positive reinforcement off the teacher.

Scenario Six

Mr. Ames has set up a reading center in his third grade classroom. As soon as students are finished with their reading and spelling workbook pages and their handwriting lesson for the day, Mr. Ames allows the students to go to the reading center to select from various books and activities. Jesse, a student who has poor handwriting, has had his eye on a book in the center for some time. On this particular day, Jesse finishes his work in about the same amount of time as two of the students who complete all tasks perfectly. As Mr. Ames sees Jesse heading for the reading center, he asks to see Jesse's handwriting before he allows him to go to the center. Looking over Jesse's handwriting, Mr. Ames notes several errors. Should he allow Jesse to go to the reading center, or should he require Jesse to redo the assignment to make his writing more legible? By the time Jesse has redone his handwriting, the free-time set aside for the reading center will probably be over.

This situation again calls for a choice between a skills-oriented activity and an affective literacy engagement. In addition, there is another issue addressed in the scenario: do students at all levels in the classroom have the same opportunities for "fun" activities in literacy? Do students who have problems with literacy skills spend more time in skill drill than those students who already possess the skill?

Gambrell and Wilson (1973) remind teachers that for a student experiencing problems in literacy, "constant focusing on his weakness cripples him as a learner and makes his learning experience intolerable" (p. 1). In a section of the book *Becoming a Nation of Readers* (Anderson et al., 1985), the authors summarize the multiple differences in how poor readers are treated in the affective domain in relation to good readers:

• Poor readers do more reading aloud and less silent reading than good readers.

• Poor readers have less of their assigned reading in meaningful context.

• Teachers correct a higher proportion of mistakes by poor readers than they do mistakes by good readers.

Scenario Seven

Ms. Cuentan, a sixth grade teacher, notices that Gerard, a superior athlete, does not read in his free time, but rather he chats quietly with his friend, Mike, who is also an athlete. Ms. Cuentan thinks to herself, "Oh well, active boys seldom like to read. At least they're being pretty quiet and not disturbing anyone." Both of these boys have acceptable achievement test scores so Ms. Cuentan feels she does not need to worry about their ability to read. Should Ms. Cuentan remain passive and allow the boys to talk quietly, or should she make serious efforts to find ways to get both boys involved in some type of literacy activities?

This scenario examines the idea of affect for all students, focusing on the belief that some students because of their sex or cultural background will never develop the same affect toward reading as other students. Some teachers believe that boys cannot have the same enthusiasm for reading as girls. What teachers must realize is that all students have unique interests related to literacy. The teacher must find the approach that fits the special needs of each student. Strickler (1977) stated,

> Just as there is no single approach that has been found to be consistently more effective than another approach in teaching children how to read, there also is no single most effective approach for developing children's interests, attitudes, and values in relation to reading (p. 7).

Teachers must know their students' interests. They must assess the types of formats for response each student enjoys most through such avenues as portfolios, diaries, and journals. Teachers need to know students' reactions to books, the number of books they have read, and whether they have a library card. In essence, they must consider records of interests as more important than records of skill achievements.

Scenario Eight

Ms. Jordan, a first grade teacher, has set up a special reward system in her classroom for students who complete their reading and writing work every day for a week. At the end of the week, the students get a special treat (a piece of candy, a small toy, or similar item). Each week there are several students who have not accomplished the teacher's goal for them. Should Ms. Jordan consider a different approach?

The reward in this scenario is for achievement-oriented activities—completion of assigned work. Could a teacher instead have celebrations focused on affective accomplishments of students? For example, could there be a treat (or celebration) when a student finds a book he really likes or when he finds a book for a friend that she enjoys reading? Could there be a celebration for everyone who enjoyed writing a story on a particular day? The focus of the treat should be on "enjoyment" of literacy activities, not for skill accomplishments.

Teachers should remember that celebrations should be a part of classroom activities. Such celebrations do not have to mark major accomplishments; minor progress is also worthy of celebration. In addition, teachers should not have a party once a week; celebrations should be held to recognize students who have reached a goal worthy of a class celebration. As the authors in Chapters 8 and 11 discussed, extrinsic rewards are not as effective when they are overused.

Roles in Promoting Reading

To summarize, the roles of teachers in fostering positive attitudes toward literacy should include the following:

• *Advocates* who promote attitudes as the top priority for any literacy activity. The attitudes of students toward literacy activities, not the skills development of students, should be a teacher's focus. If positive attitudes are not being promoted in all activities, those activities should be re-examined. Teachers should advocate positive attitudes for all students—both those with high and low literacy skills. Teachers need to believe that all students can have positive attitudes toward literacy, regardless of the students' sex, race, or culture.

• *Decision makers* who know what is best for students. Knowledgeable teachers realize that the decisions they make will influence the lifelong literacy habits of their students. It is imperative that teachers make the correct decisions about literacy instruction in their classrooms and have confidence in their ability to make the right decisions. They must search constantly for knowledge that helps them make literacy activities enjoyable.

• *Collaborators* who enlist the help of others to reinforce positive attitudes in students. Students, parents, and volunteers can help teachers in planning literacy activities and in encouraging students by providing positive reinforcement.

• *Promoters* who find time often to encourage literacy and celebrate the accomplishments of their students. No matter how small the accomplishment, teachers can help students celebrate. As students find a literacy activity enjoyable, teachers can promote ongoing enjoyment in some festive way in the classroom. Celebrations of the achievement of goals become the emphasis, not the reading and writing errors of students.

These four roles will allow teachers truly to foster positive attitudes toward literacy in their students and promote lifelong reading by people who not only use literacy but also enjoy it.

References

Anderson, R.C., Hiebert, E.H., Scott, J.A., & Wilkinson, I.A.G. (1985). *Becoming a nation of readers: The report of the Commission on Reading.* Washington, DC: U.S. Department of Education.

Gambrell, L.B., & Wilson, R.B. (1973). *Focusing on the strengths of children.* Belmont, CA: Fearon.

Hall, M. (1986). Teaching and language centered programs. In D.R. Tovey & J.E. Kerber (Eds.), *Roles in literacy learning: A new perspective* (pp. 34–41). Newark, DE: International Reading Association.

Heathington, B.S., & Alexander, J.E. (1984). Do classroom teachers emphasize attitudes toward reading? *The Reading Teacher, 37*(6), 484–488.

Huck, C.S. (1973). Strategies for improving interest and appreciation in literature. In P.C. Burns & L.M. Schell (Eds.), *Elementary school language arts* (pp. 203–210). Chicago, IL: Rand McNally.

Smith, F. (1983). *Essays into literacy.* Portsmouth, NH: Heinemann.

Strickler, D.J. (1977). Planning the affective component. In R.A. Earle (Ed.), *Classroom practice in reading* (pp. 3–9). Newark, DE: International Reading Association.

Wigfield, A., & Asher, S.R. (1984). Social and motivational influences on reading. In P.D. Pearson (Ed.), *Handbook on reading research* (pp. 423–452). White Plains, NY: Longman.

Chapter 15

Coordinating Teacher Read-Alouds with Content Instruction in Secondary Classrooms

Judy S. Richardson

●◆ Reading aloud has always been a favorite activity of readers. Many authors in this work have stressed the importance of reading aloud to children and students of all ages. Among other benefits, read-alouds provide a model of expressive, enthusiastic reading, transmit the pleasure of reading from reader to listener, and invite listeners to read. Advocates of read-alouds include Trelease (1989), who wrote *The New Read-Aloud Handbook*—his version of a read-aloud program that parents can implement. Larrick (1969) encouraged both parents and teachers to read aloud to children even after they become independent readers, because "they should have the fun of being read to as well. Furthermore, read-aloud time is ideal for introducing new books" (p. 77). Glazer (1990) implores parents to "read to your children from the day they are born and never stop" (p. 9). Norton (1992) encourages read-alouds in order to provide upper elementary and middle school students opportunities "to enjoy the classics and Newbery medal and honor award books" (p. 44). Cullinan (1987) says that "hearing good stories helps to develop vocabularies, sharpens a sensitivity to language, and fine tunes a sense of writing styles" (p. 6). Children's author Bill Martin Jr (1987), as mentioned in Chapter 5, describes his first mentor, a teacher who read to his class three times a day. Even in teacher education classes, students enjoy hearing read-alouds (Richardson, 1981; 1994).

The effectiveness of read-alouds is well documented, especially in self-contained elementary classrooms where teachers can control time and integrate instruction. Feitelson, Kita, and Goldstein (1986) conducted research that showed that first graders who were read to 20 minutes a day attained higher test scores in comprehension, active use of language, and decoding than did other students.

Resistance to Read-Alouds at the Secondary Level

Secondary teachers remain resistant to trying read-alouds in their classrooms, even though they may acknowledge the benefits. How could read-alouds work in their classrooms? Although Glazer, Larrick, and Trelease, cited earlier, encourage parents to continue read-alouds throughout their children's teenage years, their suggestions are primarily for younger children. Trelease does include some reading resources for older children, but these are very few and labeled "grade seven and up"—not very specific. Anders and Levine (1990) cite read-alouds as one activity they used in their middle school programs; however, they do not provide procedures to implement the practice.

Read-alouds are more difficult to integrate in secondary classrooms, where content must dominate instruction, and teachers are under special time constraints. High school teachers might agree theoretically to the soundness of read-alouds but argue, "I hardly have time to teach the content from the textbook as it is," "My instructional time is often too brief to include them," "High school students will think read-alouds are 'baby-stuff'," "I can't take time on activities which can't be tested," or "I don't know where I'd find appropriate read-aloud material to match my content and my students' interest."

In my classroom, I solved these dilemmas: I used read-alouds successfully while teaching tenth grade students.

Instructional Considerations

The short story unit was the first I was to teach my tenth grade class. I considered my students: grouped by the system as "average ability," they might best be described as socially active, likable, energetic, but disaffected when it came to academic tasks, especially those relating to reading (particularly when it was assigned as homework). They were a tough audience to motivate. Next, I considered the time I had to teach this unit: only three weeks because another unit had been planned by the department to start soon and guest speakers had already been scheduled. Third, I studied the stories in the unit: some were fairly interesting to this age, but many could be perceived by the students as having little relevance to their lives—a common complaint for this group. Some stories would be a challenge for me to teach and for them to understand and appreciate.

Next, I drew on theory about the reading process. What readers do before reading will often make the difference in their comprehension. Teachers who prepare their students for the assigned reading discover that students consequently read more purposefully, with greater comprehension and enthusiasm. I needed an activity that would "hook" my students, help them understand what they already knew, build their background, and help them comprehend. I decided to rely on read-alouds to motivate students during this unit.

The First Read-Aloud

"The Masque of the Red Death" by Edgar Allan Poe seemed a good story with which to start. Secondary students are usually intrigued by Poe, and they tend to like the mystery and horror associated with this particular story. Some have read Poe previously but usually understood his work only superficially. In the tenth grade curricula, students are expected to learn how this work represents basic elements of the short story: not only characters and plot, but also theme, setting, and irony.

The premise of "The Masque of the Red Death"—that a person can escape death by physically locking himself away—was alien to my students. They knew that disease is often spread by contact, that cleanliness is a factor, and that medicine—not quarantining—is effective in treating disease. Even with AIDS—perhaps analogous to the red death in some ways—we know how it is transmitted and how to avoid it. Because this story is not about the suffering that results from the disease but how one could "outsmart" it, I was not confident that a discussion about AIDS would be the best preparation. How would my students relate to a story in which the characters fear a disease but think they can lock it out? Wouldn't it seem illogical to them that Count Prospero thought he could keep the plague out of his castle? It was crucial that my students understand setting and irony in this story, but they might disregard these elements if I did not begin with some enticing preparation.

The preceding summer I had read Edward Rutherford's *Sarum*, a long historical novel about England. In one section, the author describes the transmittal of the plague from Europe to England by rats aboard cargo ships. In another section, people who are trying to avoid the plague escape to a small hut and even bar other family members from entering their haven. I remembered how clear the horror of the plague had become to me as I read the gory descriptions; I imagined how it must have been to fear an illness which one could not fight and to see loved ones die horribly. If I read sections of this book aloud to my class, the setting, as described in *Sarum*, could help my students understand Poe's setting. The irony and theme might be clearer as well. I had the perfect read-aloud.

After I introduced the book and began to read, the room was quiet. I witnessed a rapt attention and appreciation for an activity that was mostly uncommon to these students. Was the read-aloud successful? I judged success first by the reactions of the students, which were very positive. I noted interest and many enthusiastic comments. The lesson seemed to be effective because I linked an interesting affective activity (read-aloud) with the content (cognitive). I would know whether the read-aloud motivated students if they completed their assignment to read Poe's story by the next day. Indeed, class discussion the following day indicated that a majority had read the story, although I could not consider the read-aloud a total success because not all the students had done so.

An important measure of success to many secondary teachers is whether students learn material well enough to pass a test. I included two "telling" questions on the short story unit test, and the responses were encouraging. The first asked students to write a theme statement for "The Masque of the Red Death." Of 49 students, 36 received full credit for their response. One response, from a student who received a failing grade for the whole test, was "You can't escape death." Another, from a student who also failed, was "You can always run, but you can't always hide." In my judgment, these responses, even from students who failed the test, were acceptable and revealed that the read-aloud must have helped. The second question asked students to write a paragraph about what they liked about the story and why. It also asked students what they liked about the way they studied the story. A student who received a poor grade wrote,

> I liked "The Masque of Red Death" because it was interesting about when all those party animals went into the seventh room and died. What a way to end a party. I liked the way we studied it because you made it sound interesting by reading to us first about how people thought they could escape.

In this response, I could see that my student not only appreciated the read-aloud, but could restate the irony of the story. Only 16 percent of the students received a perfect score for this question, but 70 percent received passing scores.

I found that the responses to these two questions demonstrated success because, although 48 percent received failing or near-failing grades on the test, many of those students received credit for these responses, as the examples illustrate. I doubt that this success rate could have been achieved without the read-aloud.

Second Read-Aloud

"The Storyteller" by Saki presented a greater challenge. In this work set on a train, a bachelor tells a much better story to two young children than their aunt can. The irony is that the bachelor seems to know more about what will captivate the children than the Victorian aunt; his gruesome tale is more popular than her moralistic one.

While I agreed with the suggestion from the teacher's manual to read the story aloud, I selected two other read-alouds to precede it. I explained to my students that they were going to play the role of the children on the train. I was the aunt while reading a moralistic story from *The McGuffey Reader*; I was the bachelor while reading Judith Viorst's *Alexander and the Terrible, Horrible, No Good, Very Bad Day*. As I read from *The McGuffey Reader*, students were politely quiet. They tolerated this; at least they did not have to take notes or do anything but listen. As I read Viorst's story, I was delighted that they chimed in on the predictable chorus. It was obvious they were enjoying this children's story immensely. Again, judging by the classroom climate, the read-aloud was successful. Afterward, the students voted on which story they preferred. The winner was the latter story, of course.

On the same unit test I discussed earlier, I asked several questions related to this read-aloud. The first asked students to write a one-sentence description of the irony in "The Storyteller." Of 49 students, 29 received full points for their responses. One was, "The children liked the bachelor's story better, even though he doesn't have children and told a raunchy story." The second question read, "Was the story I read to you about the mother hen and her chicks more like the aunt's or the bachelor's story? Why?" Thirty-two answers were correct. The third question was the same as for "Masque"—students were to indicate what they liked about the way they studied the story. One student wrote that he liked the "confrontation" of the aunt and the bachelor and the way we read two stories first to "see how those kids would like his story better."

Overall Success of Read-Aloud Activities

I was very pleased with the success of these read-alouds. My disinterested tenth graders became more interested, which I measured by their increased attention span, appreciative comments, and even some requests to repeat the book titles and authors' names. Further, student responses about the read-aloud instruction were better than other responses on the test. I continued to use read-alouds often.

Two months after I used this teaching method, I asked students to rate several different activities I had used in instructing them. They were to respond to each activity by indicating if it had helped them a lot, some, or none. Fifty-three percent of these students checked "a lot" for read-alouds; 43 percent checked "some."

For a final writing assignment I asked students to explain two things they liked about my class. While they could select any two aspects of an 18-week experience, many identified the read-alouds, as shown by these comments:

> This semester, I liked reading the stories. I don't like reading that much, but I liked to hear you read.

> I also liked the way you'd prepare ahead of time for our short stories by reading to us.

> I liked you reading those stories out loud.

> Another thing that I liked is when you would read to us stories that you brought to class that day.

> I liked it when you read out loud in class.

> The thing I liked was just the fact that when I was in this class, I felt eager to read each story and learn more about it.

Read-Alouds in a Ninth Grade Social Studies Class

A social studies teacher tried read-alouds as an activity to help her students understand myths, legends, and fairy tales of different cultures. After listening to read-alouds, students were expected to read stories from Eastern and Western cultures and then write their own myths. These students were in a ninth grade honors class and were resistant to "baby" activities.

Every day during the first unit on India and every other day during the following units on China and Japan, the teacher read a myth, legend, or fairy tale during the last 5 to 10 minutes of class. The class then discussed the characteristics of these stories as well as their historical merit. Next they studied Ancient Greece, after which they were able to write their own myth, legend, or fairy tale from one of the civilizations explored.

Students were given two weeks to complete their writing assignment, which was graded. Students could also present their stories orally for a quiz grade. The products generated were of high quality. Although this is to be expected from honors students, the enthusiasm with which the students participated was greater than usual for this unit. Students began to remind the teacher when to start daily read-aloud time.

This teacher surveyed her students to find out how they would evaluate read-alouds. Sixty-three percent responded that they would like to have read-alouds continue for other units. She reflects on the success of read-alouds:

> I really believe more students enjoyed this than even said they did....I've had several students talk with me about the survey after we had completed it. The comments orally were much more positive.

Read-Aloud Materials for Science and Mathematics

In science, read-alouds at the secondary level might include brief articles from local newspapers. A recent article in the *Washington Post's* food section relates a food editor's experiences with readers who complain because they followed a recipe *exactly*, but the product flopped. The editor then gives some examples of readers' "exact adaptations": for instance, one cook left the cake batter—a mixture of flour, baking powder, and liquid—for 45 minutes before putting it into the oven. Of course, the baking powder began to give off a gas as soon as it was mixed with liquid; thus the cake batter had no bubbles left to make the cake rise when it went in the oven! This read-aloud could be chemistry in practice. Often, newspapers include a science section at least once weekly. The features included can become short, relevant read-alouds. *Mrs. Frisby and the Rats of Nimh* by Robert C. O'Brien is a novel example of a science experiment that worked better than expected. The scientists divide rats and mice into three groups each—control, experimental A, and experimental B—and then inject serums and conduct experiments. Whereas the serum for the control group is a placebo, the serum for the experimental groups contains ingredients the scientists theorize will make the rats and mice shorter and live longer. The serum works so well for group A that those rats and mice escape and set up their own society.

The example of infinity in Norton Juster's *The Phantom Tollbooth* has captivated mathematics students in middle and high schools. The beaver with a 30-foot tail who could build Boulder Dam, also in this novel, is a humorous look at word problems. Appendix G of *Reading to Learn in the Content Areas* (Richardson & Morgan, 1994) lists several trade books suitable for students on the topics of history, mathematics, and science. Chapter 12 of this textbook provides many ideas for infusing literature in all content areas as well. Marilyn vos Savant's column in the weekly news magazine *Parade* often contains word-problem teasers of just the right length for one- to two-minute read-alouds.

Read-Alouds *Can* Affect Secondary Students

One concern mentioned at the start of this chapter was that secondary teachers hardly have time to teach the content in their classes. Read-alouds can be *part* of the content, not an additional burden. In the examples presented, the read-alouds were integrated, not extraneous. Another concern was that instructional time is too brief to include them, but teachers who use read-alouds find that they are perfect for short instructional periods, especially when a 50-minute period is shortened to 20.

Some teachers worry that students will think read-alouds are "baby stuff," but neither the ninth nor tenth graders thought so when the read-alouds were explained in the context of the lesson objectives. In the Saki example, tenth graders enjoyed "becoming young children" again. Of course, the introduction to read-alouds must be carefully made.

Another concern was that read-alouds are not testable, but both I and my colleague found ways of measuring students' understanding: myself as part of a test as well as in essays and rating, my colleague by grading the myth written.

The last concern, that a secondary teacher will not be able to find appropriate read-alouds, was partially answered in the suggestions for science and mathematics teachers. A major resource should be the teacher's personal reading. Readers will often find relevant messages in what they enjoy reading; teachers are no different. Novels, newspapers, and magazines contain many short, interesting resources. Sources are published yearly by content area associations, the International Reading Association, and the National Council of Teachers of English. Librarians also have suggestions.

Read-alouds can work in secondary classrooms with limited intrusion on valuable instructional time, and they can have major benefits for students. Secondary students *like* being read to and show this by their attitudes—they become better behaved, alert, and interested. Students are eager to make connections between read-alouds and content material. Read-alouds help unite the affective and the cognitive domains.

References

Anders, P.L., & Levine, N.S. (1990). Accomplishing change in reading programs. In G.G. Duffy (Ed.), *Reading in the middle school* (pp. 157–170). Newark, DE: International Reading Association.

Cullinan, B.E. (1987). *Children's literature in the reading program.* Newark, DE: International Reading Association.

Feitelson, D., Kita, B., & Goldstein, Z. (1986). Effects of listening to series stories on first graders' comprehension and use of language. *Research in the Teaching of English, 20,* 339–355.

Glazer, S.M. (1990). *Creating readers and writers.* Newark, DE: International Reading Association.

Larrick, N. (1969). *A parent's guide to children's reading.* New York: Simon & Schuster.

Martin, B. (1987). The making of a reader: A personal narrative. In B.E. Cullinan (Ed.), *Children's literature in the reading program* (pp. 15–19). Newark, DE: International Reading Association.

Norton, D. (1992). *The impact of literature-based reading.* New York: Macmillan.

Richardson, J. (1981). Mind grabbers, or read aloud to college students, too! *Ad-sig Journal, 3*(1), 39–51.

Richardson, J. (1994). Great read-alouds for prospective teachers and secondary students. *Journal of Reading, 38,* 98–103.

Richardson, J., & Morgan, R. (1994). *Reading to learn in the content areas.* Belmont, CA: Wadsworth.

Trelease, J. (1989). *The new read-aloud handbook.* New York: Viking.

Literature

Juster, N. (1961). *The phantom tollbooth.* New York: Random.

O'Brien, R.C. (1971). *Mrs. Frisby and the rats of Nimh.* New York: Macmillan.

Rutherford, E. (1987). *Sarum: The novel of England.* New York: Crown.

Viorst, J. (1972). *Alexander and the terrible, horrible, no good, very bad day.* Hartford, CT: Atheneum.

Chapter 16

Writing Novels for Discouraged Readers...And Why We Must

Irene Schultz

●◆ There is a yawning abyss in the landscape of children's books, and we have got to fill it. I am going to tell you how to write a new kind of book—the enabling novel—a stepping stone that can give reading success to students who have experienced nothing in reading but hesitancy or failure since fourth grade. How do I know enabling novels work? Because I write them and see them work. Why do we need these books now more than we did before? Because, as the authors in this work have stressed, there are an astonishing number of discouraged readers.

Many young people are living lives far different from the lives of children of the past. Even though we acknowledge this, we fail to embrace the fact that the difference is bound to affect their ability to learn at the pace of previous generations. At a time when such youngsters need new insights and approaches from us, for the most part we are still trying to teach them following the patterns we used 40 years ago. We mistakenly think that for almost all children, past reading frameworks will, and should, apply—the rate at which they will learn, the methods that will reach them, and the materials to which they will respond. But many kids are truly incapable of following the old patterns at the old pace. Their inability absolutely necessitates that we take a realistic approach and form new materials built around their actual pace of development. I do not mean that we should lower our expectations but raise them; these youngsters can eventually reach high levels of reading skill.

We like to think of children nurtured, as many still are, in homes based on shared responsibilities, pretelevision family activities, one adult working at home, a fairly permanent address, and supportive extended family members living nearby. Under those conditions, most children who receive our best old-time shot at the teaching of reading learn to read. If we introduce them to sight vocabulary, oral expression, phonics skills, word

configuration, syllable drill charts, knowledge of affixes, field trips, experience with imaging, stories read aloud, basic writing activities, tactile materials, games, posters, worksheets, puzzles, alluring storybooks, and so
forth, most of these students learn to read by the end of third grade, and
they love doing it.

But how about other children? I am not speaking only of those who
have always learned more slowly due to physical and developmental problems; I am talking about children in stressful life situations. They are still in
a minority, but it is a *gigantic* minority—perhaps 30 percent and growing
larger who tend to fail at reading. Their home backgrounds almost doom
them to an irreverent view of the importance of the written word, inability
to concentrate on a printed page, a jaundiced perception of themselves as
potential readers, and ultimately, to rejection of school. For them, school is
an arena of failure. They walk out of the arena.

Listen to what they have been telling us for years:

• We've been kicked out of our apartment again.

• I've always been the dumbest in my class.

• After school I hide so my brother can't make me smoke grass.

• My folks took me to a midnight movie last night about monsters
that dig into your innards and eat you alive.

• My teacher keeps telling me how smart my brother was in her
class.

• My mother says not to talk about how my arms got black and
blue.

• My homeroom teacher wouldn't give out my birthday treat
because it's homemade.

• Ma says bad readers run in our family.

• Last night this man with a gun ran in the back door and my dad
hid him behind the furnace.

• We always have new uncles come to live with us. The last one
gave us a new color TV.

• I *hate* it when it's my turn to read aloud because the other kids
laugh at me.

• I see my dad sometimes on Sunday afternoons.

• I'm going to be a beauty-shop pin-hander, like my sisters, or a TV
actress.

- My mom's on something, so I'm late again.
- I can't button my coat. No buttons.
- No one's home and I couldn't do that homework without help.
- I live with my aunt. My mom left.
- I'm no good at reading. Anyway, I hate to read.
- Find me a big book with chapters, not a storybook. No, that one's too hard. There's nothing good to read.
- After school, I watch TV every day until my folks get home.

Consider what thoughts dominate their lives, and you begin to understand why some students cannot respond at the rate of others. They are tangled up in the bottom rungs of Maslow's Hierarchy of Needs (Maslow, 1970). Their words point out more eloquently than I can why they will probably develop at a slower pace. They cannot change their lives. It is up to us to make real changes in our teaching if we are to lead them into the joy of reading. And if they do not find the joy of reading, they will never become good readers.

By the end of third grade, discouraged readers have not conquered what Chall (1983) calls the second stage of reading, that crucial step into reading ease that allows a fourth grader to deal with novels and reference books. For them, the "confirmation, fluency, ungluing from the print, does not arrive on time. Unlike their peers, they cannot get into novels, even the so-called "hi-lo" (high interest–low vocabulary) novels; most of these are too difficult for them. They are stuck with reading storybooks with which, on a social level, they can no longer afford to be seen, and which they therefore abandon. They are nine, or maybe ten, and they do not recognize many of the key words in novels; they have not internalized a basic vocabulary.

We mistakenly feel they could have achieved more, should have achieved more. We say they are "performing below their potential." We dub them "reluctant readers" because while we regret we were unable to inspire them, we feel they were resisting our efforts and were not really trying. We taught them, but they did not learn. It is their fault, isn't it? *Wrong!* If they did not learn, we did not teach them. We simply followed useless patterns and ignored their needs.

They did try, with narrowed capacities resulting from the circumstances of their lives, and they wanted desperately to read. Point out the bad actors in a school that serves children of any social, ethnic, and economic background. Round up the villains of the hallway, the smart-alecs of the classrooms, the pinchers and pokers of the library, and I will show you a lot of kids who became outcasts because they hated themselves for being dumb. Regardless of how they scoff at reading, they *want* to read. But they have never read enough simple storybooks to get unglued from the print, because reading necessarily took second place to surviving by stealth or escaping through television.

Success, even in small increments, breeds success. We really make an effort in activities in which we can shine. Yet, some children have never succeeded in reading since their first school year. By the end of third grade, they are failures, emotional dropouts. But they once were willing to read, always wanted to read, still want to read, if only they could. So throw away the phrase "reluctant reader": call them by the more apt phrase "discouraged reader." They do not need to be blamed. They need reading success.

So what if their development is slower than we expected? So what if they cannot read award-winning children's books...or even hi-lo novels? Let's start where they are. Dolch (1953) described the necessary plan of attack: "Secure much interesting reading at present level; reading must be fun; only easy reading is fun; a quantity of reading is necessary" (pp. 46–50). So, first let's determine the discouraged readers' present level. At this point, the end of the third grade, they are too old for storybooks. They crave novels. But they need *extremely* easy-to-read novels that will help them gain what they have missed: success coupled with confirmation of their reading skills. They need escape adventures written at a storybook level and as exciting as TV, novels that will let them see themselves as successful readers so they can experience the joy of reading. And they need our approval when they read. Maybe we cannot kill TV or change their home lives, but we can give them enabling novels, excitement in adventure stories, and the warm glow of our approval—satisfaction for their affective domain.

We educators, even you, must provide these books. Outside writers probably cannot. Few authors understand the specific needs of troubled readers. We do. No one is more capable of writing to meet their needs than we. Many of us have already written for children the many times they needed simplified classroom material. We can write enabling books, and further, it is up to us to find publishers for them. We must take these two new steps, the sooner the better. I became determined to take them years ago. First, I analyzed my students' needs; then I constructed my Woodland Gang stories.

How Do You Start?

You say you want to write but you do not have time to write a whole novel? Do you have time to write 33 words of a story? Write them today. If you can average 33 words a day, by the end of the year, you will have a 12,000 word novel.

Who should your main characters be, and what should your book be about? Because many troubled readers are boys who may not respond to stories about girls, books for them should have some boy heroes with one or two girls...unless you want to write specifically for troubled girl readers, in which case reverse the mix. Have your heroes be just regular, imperfect kids so that your reader discovers that skinny kids, big-mouthed kids, disabled kids, every-colored kids, fat kids, cross-eyed kids, shy kids, or any kid can be triumphant. That is what children who have experienced a lot of failure love to think about and need to think about. So choose any plot that demonstrates that the less able or less perfect kids have courage and can win out.

Support concepts you treasure with the role models you create. Whatever qualities you would like to develop in your readers, develop them in your heroes: love for little children, independence of thought, respect for people different from themselves, curiosity, perseverance, personal warmth, interest in reading, appreciation of what one has, devotion to a hobby, family loyalty, patriotism, and so on. The world of troubled readers is often fraught with frustration and unkindness. Your story will be one of the earliest novels they will read and perhaps one of the most influential. So, be brave: accept the fact that you are not aiming at, or writing, "great children's literature"; instead, you are writing uplifting, captivating, escape literature. Create a world of dependable and kind characters, an exciting dream world on which to set one's sights, a world to which a troubled child can gladly flee.

Settings are important for several reasons. First, certain settings seem to generate excitement and their own emotional charge—for example, caves, trees, ranches with horses, zoos, circuses, tunnels, vast expanses, canyons, hills, mountains, abandoned buildings, run-down places, places at night, beaches, boats, huge cities, museums, riversides, schools, and little country houses. I am sure you can add to the list and will soon discover that various settings, invested with your own experiences, will actually initiate stories for you. Picture a place clearly in your mind; then let your characters roam about in it, and they will begin to act out a tale. Another reason settings are important is that they give readers insight into unfamiliar places. A variety of new settings for a series can instill the idea within a reader that he might eventually move on to other and perhaps better places.

The vocabulary I use comes from three groups of words. First, I use a 1000-word basic vocabulary list, which discouraged readers will internalize as they read the words over and over. Second, I add similarly spelled words that rhyme with phonetic exactness with those on the base list and have only one beginning consonant (if they can read "will" they'll be able to read "bill" but maybe not "shrill"); and third, I include words that discouraged readers have already been exposed to that have emotional impact (children who haven't a firm enough grasp to recognize "when" or "there," read "ghost" and "dinosaur" without hesitation). If you must occasionally introduce an unknown word, use it several times close together so that after someone tells the reader what it is, he or she can remember it. And, if you *have* to introduce a nonphonetic and lengthy word, use a simple system to give the pronunciation. For example, follow "Archeologist" with "(Are-key-OL-oh-jist)." Along these same lines, avoid fancy, nonphonetic names for your characters. Nothing is more discouraging to the student daring to tackle a novel than finding he or she cannot even get the main character's name straight.

Have your lead characters use standard English. Many of your readers will not have consistently encountered examples of standard English, but they do have a few chances to be exposed to it by educators, television, and your books. I have as many people as possible in my books speak "good" English. They do not use dialectical speech; nor do I give them any type of accent. Except when your plot requires a character who speaks otherwise, *stuff* your books with good English. You might increase your readers' appreciation for well-organized speech and chances for future academic success. Who cares if the language is a bit too refined? The idea that "the medium is the message" is too important to be ignored.

Compound words puzzle troubled readers and slow and distort their reading comprehension. A student might sound out "themselves" as "thems elves," and look for elves throughout the story. He or she might end up with "an yone," "now here," or "so me one" derived from "anyone," "nowhere," and "someone." Or, a reader might just take considerable time trying unsuccessfully to decode a compound word, meanwhile not comprehending the story. I realized that troubled readers need first to learn to recognize the individual parts of a compound, and I separated all but the simplest compounds in my books. No one drummed me out of the educational corps—and youngsters fly through the reading. I do not separate a compound word if doing so changes either its pronunciation or its meaning.

Avoid contractions that have counterparts written without apostrophes. Words such as "I'll," "we'll," "he'll," and "she'll" are often misread by troubled readers as "ill," "well," "hell," and "shell," and interrupt the sense of the story. For example, if you write "She'll be here," a child might read "Shell be here." Write "She will be here" instead.

Dependent clauses tend to confuse an unsophisticated reader, so I avoid them. Try to write short kernel sentences, each happening described in simple terms in consecutive order. I tended to complicate my sentence structure and had to keep reminding myself that in writing an enabling novel, I should focus on delivering these things—a sound basic vocabulary, a fast-moving story, and a bushel of self-confidence—rather than examples of the possible complexities of sentence structure.

Troubled readers lose track of who is saying what. Identify each speaker before you give his words. Here is a sample of what confuses and what seems clear on this score:

> *Confusing*
> Sammy said, "Where should we fish?"
> "Over there, near the big old tree. We've caught fish there before," said Bill.
>
> *Clear*
> Sammy said, "Where should we fish?"
> Bill said, "Over there, near the big old tree. We've caught fish there before."

This repetitive form may seem unnecessary to the sophisticated reader, but it is essential to comprehension for the less capable one. And, for the most part, I use only one easily recognized word, "said," rather than using the more descriptive words such as "asked," "exclaimed," "questioned," "explained," and so on. I want my readers to feel fly-through competency with my stories.

Paragraphs in general should be short. Many of them should even be just a sentence or two. Why? Two reasons: reading is more digestible if it is in small doses, and short paragraphs give your page more white relief. Long, descriptive paragraphs are real snore-starters for discouraged readers. Stick to action and conversation, both of which grab their attention. If you want to describe something, do it briefly or let your characters do it through their conversation. Another good rule to follow is to create a new paragraph whenever you can possibly justify doing so and sometimes even when you cannot.

Fill the starting page of each chapter with a big illustration, then use only four or five lines of writing. This makes starting a new chapter seem like a very easy thing for your unsuspecting reader to do, especially if you end each chapter with a cliffhanger.

Generous-sized type is in, but heavy or crowded-looking type is out—too threatening. Make sure the type used for your books is both ample and airy. Think of the type face, size, and weight used in the original Oz books or in the first book of the Boxcar Children series, and insist your publisher give you that. This means you have to arrange beforehand with your publisher for artistic control of your product.

Layout dictates the spacing and is all-important. Children who are not sure of how to read basic words need to be able to see those words as separated, distinct units. Therefore, spacing between letters, within letters, between words, between sentences, between lines, and around the total page of type are all important. I use a maximum—21 lines per page—and generous margins. Here, again, it is important to retain artistic control. Artistic control is not the same thing as the more usual term, artistic *approval*. The latter means that after your publisher has put the book together, you have a chance to tell him or her if you disapprove of something. By then, you are reluctant to change a ready-to-go-to-press layout. On the other hand, artistic *control* allows you to dictate specified factors beforehand. My publishers showed unusual understanding when they agreed to allow me artistic control in these issues. Other publishers will follow their example as they recognize the importance of format to troubled readers.

The length of my novels is based on the needs of my readers. I have settled on novels of about 12,000 words divided into 13 chapters on 128 pages. With this division, children feel they are reading truly full-length novels but can finish a chapter long before they become anxiety ridden. The length satisfies the often-given assignment to read a book of more than 100 pages.

Paper color, sheen, and bulk play a part in your readers' enjoyment. Use paper that is not stark white but slightly antique, and yet not brownish looking. Too-dark paper makes the pages seem old and worn. Too-white paper makes them look brittle and mean, almost threatening. Use paper with considerable bulk rather than thin, hard paper to make the novel fatter. And use a matte finish paper rather than a shiny one. It is easier on the eyes.

Pictures give the reader a chance to rest and can stimulate imaging; yet, fully detailed pictures can inhibit it. I tried to strike a balance with frequent, rather simple, undetailed silhouettes.

Book covers are important in several respects for the troubled reader. First, like any reader of novels, he or she is hoping to find excitement in a book, so the cover picture must convey the impression that something heart-thumping is going on inside. Second, the blurb on the back cover should be only a line or two long and written in large, inviting type, so that she or he receives first off the impression that the book will be easy to read. And, third, the spine of a novel from an easy-to-read series should bear an easily recognized logo that will signal for the discouraged reader all other novels belonging to the series.

Achieving the Successful Enabling Novel

Following are two examples to consider as you write for a discouraged reader. First, here is an excerpt from an unsuccessful hypothetical novel:

> As Osceolo's laughter degenerated into a blood-curdling groan, his companion leaped across the barrier, hauled him to a safe haven inside the empty mansion, and exclaimed, "We'll be in constant danger outside until someone informs the game warden and everyone converges to capture that cougar."

Now I will construct a successful example from this excerpt: first, rename Osceolo. How about the phonetic Oscar?

> Oscar was laughing. The next minute his laugh turned to a scary groan.
> His friend jumped over the fence. He dragged Oscar into the big house. Now they were safe.
> His friend said, "We will stay inside. We have to wait. Some one will tell the police. Every one will have to come together to catch that wild cat. Then it will be safe to go outside."

A final word: use every device you can think of to enable discouraged readers to experience success with your novel. After years of being constant failures, these students have learned to hate themselves. Actually, discouraged readers' greatest need by now is not to learn to read; it is to learn to love themselves, even if they never become good readers. With enabling novels available, perhaps these children can find both a love for reading and for themselves.

References

Chall, J.S. (1983). *Stages of reading development*. New York: McGraw-Hill.
Dolch, E.V. (1953). *Remedial reading*. Champaign, IL: Garrard.

Maslow, A.H. (1970). *Motivation and personality* (2nd ed.). New York: HarperCollins.

Children's Books
Schultz, I. (1989). *Woodland Gang stories.* Boston, MA: Addison-Wesley.
Schultz, I. (1995). *The Woodland Mysteries.* Bothell, WA: The Wright Group.

Chapter 17

Educating Teachers Affectively: Client-Centered Staff Development

Cara L. Garcia

●◆ "This group is going to be quite a challenge," I thought to myself. Some were clearly daydreaming, others were reading, others whispering quietly to their neighbors, and some, thankfully, were alert and ready to learn. A low-achieving class of adolescents? No, not at all: it was a middle school faculty supposedly ready for a staff development session—the classic faculty staff development scenario.

When I am invited to lead a staff development project, I am always mindful of the relevant research.

- Some teachers perceive staff development as a waste of time (Rubeck, 1978).

- The culture of the school places significant pressure to conform on teachers (Ost & Ost, 1988).

- There is a high correlation between teachers' level of need, as indexed by the Maslow Hierarchy of Needs, and their level of use of an innovation (Joyce & McKibbon, 1982).

- Teachers who are the most self-actualized do the best job of implementing an innovation. The opposite is true at the lower levels of the Hierarchy of Needs, where teachers are meeting psychological needs for safety (Hopkins, 1990).

- School change "continues to be a problem of the smallest unit"—that is, the individual teacher (McLaughlin, 1990).

Teachers' affective states are clearly a critical consideration in staff development. Any realistic leader would be well advised to expect a faculty to display a range of attitudes, just as any realistic teacher would expect a range of attitudes in a class. In this regard, the learning situation seems universal. What seems less well understood, however, is *why* people respond to change differently. In this case, why are some teachers eager while others seem threatened by new ideas when they, of all the professionals, deal daily with learning, growth, change, and the ideal of continually seeking the truth through inquiry?

Change Can Be Threatening

A core literature approach to reading, a process approach to composition, holistic scoring rubrics, emergent literacy, invented spelling, portfolio assessment, desktop publishing, and a nonlinear reading experience via hypermedia all signify changes that affect the way we organize, teach, and assess the language arts. And all of these changes are happening *now* at such a rapid pace that it takes enormous energy to keep abreast. Further, these changes are not trivial; they reflect a shift from traditional skills-based, teacher-directed instruction to student-centered instruction in which the students and teachers mutually set the direction, set the pace, and conduct the assessment of instruction and of learning. In short, they cause us to modify our self-concept as well as our teaching behaviors. This is the point at which personality theory intersects educational psychology theory— learning that affects our identity. No wonder such strong affect is associated with staff development.

Even the most enthusiastic, open-to-change, student-centered teacher among us struggles to keep up with the amount, degree, and pace of change in the profession. And the least enthusiastic, resistant-to-change, nonstudent-centered teacher among us is sure to be threatened, feel overwhelmed, and experience the abandonment of being left behind.

A Client-Centered Approach to Staff Development

Because the amount, degree, and pace of change can be threatening, successful leadership realizes that the staff development program for a faculty must be client centered if the innovations in the field are to have enduring effects in teaching practices. A client-centered approach is a term that has migrated into education from the person-centered psychology of Carl Rogers (1969). Active, or reflective, listening is the hallmark of all humanistic communication in psychology and education. It is considered the absolute requisite communication skill of anyone in the helping professions. Psychologists use active listening to be supportive when clients are expressing their problems and speculating about how they might solve them. They do not advise; they reflect ideas back to the clients by following whatever direction, at whatever pace, that the client's thinking takes and trusting that the client is ultimately the only one who has the answers to his or her problems. They check periodically to see if the client is satisfied with the resolutions arrived at in the therapy sessions, thus including the client in the assessment of the therapy.

The client-centered approach in education has been termed "student centeredness," but it maintains the same characteristics: the teacher is a supportive person, a facilitator who trusts that the students have the critical thinking potential to engage in academic problem solving with the support of the teacher. Student-centered teachers will commonly use cooperative learning groups combined with an interdisciplinary project approach to instruction. They will include the students in setting the direction of the instruction through the selection of their project topics and include students in the pacing and assessment of the work.

Using the student-centered approach in the area of staff development means that the leader includes the teachers in setting the direction of the program through needs assessment surveys, includes teachers in the pace of the program by requesting continual feedback, and includes them in the assessment of the staff development through evaluation surveys. This method of staff development implies a certain type of individualized instruction because teachers must follow their own interests, go at their own pace, and determine their own level of satisfaction with the sure knowledge that the staff development leader will provide support.

Client-Centered Staff Development: The Alhambra Schools Project

The Alhambra city schools are located east of downtown Los Angeles, California. The district is multicultural, middle class, and has a low transience rate. In 1987 the district received the first of five years of funding to establish a model technology project at Emery Park Elementary School (K–8) and Alhambra High School. The theme of the project is "student centeredness in a technology-rich environment." Pepperdine University is a partner in the project, and I have served as a staff development leader.

Staff development for the project has involved teachers as learners. We support them as they pursue the goal of shifting from teacher-directed, textbook-based instruction to student-centered instruction using cooperative learning groups and interdisciplinary projects in which technology is used as a problem-solving tool. The teachers have been overwhelmed by the simultaneous shift in philosophy and the need to integrate technology into the curriculum. The following scenario has been the most common in the project.

Mrs. Smith wants to make a videotape of a newscast with her students. As a novice, she plans the project with help from the Model Technology Schools staff. They help her learn how to run the camera and play back the tape on the VCR. They make sure that she knows which teachers and students nearby will also help her if she encounters a problem. They also cover how the project is related to various state frameworks and district objectives. The consultant asks Mrs. Smith when she thinks she will be able to begin the project with her students, and she sets a time based on her own need to be comfortable with the equipment.

When Mrs. Smith is ready, she enters the intermediate phase of her growth by taking her new knowledge to the classroom. She explains the project to the students as an assignment, puts them in small groups, and has them write their articles for the newscast. They visit the computer lab and word-process their scripts. After two lab visits, the scripts are not finished. At this point, Mrs. Smith tells the consultant that she feels disorganized and out of control; she feels the project is taking over her whole class. Further, the project is taking much longer than she had anticipated. The consultant articulates her ambivalence: she is torn between wanting to do the project, which is going well albeit slowly, and anticipating that it will take so long that she will not cover all the material that she is supposed to for her grade level. The consultant talks with her until she sets limits on the time that she will give to the project. Mrs. Smith then feels relief and in control again. They also discuss how much more the students seem to be learning in the newscast project than Mrs. Smith initially thought. This helps her realize the project's value, and at the end of the discussion, she has a plan that she feels comfortable with. Mrs. Smith also decides that she needs the consultant to come to her room on the day of the "shoot," and this seems to give her more motivation to get the students ready.

She assigns various tasks to small groups or individual students: responsibility for script, makeup, set, camera, sound, and lights. They practice, review, discuss, and then revise. It goes well, and although the amount and intensity of activity is a difficult adjustment for her, the increased enthusiasm of the students interests her. They persevere and make their tape. At the request of the consultant they have a "showing" to another class. Mrs. Smith discusses with her students how well the project went, mostly giving her own evaluation but involving them somewhat in self-assessment.

For the next unit, Mrs. Smith involves the students more in the actual planning, scheduling, and production of the videotape. They build on what they learned from their first experience, which promotes self-direction and self-pacing. When Mrs. Smith is discussing these experiences with the consultant, she states that what she learned about the students was that they could do more than she had initially thought they could. What she learned about herself was that it was more difficult to give up her teacher-directed control on the class than she thought it would be.

Mrs. Smith, after two projects, is now a self-assessed videotape "sophisticate," who is willing to guide novice colleagues through a video-taping project.

This example illustrates a client-centered staff development model. As the students in staff development, teachers are supported as they do the following:

- **Self-assess** their abilities with technology, student centeredness, and even subject matter. Using the developmental terminology of the project, Mrs. Smith declared herself a *novice*, next an *intermediate*, and finally a *sophisticate* at making a newscast.

- **Self-direct** their growth in technology, student centeredness, and subject matter by selecting areas of interest they wish to pursue. Mrs. Smith generated her own project, which led her to learn how to use the camcorder, VCR, and word-processor. She may spend considerable time on the project before learning about databases, spreadsheets, telecommunications, or any other technology or forms of student centeredness that are part of the school culture.

- **Self-pace** their growth by setting milestones within the developmental model in which they learn on their own, experiment with an innovation in their teaching, and then guide a novice colleague. Mrs. Smith decided she needed several weeks as a novice and several months for two rounds of newscast projects before she could help a colleague.

The client-centered approach follows whatever project is of immediate personal relevance to the teacher, trusts that a shift will occur in the teacher's perception of students' capacities, and considers this the major indicator of lasting change. This is a paradigm shift from positivism to relativism, similar to the shift that many teachers have made from skills-based reading instruction to a whole language approach.

The Paradoxical Nature of Change

In my staff-development projects, informal dialogue between support staff and teachers is monitored for indicators of growth toward student centeredness. The process of facilitating a teacher's growth consists of the following elements (not in any linear progression):

- Identify the teacher's position on an issue. When the position is split, discuss in such a way to clarify the pros and cons of the matter. For example, Mrs. Smith struggled with "I see the value, but this is taking too long."

- Lead discussion to see the balance of enthusiasm for each side of the issue. Mrs. Smith's ambivalence was an even split, and she might have agonized throughout the entire project if she had not resolved her dilemma and set some limits.

- Facilitate a synthesis by fully exploring each aspect of the dilemma. For example, Mrs. Smith spent time reflecting on how much the students were learning so she could appreciate the use of a project approach. Then she reflected on her imperative to cover the curriculum, and she identified with the efficiency and control of that approach.

- Let a synthesis emerge from the teacher's exploration of the dilemma; trust that the teacher is capable of generating his or her own resolution. Making suggestions or recommendations to Mrs. Smith ("The teacher next door could help you" or "Everybody is scared at first, but they get over it. You will, too") would be less effective than asking an open-ended question such as, "How can you adjust your plans to do the project at a pace that is comfortable for you?"

This model of change is informed by the paradoxical model that is common to most humanistic forms of psychotherapy in which therapists facilitate major life changes of their clients. It is still a rare model in educational contexts, however natural it might seem to teachers who are concerned with affect and process in the language arts. The change process involves examining the thesis and antithesis of a dilemma, to prompt synthesis. Gestalt theory asserts that when an experience or point of reference at one pole of a dilemma (the thesis) is closed or finished, it recedes from foreground to background, and its polar opposite (the antithesis), which serves as the context, emerges from background to foreground to be finished. Then, after shuttling back and forth between thesis and antithesis, neither of which the person can totally identify with, the person may generate a compromise—the synthesis—which is the choice that best meets the person's need (Perls, Hefferline, & Goodman, 1951). This is the paradoxical theory of change: a person changes not by becoming who he thinks he should be—that would only be one pole—but by becoming more fully who he is—that involves the synthesis of both sides of the dilemma (Beisser, 1971). The dialectic process is the model of healthy functioning used in Gestalt psychology, one of the origins of modern cognitive psychology. The dialectic may be likened to a form of conflict resolution with one important difference: one aspect of the conflict is awareness (the thesis) and one aspect is unawareness (the antithesis). Through facilitation, the antithesis can be brought to awareness, clarifying the conflict so it can be resolved.

This dialectic process is the model of health underlying Gestalt psychotherapy. It calls for facilitation rather than suggestion, for dialogue rather than advice, and for process not content. By facilitating the emergence, experience, and resolution of thesis and antithesis into synthesis, the facilitator is involved only with the person's process, not the person's content. Thus the person generates his or her own alternatives and resolution.

Often a teacher is only aware of one pole, or thesis, at the time dialogue begins. Without the intervention of a facilitator, the person might drop the matter without exploring any alternatives (antitheses) and remain unsatisfied and unresolved about it (unsynthesized, unfinished), perhaps attempting to do what he thinks he should without regard for his own interests. This is the pattern of the overly compliant and the perfectionist. In the earlier example, if Mrs. Smith had focused only on her initial feelings of disorganization, lack of control, and concern about time, she might have decided that she was "no good" with technology or that technology is too demanding. She might then have stuck with her original schedule simply to comply with it and curtailed or abandoned the project "due to technological difficulties." Instead, she worked with the staff development facilitator to discover that she was equally concerned with her learning goals for the project. When she considered time versus learning, she modified her timeline and resolved her conflict. Her conflict is not uncommon: teachers do lose track of learning goals because they believe they should cover the curriculum as originally planned.

To facilitate the resolution of the dilemma, the facilitator seeks to heighten the person's experience of whichever aspect of the matter the person is aware of, which means starting from where the teacher is and moving from there to antithesis and synthesis.

Validating Student Centeredness

Here is an example of facilitating a primary grade teacher's awareness of how she is intuitively student centered. This teacher has never expressed any difficulty using a project approach to the curriculum in which she integrates language arts, math, science, and social studies, nor has she had difficulty in involving students in self-direction, self-pacing, and self-assessment. Occasionally she complains good naturedly, wondering why she teaches this way.

Facilitating this teacher's experience of instructional change is a matter of validating her professional decisions and providing a theoretical basis for her actions, bringing intuition to conscious level. It is assumed that such facilitation will promote her independence from the support staff. Change for this teacher involves her integrating technology into her usual project-based instructional program.

This excerpt in the following dialogue (indicating the conversation between the teacher and consultant with occasional explanations of the questions or comments in the righthand column) is similar to a therapy session during which the client asks the therapist to listen, articulate, and thereby confirm the client's perceptions. Dreyfuss and Dreyfuss (1986) have indicated that the difference between experts in any field and nonexperts is that the former can articulate the theory by which they act.

Scenario: The teacher has just finished describing a project on space that she and her students have completed. They read books about space and discussed life in space; they discussed space clips from laser discs; they visited Rockwell Space Systems in California and went in a capsule; they collaborated with another class on a huge space station mural.

Consultant: Let's see, there was a lot of student choice, so that would cover self-direction. [*Seeking to identify the aspects of student centeredness and perhaps elicit any ambivalence that the teacher has with the philosophy of student centeredness.*]

Teacher: Yes...

Consultant: Self-pacing, um...How do children let you know they need to speed up or slow down? They must have their own way of communicating their pacing needs to you.

Teacher: Slow down is, "Again?" when I tell them what we're doing. And I say, "Okay, okay, what do you need?" "I'm bored," they'll say.

So I say, "Okay, let's go look and see." I mean you have to go see why they're bored. Maybe some kid is hogging all the material and not letting this kid do something.

So you just really can't take their word for it; I mean, not that they're not telling you the truth....[*No hesitation here: she knows exactly how this is communicated by her students and exactly how she responds.*]

Consultant: You just want to look into it.

Teacher: Yes, and then maybe you feel, "Yes, that's pretty nice. That's as far as you can go." Or maybe they're thinking along a bigger line, and they can't do that, and you have to say, "That's too much." It can be too intricate for them.

Consultant: Or maybe they're lost in the parts and can't see the bigger picture.

Teacher: Yes, and you have to keep in mind that each class is different, too. Like last year's class really liked getting into details, but this one doesn't. [*Here again, she shows that she has a strong, integrated focus for teaching primary level.*]

Consultant: In a way, there's an element of self-assessment built into their statements of self-direction. In order to make a choice, you have to decide if something is preferable to something else, same with self-pacing. There's preference built into the pacing—"Do we have to do that again?"

Teacher: You have to ask, "Do you think this is finished? Does this look done? Is this like what we saw at Rockwell or on the laser disc?" I say, "We have to talk about what you want to do, what you need." They try more, and then they say, "Yeah, that does look better." I probably should have brought the laser disc out again to show them, but I didn't.

Consultant: Well, that's the next thing I wanted to ask you about. What would you do differently if you had it to do over again?

Although the consultant's work with this teacher required no exploration of a dilemma, no long dialogue to elicit contradictions, and no struggle to resolve thesis and antithesis into synthesis, such is not always the case.

Double Message or Not?

The next episode will show how subtle the dilemma can be and implies that it can take considerable time and an extended dialogue to elicit thesis and antithesis before any synthesis begins.

In the teacher's lounge, the consultant broaches the topic of student centeredness with a high school language teacher who, in the course of working with the consultant on developing a module, had made a comment about student centeredness being of limited value for certain disciplines.

Consultant: Could I talk to you for a minute about something that's been puzzling me ever since we worked together on your module? [*Stating an honest "I message" on the assumption that any contrived reason would be sensed by the teacher.*]

Teacher: Sure. I want an excuse not to grade these papers anyway.

Consultant: Well, a comment you made has been on my mind. I think I understood you to say—correct me if I'm wrong—that student centeredness is of limited value for some subjects. That puzzles me because you keep coming up with student-centered projects. Enlighten me! [*Seeking to get more information, to explore the objections to student centeredness.*]

Teacher: [laughing] Well, student centeredness takes so much time to do the projects. The students get a lot but they're not learning the language. The projects are more cultural things. [*It appears that there are two different "tracks" in the class—a project track and a learning-the-language track—and each has its own philosophy.*]

For example, when I take my students to the Mac lab, they write in English because they are not ready to write in the foreign language. Their foreign language would be horrible. [*No evidence of a belief that writing as a process might bring about improved skill with the foreign language, perhaps getting students to use their texts as a reference in the lab.*]

As a teacher, I've always done the outside thing. Learning the language is only a part of the course. I've always done films, field trips, and reports to make it interesting. [*Here's the confirmation that there are two tracks—the projects are "outside."*]

I don't know if I'm getting this across.

Consultant: [nodding in agreement] I think I understand.

Teacher: I've done student-centered things on the perimeter. I can't make a lot of the class student centered. I have to do grammar, too. I don't like cooperative learning for language skills. They need an expert to correct their mistakes before they become a habit. [*Here are the reasons for dual philosophies: 1. Student centeredness is too slow and makes it difficult to cover the content of the course. 2. Language learning requires a teacher-directed approach, implying that the students are not capable of peer teaching.*]

Consultant: So you're a middle-of-the-roader—philosophically between student centeredness and teacher directedness. [*Trying to reflect back what the teacher had said. This is not quite accurate, in retrospect.*]

Teacher: Well, I've taught for 30 years in California, and I believe that this will pass, too. We can take what's good from it. It will help students prepare for the new society. Actually, I only accept typed papers in class now, and most of them are word-processed. [*The content of this response seems defensive, but the teacher's voice was not at all defensive, more reflective and still warm.*]

At the same time, I don't throw out vocabulary and grammar: those are shortcuts to learning the language. And I don't like the oral approach.

I think I've been student centered all along. My record over the years shows I've been doing cooperative learning before it was even called that. [*Here's an area to pursue: some ambivalence in her opinion of cooperative learning. Earlier she criticized it but now is identifying with it.*]

I just don't advertise myself. I have a reputation for being a hard teacher, and the students say that the class is hard because there's so much besides the foreign language. [*Again, the content seems defensive, but the tone was not.*]

I think that they have to know the grammar, but they also have to play with the language.

Consultant: [pause] I think I understand your thinking. I'd like to think over what you've said and come back another time to talk more. Would that be okay with you? [*Feeling appreciative that the teacher has opened up but rather confused at how the teacher perceives the curriculum and the students.*]

Teacher: [shrugging] Sure.

At a deep level, this teacher seems to believe that students need an expert, a teacher-directed approach for language skills. She appears to believe in language instruction through habit formation, a position popularized by behaviorism. If she were asked to consider that all students are thought by cognitive psychologists to learn their native language without experts and with the assistance of their peers, she would probably raise the counterpoint of the time issue in the class. In other words, she would most likely concede that it is possible to learn a language in a student-centered fashion but not in the time she has in a high school class.

Facilitating this teacher's coping with instructional change for foreign language instruction will be a challenge. She is not like other teachers who have always wanted permission to be more student centered in their teaching: she has already decided what its place is. Yet she requested that the consultant arrange for her students to telecommunicate in the foreign language to the elementary site. She gave them an assignment to "write a letter to someone that they don't know." The consultant will monitor the telecommunication project to determine if the students show signs of learning grammar and vocabulary as they prepare their letters. The consultant believes that this will indeed happen and will discuss with the teacher how a project might cover less systematically what the teacher systematically covers through direct instruction.

The consultant is getting a double message from this teacher, who is acting more and more student centered while simultaneously insisting that these activities are "outside" and "peripheral." Ongoing dialogue will be essential for both the consultant and teacher to clarify when, where, and how much student centeredness this teacher really wants in her classes.

Growing Pains

The next example shows how threatening and painful it can be for a teacher to go through the change process when direction is not truly self-direction.

The site coordinator has asked the consultant to meet with a special education teacher whose students want to use the computer in her room. The site coordinator mentions that the teacher may be interested in a language experience software program, which the consultant has shown to some of the primary teachers.

Scenario: *The consultant approaches the teacher in the teacher's lounge.*

Consultant: Hi! I heard that you are interested in looking at some software for your students, something with a language experience approach?

Teacher: Oh, I don't know. I don't see that these kids are ever going to have computers in their lives. [*Here is a clear statement of resistance to involvement in the project.*]

Consultant: Well, if they have jobs, they'll probably have to deal with computers. [*Caught off-guard, feeling defensive.*]

The situation that we're in right now is that the visitors will be asking for what we are modeling in special ed, and we need to have something to tell them. [*Makes a mildly threatening statement.*]

Teacher: Yes, I know. [*Tone of reluctance in voice.*]

Consultant: Kath said you were interested in language experience. Would you like a program that lets you take dictation from a group of your students, print it out as a booklet, and use that to work on a basic sight-word vocabulary instead of worksheets? [*Attempting to refocus on the purpose of this conversation.*]

Teacher: No, most of my kids can read. They know word-processing.

I have to follow my program with them. That's mostly individual work with them that they bring from their teacher, but I do have a "citizenship" project where they write an essay. Most of them got that done. [*Here's an "I'm different" statement that often implies a request for different treatment, resisting conforming to the project goals.*]

Consultant: Well, would you like to try the language experience software when you do that project the next time, and see if you like that approach any better? Maybe the kids who didn't do the assignment could do it using a language experience approach where they dictate their ideas to you. [*Trying to point out how her strategy left some needs unmet and how these needs might be met next time.*]

Teacher: Yeah, that sounds all right. I don't know when I'll be doing that again. [*Voice dead, content says, "Yes...no"— clearly ambivalent.*]

Consultant: Do you not want to do this? [*Here is an attempt to reach "no" or "not yet" to clarify at least one pole of the ambivalence.*]

Teacher: [quietly, looking down at the table] No. [*The clarification was successful because the other pole, the antithesis, emerges. Now we have the classic Gestalt split between want and should. Resolution is possible.*]

Consultant: I see you want to do this but are concerned about how this fits in. [*Articulating her perceptions of the poles of the dilemma. She can identify with both want and should but not with either completely. She needs to generate her own synthesis, something she can relate to.*]

Teacher: [nods and shrugs]. *Confirmation.*

Consultant: Would you like to try an experiment, and we can talk about how it goes for the kids and for you? You can see if it is easy enough to do and fits your program. If it doesn't, we can stop and regroup. [*This is a suggestion, but a process-oriented one rather than a content-oriented one such as "Why not try 'My Words.' Your kids will love it." It is also an honest, open-ended experiment to be facilitated with unknown results.*]

Teacher: [nods.] [*Looking at her lunch.*]

Consultant: There's a program that gets kids involved with real-life issues such as drinking, child abuse, stealing, AIDS, and so on. The kids have to decide how to handle these issues. Would that be something that you'd be interested in? [*Showing that I'm not giving up and going away, nor am I telling her what to do. My voice gets very low and soft as I imagine the discomfort and pain that she is feeling. When I mention the issues, she catches my eye, and I see a flash of interest.*]

Teacher: Now that's something that my kids would like.

Consultant: I'll be here again on Friday. Can I run it with you in your room at 10:00?

Teacher: Yes, okay, sounds good. [*Not sure if she's responding to the idea of the software or to her idea that I am persisting until I get a response. Sounds somewhat sincere... maybe relieved.*]

Consultant: Great! See you then!

This teacher's experience of change was facilitated by taking her further in the direction that she was going until she had enough of that direction and the opposite emerged. This is the paradoxical change as it occurs. The experiment may give her the safety to look at both poles of her dilemma and create a middle ground for herself, neither capitulating to the project simply because she made a commitment nor continuing with the hope that the project will all go away. She may find a way to involve herself comfortably so she is participating in a way that makes sense to her.

Since the time this dialogue took place, this teacher has used the suggested software with her students in groups. She told the consultant that the students are doing well with the program. Such satisfaction implies that she has reached a synthesis, resolving her split. Since then, the site coordinator reports that this teacher has scheduled two visits to other sites and spent several hours previewing software in the lab on a Friday afternoon after school.

This teacher's experience of change appeared to be confusion until dialogue helped her identify, articulate, and confront her own doubts and her response to what was expected of her. Her experiment appears to have been successful.

A Conflicted Teacher?

The next segment shows a dialogue where a synthesis appears to happen so quickly that it leaves the consultant puzzling over what the dilemma must have been.

Scenario: In the computer lab, the clerk has directed the teacher to a drill-and-practice program. The teacher is thumbing through the manual. The training consultant is seated nearby and overhears the following dialogue.

Teacher: Do you have anything that's marked for special education?

Clerk: Not really.

Consultant: The special ed. teacher likes this one—it's language-experience based. Are you looking for something for language or speech? [*Fears that the teacher wants to assign drill-and-practice software instead of tool software; would only recommend drill-and-practice software if the students were choosing to use it to drill themselves.*]

Teacher: Well, I'm looking for something that special ed. kids can do. [*I infer that she believes that special ed. kids can't use the "tool" software that we recommend.*]

Consultant: Most of the research indicates that special education kids do okay with regular software. [*I make a poor argument for why we don't have any software marked special ed. A more honest response would have been to say what was on my mind—we recommend tool software for everyone. At the moment it was difficult for me to articulate my belief directly.*]

> Teacher: Anything in verbal reasoning? Like verbal analogies? [*Suddenly the teacher asks for software that would likely be much more open ended, much more student centered. Did she shift from what sounded like a teacher-directed preference, or was that what she thought she should ask for when all along what she wanted was student centered? Was my remark pertinent to any shift she may have made?*]
>
> Consultant: Yeah, I think Sunburst Software specializes in that. [Shows copy of software on critical attributes]. How about this? [*I'm playing it cool, but my mind is reeling.*]
>
> Teacher: Yes, this is great!
>
> Consultant: Could we talk more later about what you're looking for? [*I promise myself to be more honest—later.*]
>
> Teacher: Okay.

It is not easy to change, and it is not easy to facilitate change. The facilitator, who has his or her own agenda in a project such as the one going on in Alhambra, can be defensive or confused until there is a dialogue that explains what both parties—teacher and facilitator—are thinking and feeling.

A Look Toward the Future

When the change process inherent in staff development becomes threatening, staff development leaders can employ a client-centered approach to reduce or resolve the threat. In this chapter, the dialectical dialogue was presented as a means for leaders to facilitate conflict resolution on an individual basis. Dialectical dialogues from the Alhambra project were analyzed to point out the complexities that teachers experience as they change.

I recommend that staff development leaders experiment with dialectical dialogues in conducting informal staff development in their projects. Such dialogues can help us document how complex the change process is; when we can point to the hard-won resolutions of individuals, we are indeed pointing to reform efforts at the most fundamental level, showing the progress on a person-by-person basis toward the larger goals at which staff development is aimed.

References

Beisser, A. (1971). The paradoxical theory of change. In J. Fagan & I.L. Shepherd (Eds.), *Gestalt therapy now* (pp. 77–80). New York: HarperCollins.

Dreyfuss, H., & Dreyfuss, S. (1986, January). Why computers may never think like people. *Technology Review, 89*(1), 42–61.

Garcia, C.L. (1986). Extending reading tradition: An educational therapy approach. *Reading Psychology, 7*(4), 305–311.

Hopkins, D. (1990). Integrating staff development and school improvement: A study of teacher personality and school climate. In B. Joyce (Ed.), *Changing school culture through staff development.* Yearbook of the Association for Supervision and Curriculum Development. Alexandria, VA: Association for Supervision and Curriculum Development.

Joyce, B., & McKibbon, M. (1982). Teacher growth states and school environments. *Educational Leadership, 40*(2), 36–41.

McLaughlin, M.W. (1990, December). The Rand change agent study revisited: Macro perspectives and micro realities. *Educational Researcher, 19*(9), 11–16.

Ost, D.L., & Ost, L.J. (1988). The culture of teaching: Implications for staff development. *Journal of Staff Development, 9*(3), 50–55.

Perls, F.S., Hefferline, R.E., & Goodman, P. (1951). *Gestalt therapy: Excitement and growth in the human personality.* New York: Dell.

Rogers, C.R. (1969). *Freedom to learn: A view of what education might become.* Columbus, OH: Merrill.

Rubeck, P. (1978). How to conduct effective inservice reading programs. *Reading Improvement, 15*(3), 170–171.

Acknowledgments

Preparation of this article was supported in part by the Alhambra Model Technology Schools project, California State Department of Education #03751316.

EPILOGUE

The Need for Affective Literates

*A truly good book teaches me
better than to read it. I must
soon lay it down and com-
mence living on its hint....
What I began by reading,
I must finish by acting.*

H.D. Thoreau

The Need for Affective Literates

Larry Mikulecky

●◆ The preceding chapters have examined the lifelong love of reading from many perspectives, from societal demands to theoretical models for acquiring positive literacy attitudes to a host of teacher-tested methods for developing positive literacy habits and attitudes. Parents, teachers, adolescents, children, and society have all been examined for the roles they play in fostering a love of literacy.

Research I have done over the past decade with adolescents and adults suggests a few additional reasons and perspectives for giving high priority to developing lifelong literacy habits and a love of literacy. These reasons involve the concepts of learning loss and perceived self-efficacy with literacy—each of which is related to the regular practice and enjoyment of literacy.

Learning Loss

A few years ago, I was involved with a program to help stem literacy loss among adolescents two or more years behind their peers in reading ability (Mikulecky, 1990). We found that students from the bottom 25 percent of classes read very little during school, did little reading in the evenings, and read virtually nothing during the summers when they could choose how their time was spent. As a result, test scores during a two-year period actually showed a decline in reading ability. Students improved slightly while in school when they were forced to read the small amount they could not avoid. Over the summers, the modest reading abilities they possessed declined rapidly to the point where they lost more over the summer than they had gained the previous year. Sixteen-year-olds who chose not to read were better readers when they had been two years younger.

This learning loss is not surprising when one looks closely at how reading is used in school and after school. Numerous studies document the fact that most adolescents engage in almost no literacy in school and even less for homework. Data that indicate that most high school students perform little reading and writing related to class work have been consistent for more than a decade. In 1981 Applebee reported that only 3 percent of student writing was as long as a paragraph, and the majority of writing was in response to text or worksheet questions. Most of the information in school is distributed through lecture or teacher-dominated discussion, and what reading does occur is primarily for the purpose of answering short worksheet or end-of-chapter questions. Goodlad's (1983) observations of more than 1000 classrooms indicate that at least 70 percent of student time is spent listening, and the majority of this listening is to teacher talk. There is very little time for practicing reading or writing, let alone enjoying it.

Some teachers suggest hopefully that literacy practice occurs at home during homework. Recent results of the U.S. National Assessment of Educational Progress survey of adolescent homework patterns suggest this is misplaced hope for most students (Langer et al., 1990). Nearly 30 percent of 8th graders do less than a half-hour of homework daily, and by grade 12, nearly 40 percent of students do less than a half-hour of homework daily. The assessment also surveyed the amount of homework reading completed each day: for all their classes combined, 61 percent of 8th graders reported reading fewer than 10 pages each day; more than 30 percent read fewer than 5 pages. These figures remain essentially the same for 12th graders. Fifty-six percent reported reading fewer than 10 pages daily with more than 30 percent reading fewer than 5. The majority of students currently do not receive very much literacy practice either in school or while doing homework. Discussion of the quality of the 5 to 10 pages of daily reading engaged in by these students is another issue, which has been addressed throughout this book.

For the 30 percent of students who read fewer than 5 pages daily during the school year and virtually nothing during summers, the decline in abilities appears likely to continue. No positive reading habit has been developed, and literacy is, to a great extent, a "use it or lose it" capability. One-sided education that does not address both attitude and habit on the one hand and skills on the other appears to be a waste of time. Gains are minimal, they do not last, and the side effects of learning to dislike literacy may be detrimental to a society that requires lifelong learning.

In addition to working with adolescents, I work regularly with adults in workplaces and adult literacy programs. In each of these settings, I have had many opportunities to talk with high school graduates whose literacy abilities have declined—many to the point where they read less well than an average 12-year-old child. Some have read little beyond minimal requirements for decades. These adults often mention not practicing reading much since school, hating to read, and feeling particularly inadequate about succeeding in print-centered activities. As society's literacy demands increase, these adults find themselves ill prepared, both intellectually and emotionally, for what they must do to lead productive, balanced lives. Their education has failed them, in part, because they have never developed a literacy habit.

Attitude, Habit, and Perceived Self-Efficacy

During the past three years, I have worked extensively on a model to evaluate the broad impact of adult literacy programs. The model is partially based on a conception of literacy that embraces not only literacy skills, but also literacy beliefs, practices, and aspirations. Lytle's (1990) Beliefs, Practices, Processes, and Plans framework for categorizing changes in adults' relationships to literacy serves as a major element of the model, which directs programs to assess literacy behaviors, skills, and attitudes. This broad framework makes it possible to determine the effect of literacy education throughout life. This model is discussed in detail in Mikulecky and Lloyd (1992). Interviews, questionnaire items, and custom-designed literacy tests assess learner changes in various areas, which are outlined following.

Beliefs

- perceptions of what is a literate individual
- perceptions of self as literate
- aspirations toward becoming more literate

Practices

- amount and types of reading and writing at home
- amount and types of reading and writing at work

Processes and Abilities

- literacy strategies employed in think-aloud scenarios (for example, "When reading this newsletter or this graph, what would you do first, then next?")
- literacy comprehension of a range of materials using questions developed following a pattern for custom-designing literacy tests
- cloze test scores derived from learner-specific materials

- standardized tests, if general literacy is a program goal

Plans

- plans for self at one-, five-, and ten-year intervals
- perceptions of literacy and education in those plans

Family Literacy

- literacy materials available in the home
- literacy practices with one's children
- general literacy practices and modeling at home

In workplace programs, the following areas are also assessed:

Productivity

- anchored supervisor ratings of job performance related to literacy and basic skills
- attendance
- safety
- productivity suggestions made and approved
- disciplinary measures and grievances

The framework involves a mixture of interview and questionnaire items that are common across sites and are clear guidelines for developing parallel custom-designed assessments of learner literacy performance.

There is a twofold rationale for assessing attitudinal changes in relation to literacy *beliefs* and *plans*. What learners believe about their own literacy matters. Bandura's (1989) research on self-efficacy indicates that learners with high perceptions of their own abilities tend to try harder, continue in the face of obstacles, and succeed more often than learners of comparable tested ability but lower senses of personal effectiveness with literacy. Learners with low perceptions of personal effectiveness tend to subvert their own efforts with self-doubt and excuses for quitting. Low-literate adults tend to have exceptionally low and narrow visions of their own literacy abilities. These perceptions were nearly always developed in schools. Programs that help learners develop broader, more accurate senses of what it means to be literate and more detailed personal educational plans are more likely to encourage those learners to use literacy outside of classrooms and continue learning after the completion of a brief class.

In the areas of *literacy practices* and *family literacy,* questionnaire and interview items assess literacy activities over a specified period (usually seven days). It is possible to quantify results in terms of breadth, depth, and frequency of activities. Because literacy improvement takes much time, it is very important to determine if instruction increases literacy practice in the workplace, the home, and with one's family. Schools might also do well to examine their effect on these literacy habit areas. Programs that foster literacy practice only in classrooms are severely limited in terms of expected learner gain; they simply cannot provide enough practice time to accomplish very much.

This model has now been used with several hundred adults in adult literacy programs and workplace literacy programs across the United States. The most effective programs, in terms of learner gains, address attitudes and practices as well as skills. Learners who receive regular feedback on their growing competence and who read outside of class in areas they care about develop stronger senses of their own effectiveness. They practice more, expand their aspirations for more education, and improve in ability. In fact, Bandura's (1989) research indicates that learners' own changed self-images lend them the attitudinal strength to keep trying with difficult tasks and to eventually outperform their less confident but slightly more skilled colleagues.

The Importance of Working in the Affective Domain

Love of literacy makes life richer, but it is much more important than that. Developing the habit of lifelong literacy helps ensure that our educational efforts are not wasted and that short-term literacy gains in school are not lost through disuse over summers and indeed throughout life. One-sided education that ignores fostering positive reading habits and attitudes is a potential danger to us all. It squanders resources through attempting to teach narrow skills, which will be rapidly lost by a large percentage of students. It also develops negative literacy habits and attitudes, which nearly guarantee that many students will be ill suited for life in a developed nation.

When we take part in shaping adults and adolescents who avoid reading, who are convinced they are not very good at it and who do not plan to change, we help develop people who have few choices in our global economy. Their problem is not theirs alone, because they are condemned to no jobs or very low-wage jobs that cannot pay the taxes communities need to prosper. In addition, the ambiguous to negative literacy models they provide their children make the challenge faced by elementary school teachers even greater. As has been the case in schools for the past several decades, *what we do matters*. We daily sow the seeds of our future problems and solutions. Improving literacy habits and love of literacy is clearly an integral part of the solution and central to the world most of us want to inhabit.

References

Applebee, A. (1981). *Writing in the secondary school.* Urbana, IL: National Council of Teachers of English.

Bandura, A. (1989). Regulation of cognitive processes through perceived self efficacy. *Developmental Psychology, 25*(5), 729–735.

Goodlad, J.I. (1983). *A place called school.* New York: McGraw-Hill.

Langer, J., Applebee, A., Mullis, I., & Foertsch, M. (1990). *Learning to read in our nation's schools.* Princeton, NJ: National Assessment of Educational Progress, Educational Testing Service.

Lytle, S.L. (1990). *Living literacy: The practices and beliefs of adult learners.* Paper presented at an Invited Symposium of the Language Development Special Interest Group entitled "Adult literacy/Child literacy: One world or worlds apart," American Educational Research Association Annual Meeting, Boston, MA.

Mikulecky, L.J. (1990). Stopping summer learning loss among at-risk youth. *Journal of Reading, 33*(7), 516–521.

Mikulecky, L.J., & Lloyd, D.P. (1992). *Evaluating the impact of workplace literacy programs: Results and instruments from the National Committee for Adult Literacy Workplace Literacy Impact Project.* Bloomington, IN: Indiana University School of Education.

Bibliography

ADLER, M.J., & VAN DOREN, C.L. (1972). *How to read a book* (rev. ed.). New York: Simon & Schuster.

ANRIG, G., & LAPOINTE, A.E. (1989). What we know about what students don't know. *Educational Leadership, 47*(3), 4–5, 7–9.

ARNOLDSEN, L.M. (1982). Reading made necessary, naturally! *Journal of Reading, 25,* 538–542.

ATHEY, I. (1970). Affective factors in reading. In H. Singer & R.B. Ruddell, (Eds.) *Theoretical models and processes of reading.* Newark, DE: International Reading Association.

BEAVEN, M.H. (1974). Beyond language arts and reading: Self-disclosure. *Elementary English, 51*(3), 437–439.

BETTMAN, O.L. (1987). *The delights of reading.* Boston, MA: Godine.

BIBERSTINE, R.D. (1977). Affective dimensions of reading instruction. *Contemporary Education, 48*(3), 165–167.

BLOOME, D. (1985). Reading as a social process. *Language Arts, 62*(2), 134–142.

BRANN, E.T.H. (1991). *The world of the imagination: Sum and substance.* Lanham, MD: Rowman & Littlefield.

BURGESS, J.R. (1985). Modifying independent reading habits at home. *The Reading Teacher, 36,* 845–848.

CARTER, S. (1978). Interests and reading. *Journal of Research and Development in Education, 2*(3), 61–68.

CECIL, N.L. (1987). *Teaching to the heart.* Salem, WI: Sheffield.

CENTRAL MIDWESTERN REGIONAL EDUCATIONAL LAB. (1978). Reading enjoyment and affective development. *Reporting on Reading, 4*(3).

CIANI, A.C. (Ed.). (1981). *Motivating reluctant readers.* Newark, DE: International Reading Association.

COMPAINE, B.M. (1983). The new literacy. *DAEDALUS, 112,* 129–142.

CONDON, M.W.F. (1978). Consideration of affect in comprehension: The person belongs in reading. *Viewpoints in Teaching and Learning, 54*(3), 107–116.

COOPER, C.R. (1972). *Measuring growth in appreciation of literature.* Newark, DE: International Reading Association.

CRAMER, E.H. (1993). ICARE: Developing positive attitudes toward reading. In J.L. Johns (Ed.), *Literacy: Celebration and challenge* (pp. 125–131). Bloomington, IL: Illinois Reading Council.

CRAMER, E.H., & BLACHOWICZ, C.L.Z. (1980). Teachers as readers: An extension of the "impact on reading" survey. *Reading Horizons, 20,* 285–291.

CRISCUOLO, N.P. (1980). Activities to generate enthusiasm. *The Reading Teacher, 33*(4), 467–468.

DECKER, B.C. (1986). Aliteracy: What teachers can do to keep Johnny reading. *Journal of Teacher Education, 37*(6), 55–58.

DIEDERICH, P.B. (1973). *Research 1960–1970 on the reading problem in the United States, Part II.* Princeton, NJ: Educational Testing Service.

DIETRICH, D.M., & MATTHEWS, V.H. (Eds.). (1968). *Development of lifelong reading habits.* Newark, DE: International Reading Association.

DILLNER, M.H. (1974). Affective objectives in reading. *Journal of Reading, 17*(8), 626–631.

FAGAN, W.T. (1987). Emergent literacy: Avoiding the plateau effect. *Reading Horizons, 27*(4), 232–237.

FITZPATRICK, K. (1977). Effects of values clarification on self concept and reading achievement. *Reading Improvement, 14*(4), 233–238.

FRAGER, A. (1987). Conquering aliteracy in teacher education. *Journal of Teacher Education, 38,* 16–19.

GENTILE, L.M., & MCMILLAN, M.M. (1990). Literacy through literature: Motivating at-risk students to read and write. *Journal of Reading, Writing, and Learning Disabilities International, 6*(4), 383–393.

GREANEY, V. (1980). Factors related to amount and type of leisure time reading. *Reading Research Quarterly, 15*(3), 337–357.

GUTHRIE, J.T. (1981). Reading in New Zealand: Achievement and volume. *Reading Research Quarterly, 17*(1), 6–27.

GUTHRIE, J.T. (1981). Research views: Reading interests. *The Reading Teacher, 34*(8), 984–986.

HALE, R. (1986). Musings. *Horn Book Magazine, 62*(3), 352–353.

HEATHINGTON, B.S. (1979). What to do about reading motivation in the middle school. *Journal of Reading, 22,* 709–712.

HEINS, E.L. (1984). A challenge to young and old adults. *Horn Book Magazine, 50*(4), 426–427.

HONIG, B. (1988). The California reading initiative. *The New Advocate, 1*(4), 235–240.

HORNIK, R. (1981). Out-of-school television and schooling: Hypotheses and methods. *Review of Educational Research, 51*(2), 193–214.

HOULIHAN, B. (1980). Reading treasuries or literary graveyards? *Curriculum Review, 19*(5), 463–464.

HUNTER, J. (1980). Hooks to catch "on level" readers. *The Reading Teacher, 33*(4), 467–468.

JACOBS, H.C. (1985). Readers—an endangered species? *Vital Speeches of the Day, 51*(14), 446–448.

JOHNS, J.L. (1978). Motivating reluctant readers. *Journal of Research and Development in Education, 2*(3), 69–73.

KLINE, L.W. (1985). *Learning to read, teaching to read: For those who cherish reading.* Newark, DE: LWK Enterprises.

KRATHWOHL, D.R., BLOOM, B.S., & MASIA, B.B. (1964). *Taxonomy of educational objectives, Handbook II: Affective domain.* White Plains, NY: Longman.

LAMME, L.L. (1976). Are reading habits and abilities related? *The Reading Teacher, 30,* 21–27.

LAPOINTE, A.E. (1987). Is there really a national literacy crisis? *Curriculum Review, 27*(1), 12–15.

LEHR, F. (1985). A portrait of the American reader. *Journal of Reading, 29*(2), 170–173.

LESESNE, T.S. (1991). Developing lifetime readers: Suggestions from fifty years of research. *English Journal, 80,* 61–64.

LUNSTRUM, J.P. (1981). Building motivation through the use of controversy. *Journal of Reading, 24,* 687–691.

MANGIERI, J.N., & CORBOY, M.R. (1981). Recreational reading: Do we practice what is preached? *The Reading Teacher, 34,* 923–924.

MANNING, G.L., & MANNING, M. (1984). What models of recreational reading make a difference? *Reading World, 23,* 375–380.

MELLON, C.A. (1987). Teenagers do read: What rural youth say about leisure reading. *School Library Journal, 33*(6), 27–30.

MIKULECKY, L. (1978, May). *Aliteracy and a changing view of reading goals.* Paper presented at the annual meeting of the International Reading Association, Houston, TX. (ED 157 052.)

MIKULECKY, L. (1987). The status of literacy in our society. In J.E. Readence, R.S. Badwin, J.P. Konopak, & H. Newton (Eds.), *Research in literacy: Merging perspectives* (Thirty-sixth Yearbook of the National Reading Conference, pp. 211–235). Rochester, NY: National Reading Conference.

MILLER, J.W., & MCKENNA, M.C. (1989). *Teaching reading in the elementary classroom.* Scottsdale, AZ: Gorsuch Scarisbrick.

MOLDENHAUER, D.L., & MILLER, W.H. (1980). Television and reading achievement. *Journal of Reading, 34*, 615–618.

MORROW, L.M. (1986). Voluntary reading: Forgotten goal. *The Educational Forum, 50*(2), 159–168.

MORROW, L.M., & WEINSTEIN, C.S. (1986). Encouraging voluntary reading: The impact of a literature program on children's use of library centers. *Reading Research Quarterly, 21*(3), 330–346.

MORROW, L.M., & WEINSTEIN, C.S. (1982). Increasing children's use of literature through program and physical design changes. *Elementary School Journal, 83*(2), 131–137.

MOORE, J.C., JONES, C.J., & MILLER, D.C. (1980). What do we know after a decade of sustained silent reading. *The Reading Teacher, 33*(4), 445–450.

NATIONAL ASSESSMENT OF EDUCATIONAL PROGRESS. (1985). *The reading report card: Progress toward excellence in our schools: Trends in reading over four national assessments, 1971–1984* (Rep. No. 15–R–01). Princeton, NJ: National Assessment of Educational Progress/Educational Testing Service.

NELL, V. (1988). The psychology of reading for pleasure: Needs and gratifications. *Reading Research Quarterly, 23*(1), 6–50.

NEUMAN, S.B. (1984). Teletext/videotex: The future of print media. *Journal of Reading, 27*, 340–344.

REED, A.J.S. (1988). *Comics to classics: A parent's guide to books for teens and preteens*. Newark, DE: International Reading Association.

REED, K. (1978, August). *Reading instruction: The affective domain "measuring affective growth in reading."* Paper presented at the 7th Annual Meeting of the International Reading Association World Congress on Reading, Hamburg, Germany. (ED 160 990)

ROBINSON, H.M. (Ed.). (1956). *Developing permanent interest in reading*. Chicago, IL: University of Chicago.

ROETTGER, D. (1980). Elementary students' attitudes toward reading. *The Reading Teacher, 33*(4), 451–454.

SADOSKI, M.C. (1982). *SSR, accountability and effective reading instruction* (Technical paper number R82001). College Station, TX: Texas A&M University. (ED 222 863)

SANACORE, J. (1988). Schoolwide independent reading: The principal can help. *Journal of Reading, 31*(4), 346–353.

SANDERS, M. (1987). Literacy as passionate attention. *Language Arts, 64*(6), 619–633.

SCHULTZ, I. (1987). The discouraged reader. *Curriculum Review, 27*(1), 26.

SHUMAN, R.B., & FOX, B. (1980). Professional concerns: Remedial programs: Some strategies for creating a supportive learning environment. *Reading Horizons, 20*(2), 147–149.

SITTIG, L.H. (1982). Involving parents and children in reading for fun. *The Reading Teacher, 36,* 166–168.

SPINK, J. (1989). *Children as readers: A study.* London: Bingley.

STEINBERG, H. (1983). Reading and TV viewing—complementary activities. *Journal of Reading, 27,* 510–514.

STEVENS, K.C. (1980). Trivia content stimulates enthusiastic reading. *The Reading Teacher, 33*(4), 466–467.

STRICKLER, D.J. (1977). The affective component of the reading process. *Contemporary Education, 48*(3), 161–164.

SUHOR, C. (1987). ERIC/RCS report: Understanding literacy—an overview. *Language Arts, 64*(6), 659–662.

SULLIVAN, J.L. (1985, March). *An antidote for aliteracy: Aliteracy—people who can read but won't.* Paper presented at the annual meeting of the National Council of English Teachers, Houston, TX. (ED 255 934)

THIMMESH, N. (Ed.). (1984). *Aliteracy: People who can read but won't.* Washington, DC: American Enterprise Institute for Public Policy Research.

THOMAS, J.L., & LORING, R.M. (Eds.). (1983). *Motivating children and young adults to read.* Phoenix, AZ: Oryx.

THOMAS, K., & MOORMAN, G. (1983). *Designing reading programs.* Dubuque, IA: Kendall/Hunt.

TREAT, J. (1977). Affective objectives in reading: The self concept. *Reading Improvement, 14*(4), 229–232.

TUNNEL, M.O., CALDER, J.E., & JUSTEN, J.E. (1988). A short form reading attitude survey. *Reading Improvement, 25*(2), 146–151.

WAGNER, L. (1980). The effects of TV on reading. *Journal of Reading, 34,* 201–206.

WEBB, C.A. (1985). Modeling recreational reading: A model. *English Journal, 74*(5), 82–83.

WEINER, B. (1990). History of motivational research in education. *Journal of Educational Psychology, 82*(4), 616–622.

WINKELJOHANN, R. (1974). ERIC/RCS report: Children's affective development through books. *Elementary English, 51*(3), 410–414.

WINKLE, A.W. (1988). Research on aliteracy: Why Johnny doesn't read. *Ohio Reading Teacher, 22*(2), 40–47.

Author Index

Note: An "f" following a page number indicates that the reference may be found in a figure; a "t" that it may be found in a table.

A

Adams, M.J., 93, 103
Adler, M.J., 255
Aiton, G.B., 9
Ajzen, I., 25, 26f, 26–27, 32, 38
Alderman, M.K., 163, 164
Alexander, J.E., 6, 9, 19, 21, 38, 199, 208
Allen, J., 82, 83, 85
American Association of School Administrators, 68, 73
Anders, P.L., 210, 216
Anderson, A.B., 75, 76, 79, 84
Anderson, M.A., 32, 33, 34, 38
Anderson, R.C., 1, 5, 9, 37, 38, 63, 74, 84, 96, 103, 146, 149, 150, 165, 205, 208
Anrig, G., 255
Apfel, N., 75, 83, 85
Applebee, A.N., 145, 165, 250, 254
Apter, M.J., 42, 51
Arendt, H., 46, 51
Arizona Department of Education, 110, 115
Arnold, H., 75, 81, 86
Arnoldsen, L.M., 255
Asher, S.R., 75, 77, 87, 204, 208
Athey, I., 18, 24, 38, 255
Atwell, N., 185, 193
Ayres, G.A., 60, 64

B

Bacharach, N., 187, 193
Bader, L., 163, 167

Baldwin, J., 63
Bandura, A., 252, 253, 254
Banks, C., 46, 51
Barchers, S.I., 99, 103
Barr, R., 190, 193
Barrett, T.C., 114, 117
Bauer, W.W., 144, 166
Bear, G.G., 33, 40
Beaven, M.H., 255
Beisser, A., 234, 244
Berelson, B., 50, 51, 57, 58, 63
Berglund, R.L., 91, 101, 103
Berlyne, D.E., 50, 51
Bettelheim, B., 70, 73
Bettman, O.L., 255
Biberstine, R.D., 255
Bissett, D., 94, 103
Blachowicz, C.L.Z., 182–193, 256
Bloom, B.S., 257
Bloome, D., 82, 84, 255
Boorstin, D.J., 43, 51
Bower, G., 114, 115
Boyer, E.L., 107, 115
Brann, E.T.H., 255
Brazee, P.E., 183, 193
Breedlove, W.G., 172, 179
Brophy, J.E., 69, 70, 73, 92, 93, 103, 163, 165
Broudy, H.S., 108, 110, 112, 115, 116
Brown, D.H., 34, 40
Budinsky, M., 174, 179
Burgess, J.R., 255

Subject Index

Note: An "f" following a page number indicates that the reference may be found in a figure; a "t" that it may be found in a table.